Connecting Leadership to the Brain

To the mindful leaders
who have been and must be

Connecting Leadership to the Brain

Michael H. Dickmann
Nancy Stanford-Blair

CORWIN PRESS, INC.
A Sage Publications Company
Thousand Oaks, California

For information:

Corwin Press, Inc.
A Sage Publications Company
2455 Teller Road
Thousand Oaks, California 91320
E-mail: order@corwinpress.com

Sage Publications Ltd.
6 Bonhill Street
London EC2A 4PU
United Kingdom

Sage Publications India Pvt. Ltd.
M-32 Market
Greater Kailash I
New Delhi 110 048 India

Printed in the United States of America

Library of Congress Cataloging-in-Publication Data

Dickmann, Michael Haley.
  Connecting leadership to the brain / by Michael H. Dickmann and Nancy
Stanford-Blair.
     p. cm.
  Includes bibliographical references and index.
   ISBN 0-7619-7667-1 (cloth) — ISBN 0-7619-7668-X (pbk.)
   1. Leadership. 2. Intellect. I. Stanford-Blair, Nancy. II. Title.
   HM1261 .D53 2002
    303.3'4—dc21   2001004072

This book is printed on acid-free paper.

01   02   03   04   05   10   9   8   7   6   5   4   3   2   1

Acquisitions Editor:	Robb Clouse
Corwin Editorial Assistant:	Erin Buchanan
Associate Editor:	Kylee Liegl
Production Editor:	Diane S. Foster
Typesetter/Designer:	Denyse Dunn
Proofreader:	Scott Oney
Indexer:	Teri Greenberg
Cover Designer:	Michael Dubowe
Permissions Editor:	Anna Howland

Contents

Preface:
In Defense of Simplicity

*Leadership is one of the most observed and least
understood phenomena on earth.*

—James MacGregor Burns (1978, p. 2)

This book aspires to respond to Burns's decades-old observation about "the crisis of leadership" (1978, p. 1). It is a response enabled by a phenomenon not uncommon to human experience, that of a breakthrough in knowledge that advances resolution of intimidating challenges. Notably, such breakthroughs are most dramatic in effect when distillation and interpretation of patterns of information transform understanding and, thereby, behavior. The breakthrough in knowledge, in this instance, pertains to the nature of the human brain and the intelligence it enables. This new knowledge has widespread implications for human understanding and behavior, including Burns's concern for a failure to "grasp the essence of leadership that is relevant to the modern age" (1978, p. 1). Indeed, emerging information about the brain presents unparalleled opportunity for insight into the essence of leadership, insight such as that anticipated in John Archibald Wheeler's reflection:

> To my mind there must be, at the bottom of it all, not an equation, but an utterly simple idea. And to me that idea, when we finally discover it, will be so compelling, so inevitable, that we will say to one another, "oh, how beautiful. How could it have been otherwise?" (quoted in Wheatley, 1992, p. xiv)

The task we have set for ourselves in this book is the creation of a framework that bridges reflection about effective leadership practice to breakthrough knowledge about the nature of human intelligence. To that end, we propose a structure that facilitates alignment of leadership behavior to the nature and nurture of human capacity to learn and achieve. It is a simple framework, but one that both mirrors and accesses the natural and powerful operations of the human brain.

Is this a framework that supports the distillation of essential insights that will transform leadership behavior? Does the framework itself represent a breakthrough in perception about leadership purpose and practice? The answers to these questions reside in the mind of the reader—answers that will unfold in your mind as you process and apply the information that follows in *Connecting Leadership to the Brain*.

Acknowledgments

This work benefited from the inspiration, example, and support of many sources. Close to home, parents Alfred and Jean Dickmann and Kenneth and Helen Stanford instilled in their children the disposition to learn through inquiry, dialogue, debate, and collaboration. Evelyn and Ron graciously provided spousal encouragement and feedback throughout the project. Most important, children Amelia, Emily, Abigail, Alexis, and Nick provided ongoing orientation to what is truly worth being mindful about.

An extended family of exceptionally creative and dedicated colleagues in the Department of Educational Leadership at Cardinal Stritch University formed the supportive community in which leadership connections to human capacity to think, learn, and achieve were progressively explored. Beyond that direct collegial interaction, a greater community of scholars collectively contributed a rich knowledge base about leadership and the nature and nurture of intelligence as enabled by the human brain.

Then there are those who laid eyes and hands on the pages of the book as it evolved. Dale Weis provided copy feedback for early content drafts. Robb Clouse struck an admirable balance between pressure and patience in his editorial role. In this, he was ably assisted by the production editing of Diane Foster.

Finally, Robert Sylwester critiqued content and provided encouragement and direction throughout the drafting and editing process—all the while, claiming that he knew a bit about the brain but not much about leadership. Given that leadership is generally defined as a process of influencing others in the achievement of a goal, Bob performed admirably in helping to lead the authors to the conclusion of this work.

About the Authors

Michael H. Dickmann, PhD, and **Nancy Stanford-Blair, PhD,** are Associate Professors at Cardinal Stritch University in Milwaukee, Wisconsin, where they teach, advise, and conduct research in the areas of leadership, learning, and service. They are also consultants to education, business, and service organizations in matters of leadership, learning, planning, and development. They can be contacted at mhd@stritch.edu and nsblair@aol.com

Introduction:
Is There a Connection?

*Except for the neural engine we carry under our
skulls, the experiential and reflective intelligence housed
by that engine, and the products of past intelligence
in the form of an immense support structure of culture
and language and artifacts that lets each generation
capitalize on the advances of the previous, we human
beings are unimpressive organisms.*

—David Perkins (1995, p. 319)

Perception of Connections

The universe in which humanity resides and thrives is an endless system of systems
within systems in which everything is connected to something. As Wheatley (1992)
advises, "We inhabit a quantum universe that knows nothing of itself, independent
of its relationships" (p. 39)—be it the relationships within and between atoms, molecules, ecosystems, galaxies, machines, families, corporations, governments, or ideas.
Two exemplars of this universal pattern are the relationships that exist between leaders and the people they lead and the relationships that comprise the most intricately
connected system in the universe—the human brain. What, then, of the relationship
between leadership and the brain?

A True Story

We had finished our presentation and were responding to questions from linger-
ing participants while packing materials and making way for the next conference activity. The program had been well received. As had been our experience with prior
presentations, the examination of leadership in the context of emerging knowledge

about the human brain had struck a nerve. We were particularly pleased with the connections and insights generated by our audience.

As we made our way to the exit, a woman who expressed interest in communicating with us further and perhaps collaborating in our work approached us. She had designed a master's thesis proposal addressing emerging knowledge about the brain and the implications of such revelations for leadership practice. It pleased her to know that we were investigating the same issue, given that her initial review of the literature had revealed few sources focused on a relationship between the two topics. She also expressed concern that her proposal had received a less than enthusiastic response from her graduate adviser, as demonstrated by his comment, "What makes you think that there is a connection between leadership and the brain?"

A Reasonable Question

The adviser's question may have been Socratic, sarcastic, or cynical in intent. Perhaps it was merely an attempt at *Dilbert*-style humor, that is, an observation that the collective behavior of individuals in positions of authority suggests that leadership—by tradition if not nature—is, indeed, most often a brainless exercise. Whatever its intent, the question is both legitimate and revealing: legitimate because it is human nature (i.e., the nature of the human brain) to inquire about the what, why, how, when, and where of things—including, certainly, the suggestion of a relationship between leadership and the brain, and revealing because it suggests that the implied relationship between leadership and the brain has not been adequately investigated, much less deeply understood or appreciated.

An Underlying Question

The significant question lurking beneath the adviser's inquiry is not whether leadership is connected to the brain. The answer to that question is obvious, given the brain's physiological presence and mediating role in all human activity—that is, the brain is always at the party and leadership always dances to the tune of the brain. This natural connection may operate ineffectually, however, if not understood and judiciously acted on. Accordingly, the more important *connection* question is how the brain is accessible at a conscious level to leaders who seek to most effectively engage it in the achievement of important goals.

A Question to Be Refined

It might also be anticipated that the adviser, in the responsible manner of an academic mentor challenging and guiding proposed scholarship, would have further questions for his graduate student. One such question would surely be "how are you interpreting the term *brain?*" Again, this is a reasonable question. If one is going to explore the connection of leadership to something, it is best to know what the interpretation of that something is—and here arises a bit of a problem.

The good news is that the beginning of the 21st century is witnessing a convergence of information from investigations in diverse fields of study (neurophysiology, neuropsychology, cognitive psychology, developmental psychology, evolutionary psychology, evolutionary biology, primatology, ethology, linguistics, psychophysics, mathematics, philosophy, anthropology, archaeology, and computer science—to name a few) that sheds considerable new light on qualities of the human brain. The downside of this information explosion is that it is generating as many questions as it does answers. The result is considerable debate and ongoing interpretation of brain physiology and processes—particularly the relationship of the brain to conceptualizations of human mind and intelligence.

This text embraces a general interpretation of the human brain as a collection of physiological structures that support electrochemical communications within neural networks—thus enabling, among other things, consciousness and intelligence. This is an orientation to the brain that is both compelling and useful for the exploration of leadership-brain connections. It is also an interpretation that is in alignment with observations rendered by investigators in diverse fields, including these:

- The neurological description by Marian Diamond (Diamond & Hopson, 1998) of the multiple lobes of the brain neocortex "that collectively interpret our sensations, initiate our movements, and enable us to think, speak, write, calculate, plan, create, organize, and do all the other things that make us human" (p. 41)
- The hypothesis of physiologist Francis Crick (1994) that our brains are responsible for our mental lives through "the behavior of a vast assembly of nerve cells and their associated molecules" (p. 41)
- The theoretical perspective of neurophysiologist William Calvin (1996) that intelligence is "the high-end scenery of neurophysiology—the outcome of many aspects of an individual's brain organization that bear on doing something that one has never done before" (p. 11)
- The thesis of philosopher John Searle (1997) that brain processes cause consciousness but "consciousness itself is a feature of the brain" (p. 8)
- The neuropsychological view of Michael Gazzaniga (1998) that "How the brain enables mind is *the* question to be answered in the 21st century" (p. xii)

A holistic orientation to the overall architecture of the brain and its broad modes of operation also echoes the position of Leslie Hart (1983) on the relative importance for nonneuroscientists to understand the brain at a broad (i.e., macro) level as opposed to a molecular, cellular, or synaptic (i.e., micro) level. Hart's passion focused on bridging the gap between knowledge about the nature of the human brain and the organization of effective learning systems. Similarly, leaders might productively focus on bridging broad and essential knowledge about the brain to effective leadership practice in organizations. To paraphrase and further adapt Hart's sentiments about the brain and learning to similar sentiments about the brain and leadership—the construction of

such leadership-brain connections should recognize that leaders are not ineffective because they do not know what happens at synapses or the chemistry of neurotransmitters, but rather because they have yet to address the brain as the organ that enables complex thinking and intelligence. Thus, while it is important to be grounded in
general knowledge about the physiology and functions of the brain, the ultimate task is
to fit the practice of leadership to the nature and nurture of the intelligence the brain
enables.

A Timely Question . . .
and a Question for the Ages

How and to what purpose leadership is connected to the brain is a question that is
appropriate to ask in the context of the challenges confronting leaders at the beginning of the 21st century—such as those of equity, justice, peace, and sustainable environments. From this perspective, emerging knowledge about the brain begs for examination of the implications for leadership practice. Indeed, human survival in an
ever more complex and interconnected global society mandates the investigation of
leadership practice aligned to the nature and nurture of human intelligence. It is a
question that merits a response.

Timely as it may be, however, examination of leadership-brain connections is not
new. Plato's advocacy of the philosopher king prescribed leadership that was both
intellectually able and disposed to seek wisdom. Eastern philosophy, as represented in
Buddhist, Taoist, and Confucian teachings, also valued a leadership capacity for reflection and, thereby, discernment of wise actions. Thus contemporary explorations
of the mental dimensions and demands of leadership, such as Gardner's (1995)
Leading Minds: An Anatomy of Leadership and Goleman's (1998) *Working With Emotional
Intelligence* extend a historic human interest in the leadership-brain connection.

How We Came to This

The authors' formal exploration of the relationship between leadership and the brain
emerged from work with colleagues at Cardinal Stritch University in the design of a
doctoral program in leadership. Aspiring doctoral students had expressed need for a
program that would align their leadership experience, context, and scholarship. As
individuals already occupying leadership positions, they lobbied for a program of
scholarship that would have direct impact on the organizations they were leading.

With an orientation to the contextual challenges of leaders in an era of profound
change, the design team created a program of study based on an underlying assumption that leadership engages the collective capacity of a group to think, learn, and
achieve important purpose. It was this process of composing a theoretical foundation
for a doctoral program in leadership—particularly perception of the relationship between leadership, organizational intelligence, and the achievement of organizational

goals—that prompted an initial conceptualization of how and to what purpose leadership is connected to the brain.

There is, however, a more basic and precedent incentive for this inquiry. It is human nature to want to know and understand. The professional experience of the authors spans three decades of studying, practicing, and facilitating leadership and learning in diverse organizations. Such experience provokes the exploration of promising leads to a deeper understanding of leadership, learning, and the relationships therein. Interest in insights that might be gleaned from emerging brain theory and research is, therefore, a given for serious students of leadership. Indeed, failure to pursue such an investigation would be equivalent to the medical field ignoring the implications of emerging information about the human genome for health maintenance and treatment. Accordingly, this inquiry is motivated by a fundamental human disposition to integrate and capitalize new knowledge—a disposition that leads herein to the formulation of a framework for aligning leadership behavior to emerging knowledge about the human brain.

What This Book Is About

This book intends to facilitate the formulation of new leadership perception and behavior. In attempting to do so, it does not present prescriptive formulae, recipes, or directives. Rather, it presents a framework for constructing personal understanding of the implications of emerging knowledge about human intelligence for leadership practice. Specifically, it presents a framework designed to advance leadership that is *mindful* (i.e., attentive) rather than *mindless* (i.e., heedless) of the nature and nurture of intelligence. In essence, it is a framework for aligning leadership behavior to the advancement of the collective capacity of individuals in organizations to think, learn, and achieve purpose. This framework is motivated by three assumptions:

1. **A new day requires a new perspective.** Given a convergence of new information about the nature and nurture of human intelligence emerging from investigations in neuroscience, cognitive science, and many other fields, it is both appropriate and necessary to reassess many aspects of human behavior, including leadership.

2. **A framework for reflection facilitates perceptual shift.** Refinement of understanding about intelligence and its implications for leadership practice is assisted by a framework that structures active reflection and planning.

3. **There is no universal prescription for leadership.** There is no universal prescription for how leadership engages the collective capacity of a group to learn, evolve, and achieve. There are, however, procedures for formulating general principles and practices of mindful leadership—as well as planning situation-specific leadership behaviors aligned to said principles and practices.

Questions That Will Be
Answered Along the Way

The reader will be guided through responses to seven questions as a means to construct personal understanding about leadership connections to the brain:

1. What is the relationship between information, perception, and behavior?
2. What is intelligence and how might emerging information about its nature be most effectively organized to inform leadership, perception, and behavior?
3. What is essential for a leader to know about the nature of human intelligence?
4. What is the nature of leadership, and how should it be practiced in the context of the 21st century?
5. What is the nature of perception, and how might it proactively adjust to new information?
6. What are the important components of a framework for aligning leadership behavior to the nature and nurture of intelligence and the achievement of purpose?
7. What is mindful leadership?

Chapter Format

Each chapter will sequentially provide an orientation to chapter content, presentation of relevant concepts and constructs, and summary observations. Chapter formatting will also provide opportunities for active reader reflection about content.

Chapter Content

Chapter 1 addresses the interactive relationship between information, perception, and behavior. The influence of contemporary advances in information about the human brain on perceptions of appropriate leadership behavior is introduced as an example of this phenomenon. *Main idea:* Informed by a convergence of significant new insights about the human brain and the intelligence it enables, leaders at the threshold of the new millennium are presented with an extraordinary opportunity to inform and restructure their perceptions about leadership purpose and behavior.

Chapter 2 targets intelligence as the brain connection of primary concern to leadership practice. Parallel developments in microtechnology, brain research, and intelligence theory have generated an explosion of new information. Paradoxically, leaders cannot act with assurance about the accuracy of current interpretations of the nature of human intelligence, yet they must respond to new information as it becomes available to them. Given this dilemma, it is important for leaders to engage and organize this evolving knowledge base in a focused and useful manner. With this need in mind, Chapter 2 advocates a practical process for distilling essential knowledge about the nature of human intelligence. *Main idea:* Leadership is most interested in connecting to how the brain enables and exercises intelligence, because intelligence is the means to achieving goals. If this connection is to be effectively explored and engaged, however, leaders must first commit to practical strategies for accessing and processing essential knowledge about the brain and the nature and nurture of intelligence.

Chapter 3 demonstrates a structure and process that organizes information about the physiological, social, emotional, constructive, reflective, and dispositional nature of the brain in the exercise of intelligence. This construction of a personal knowledge base is a prerequisite for informed perception about leadership influence on natural human capacities to think, learn, and achieve. *Main idea:* Given that most leaders are not and will never be neuroscientists or cognitive psychologists, the technical and rapidly evolving knowledge base about the brain and human intelligence must be focused and organized if it is to be useful to reflection about leadership purpose and practice.

Chapter 4 examines the nature of leadership, with particular attention to the influence of context. A case is made for an emerging stage in the evolution of leadership practice in which leaders consciously align their behavior to knowledge about the nature and nurture of intelligence—are mindful about behavior that might favorably influence the capacity of individuals and organizations to achieve purpose. *Main idea:* Leadership practice in human societies has evolved over millions of years at the influence of changing environmental contexts. A new stage is emerging in which leaders cultivate understanding about the nature and nurture of intelligence in self and others. Such leaders are potentially mindful in the alignment of their behavior to the advancement of organizational intelligence and purpose—as opposed to leaders who are mindless of such perception or behavior alignment and, thereby, less effective in their influence on organizational success.

Chapter 5 interprets perception as the mental process by which humans see and understand their world. Perceptions evolve from experience and a natural accumulation of information patterns that continually interact with values and behavior patterns. Importantly, perceptual shifts and the extraction of meaning from experience are facilitated by proactive reflection about new information in relation to behavior. Emerging information about the human brain at the beginning of the 21st century presents leaders with a unique opportunity to reflect on their understanding of the nature of human intelligence and, thereby, to restructure their understanding of effective leadership behavior. *Main idea:* The convergence of new discoveries about the brain and the intelligence it enables, coupled with the challenges confronting humanity at the threshold of the new millennium, both accommodate and require proactive reflection about leadership purpose and practice.

Chapter 6 presents a framework that provides structure and support for aligning leadership behavior to the nature and nurture of human capacity to achieve needs. The framework is designed to both mirror and access the natural and powerful processes of the human brain. To that end, the framework is organized by four components of mindful leadership:

1. **Arousal of brain attention** to leadership-intelligence connections and the potential of mindful leadership

2. **Acquisition of knowledge** about the nature and nurture of intelligence

3. **Application of knowledge** about the nature and nurture of intelligence to leadership behavior that influences human capacity to achieve needs

4. **Adjustment of knowledge** about the nature and nurture of intelligence and mindful leadership behavior in response to application experiences

The *application* component is the action platform within the framework. It provides a four-step structure for applications of mindful practice to self, systems, and situations:

1. Clarification of an achievement **need,** that is, clarity about the goal or purpose to be achieved

2. Assessment of the **nature** of the intelligence required for achieving the identified need

3. Assessment of options for the **nurture** of the intelligence required to achieve the identified need

4. Composition of a **narrative** plan for the nurture of the nature of intelligence required for the achievement of the identified need

Main idea: A framework provides structure and support for diagnosing and planning mindful leadership behavior that nurtures the nature of human capacity to achieve needs.

Chapter 7 advocates for leaders who lead with the brain in mind. Adherence to mindful leadership principles, cultivation of mindful leadership practices, and orientation to mindful leadership purpose is important to that end. Examples of such principles, practices, and purpose are provided as defining attributes of a mindful leader. The reader is also invited to construct summary interpretations of the implications of mindful leadership for personal perception and practice. *Main idea:* Adherence to mindful principles and cultivation of mindful practices represent the path by which a leader influences the achievement of mindful purpose.

A Journey to New Perception

A Shared Journey

Leadership is a natural and broadly practiced phenomenon. Accordingly, a broad view of leadership is in order as one proceeds through this book. If it is important for leadership perception to be informed about the nature of the brain and its capacity for intelligence, such information is valuable to both formal and informal leaders—whether they be politicians, CEOs, school administrators, directors, teachers, coaches, health officials, parents, or anyone else in a position to influence others in the achievement of a goal or purpose. The information presented herein, then, is intended to guide an investigative journey that holds promise for deepening understanding of connections between leadership and the brain—an opportunity to think about and see leadership from a different vantage point. It is a journey that invites the companionship of all who seek to understand what it might mean to be a mindful leader.

Prepare to Pay Tolls

This journey requires the exercise of the very intelligence that is the focus of mindful leadership. Specifically, participants are required to engage the complex reflective reasoning capacities of the prefrontal lobes of their cerebral cortex—to think their way to new understanding. Accordingly, chapter narratives will speak directly to *you* and your reflective search for new perceptions of leadership.

Part One

Breaking Through

1

A Louis Moment

May you live in interesting times.

—Anonymous

Chapter Orientation

The Wonder of It All

The universe and all its content are a constant source of wonder to humans—the self-proclaimed most-intelligent inhabitants of the planet Earth. Indeed, to be human is to be intrigued with the objects, events, processes, and other life forms that surround. This quality is easily observed in infants and toddlers as they investigate the inhabitants, artifacts, and systems of their environment. It is a quality born of the evolution of conscious thought in ancient ancestors who first questioned matters of life and death and the nature of the moon and the sun and the stars. It is a quality that has evolved as a hallmark of the human species, exhibited as a constant questioning of the nature of things: What is this? Where did it come from? How does it work? What just happened? Why did it happen? Who are we? Where are we? Why are we here? Where are we going? What if . . . ? Inevitably, this human inquisitiveness about the infinity of mysteries near and far has fostered a strong species interest in finding answers to the questions wonder raises.

A Defining Disposition

It is human nature to complete the puzzle, find the answer, solve the mystery, improve conditions—to figure it out. Indeed, human success as a species is defined by a prodigious disposition and ability to analyze and create on many levels.

At a basic level, to be human is to engage in involuntary, pervasive, and continuous inquiry. Humans construct patterns, compare, question, induce, deduce, judge, classify, predict, and plan. You do this when you shop, exercise, fix the plumbing, visit the doctor, converse, plant the garden, or organize a social event. You cannot not do it because it is behavior that is encoded and reflexive. It is your nature . . . and it serves you well. This analytic and creative capacity is exercised at more advanced levels when it is consciously committed to the resolution of complex problems and tasks. People become more formal and systematic when attempting the completion of a course of study, pursuing the cure for a disease, or planning a voyage to Mars. At this formal level of inquiry, humans become more reflective in generating, accumulating, and organizing knowledge for specific purposes. It is at this level also that humankind becomes aware of the challenges, frustrations, and breakthroughs associated with inquiries of great magnitude.

Breaking Through

The focus of this chapter is the nature and implications of significant break-throughs in understanding that occur at the prodding of human inquiry—with specific reference to the magnitude of recent discoveries about the human brain and intelligence. Specifically, chapter content will address:

- The nature and influence of significant moments of discovery, breakthrough advances in human knowledge that energize the relationship between information, perception, and behavior
- The significance of contemporary breakthroughs in knowledge about the human brain at the dawn of a new century
- The implications of emerging knowledge about the human brain and the intelligence it enables for a breakthrough in leadership theory

Moments of Discovery

Given the engagement of billions of people over millions of years in the interpretation and generation of alternatives for successful interaction with their environment, the collective growth of human knowledge is inevitably exponential in character. In fact, the growth of human knowledge—by virtue of persistent contributions from a large and highly social population over time—is a good example of compound return on investment. New knowledge is connected to prior knowledge, thus generating more new knowledge to be connected to prior knowledge that, again, generates new knowledge ad infinitum. In this fashion, human knowledge always advances. There may be plateaus and momentary setbacks—the Middle Ages and the Spanish Inquisition come to mind—but the big picture of knowledge acquisition is one of continuous and dramatic growth. Similar to an economic market, it is also marked by exhilarating advances as expressed in singular insights or periods of general intellectual prosperity.

The most spectacular advances in human understanding are represented by moments when critical new knowledge emerges and original ideas are formulated. Such moments are, in effect, comparable to discovering a key or combination to a lock. Possession of such a key opens a door to a wealth of new knowledge that, in turn, produces a surge in the generation of more knowledge. The signature of such a dramatic advance in knowledge is a shift in how the world is perceived and, subsequently, how people act in accordance with the new worldview. Louis Pasteur is representative of this phenomenon.

Shift Happens

In 1857, Louis M. Pasteur and his associates were engaged in investigations addressing the problem of wine spoilage, as well as other food and health-related issues. In conducting his inquiry, Pasteur devised a simple experiment that provided proof of the biogenesis of life (i.e., life comes from life), thereby establishing an empirical base for the theory of the spread of contagious disease by microorganisms (i.e., bacteria). This scientific knowledge was in itself a dramatic revelation of what had been, up to that point in time, an unperceived universe acting on the human condition. The ultimate impact of this scientific breakthrough, however, was revealed through significant changes in diverse human behaviors. As people constructed personal understanding of the basic concept of disease spread by germ hosts, they began to alter their practices of personal hygiene, food preparation, and environmental sanitation. Food producers and processors implemented new practices consistent with their perception of an unseen world of potentially harmful bacteria. The medical field developed operational policies for washing hands, covering faces, and sterilizing instruments. Scientists embarked on vast and ongoing investigations that produced vaccines, antibiotics, and other contributions to improved human health.

The Relationship Between Information, Perception, and Behavior

The impact of Louis Pasteur's scientific discovery exemplifies the phenomenon of information influencing perception that, in turn, influences behavior (see Figure 1.1). In Louis's case, significant new information (i.e., revelation that microscopic organisms transmit disease between other organisms) refined perception (i.e., of disease as spread by germs rather than by curse, changes in weather, bathing too frequently, etc.) that, in turn, directed modification of behavior (i.e., improved personal hygiene, medical practice, sanitation systems, and food processing and storage). In other words, after the scientific revelation of information about the existence and nature of germs, there was no going back—there was no other option but to adopt behavior that was compatible with the resulting perceptual shift in understanding about the nature of disease.

Figure 1.1. The Relationship Between Information, Perception, and Behavior

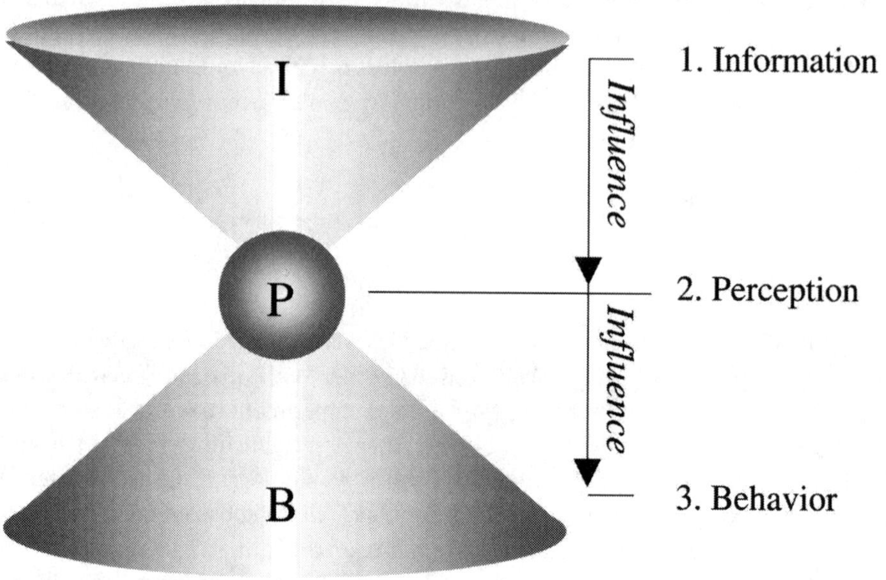

Information processed by the brain influences perception that, in turn, influences behavior.

1. A body of information within the field of all possible information is engaged and processed by the brain:

2. The processing of this information forms and refines perception (i.e., knowledge, understanding):

3. Perception influences an array of behavior patterns and choices within the field of all possible behavior options:

Distillation of Essential Understanding

The legacy of Pasteur's scientific breakthrough is, of course, much greater than that briefly outlined above. His discovery, combined with the subsequent scientific research and development it spurred, ultimately resulted in enhanced health and life expectancy for much of humankind—an extraordinary return from rather simple experiments that empirically proved the biogenesis of disease-bearing microorganisms.

It should be acknowledged, however, that Pasteur's confirmation of microscopic disease agents did not come as a complete surprise. Louis's scientific inquiry provided both revelation and verification. It revealed information that had previously not been known. It also verified intuitive conclusions about the spread and prevention of disease (e.g., over 2,000 years earlier, Aristotle suspected microscopic "seeds" as the transmitters of illness). In this sense, the results of Louis's experiments provided reinforcement for the expansion of hygienic and sanitary practices that were already in effect by virtue of individual or cultural intuition. Nevertheless, whether minds were opened to a new reality or intuition confirmed, Pasteur's revelations ultimately had the perceptual-shift effect of advancing how people understood their world and, subsequently, how they acted in it.

The Importance of Gist

It is worth noting at this point that extensive knowledge of Louis Pasteur and his work is probably not of the highest priority for most people living today—unless, perhaps, they have a personal or professional interest in the history of biological science. At the same time, however, it might be safe to conclude that most adults are able to retrieve some textbook memory of Monsieur Pasteur as a French scientist associated in some manner with important scientific discovery.

If one were to be completely honest, he or she would be likely to admit that most people survive rather well with limited knowledge of Louis Pasteur, the man. It would be somewhat difficult, however, to locate anyone, from young children on, who do not have a grasp of the essential knowledge derived from Pasteur's experiment and did not act in accordance with that understanding. Thus we have an example of people distilling the *gist* (i.e., the essential points or general sense) of an important body of knowledge. They have distilled essential knowledge from the quantity that is available, knowledge that is important to know in a fundamental fashion—knowledge of the *big idea*.

At the Break

The 20th Century Remembered

Pause and reflect for a minute about what significant issues and events, in your opinion, the latter part of the 20th century will be remembered for?

> *Reflection Time*

There are, of course, many possible responses to the above question. It is somewhat predictable, however, that you might consider issues and events, such as computer technology, space exploration, genetic engineering, civil rights, the feminist movement, the spread of democracy, environmentalism, and globalization of economic markets and communications as possible candidates. Whatever your choices, a listing of significant events and issues that are transpiring during your time on the planet might well have an intimidating effect. They collectively describe a unique historical period of concurrent developments in technology and social, political, and economic systems. This circumstance suggests that you do indeed live in an interesting time of great change and challenge—a time that places a high premium on human disposition and capacity to figure it out.

Historical Convergence

In terms of quantity, degree, and speed of change, it is not unreasonable to consider the years leading into the 21st century as rivals to any previous historical period. It is, of course, easier to recognize the convergence of significant historical developments from a distance. It is relatively easy, for example, to observe and analyze the integrated surge of technological and humanistic change that evolved during the Renaissance. It is more difficult, in comparison, to fully appreciate the unique status or magnitude of change in the present. Preoccupied with the developments and demands of the moment, we are required to make a conscious effort to perceive the collective effect and direction of significant changes that are occurring concurrently—that is, to see the forest for the trees. The difficulty one might experience in appreciating the historical significance of events in the making, however, does not absolve one of the need to understand what is happening.

Senge (1990) provides an example that helps us understand the phenomenon of historical convergence in his description of the merging of five technologies (i.e., the variable-pitch propeller; retractable landing gear; lightweight, monocoque body construction; radial, air-cooled engine; and wing flaps) that made commercial air travel possible in 1935—30 years after Kitty Hawk. A comparative pattern in the latter half of the 20th century is that of a merging of advancements in microtechnology with advances in biological science, space exploration, communication systems, and the like. In such a convergence, one significant development connects with another . . . that connects to another . . . that connects to another—thus exponential change is engaged.

A Louis Moment

Within the big picture of significant contemporary changes and developments are the information breakthroughs occurring in neuroscience and related fields of brain research and theory. This surge forward in understanding about the human brain and the intelligence it enables is comparable to the dramatic breakthrough of Louis Pasteur's scientific discovery of micro-organic contagion in the mid-19th century. Indeed, contemporary scientific progress in revealing information about the nature of human intelligence represents, in effect, a *Louis Moment* of discovery—discovery that is facilitated by converging advancements in technology at the beginning of the 21st century. Furthermore, as was the case in Louis's revelations about the nature of contagious disease, as the "black box" of intelligence is opened and its nature revealed, there can be no going back to a less informed understanding or alignment of appropriate behavior in the conduct of human affairs.

Moving Leadership Upstream

A Louis Moment of breakthrough advances in knowledge about the human brain and intelligence creates pressure to reflect about many aspects of human behavior, including leadership. Accordingly, leaders are well-advised to explore the headwaters of intelligence—that is, the three-pound physiological mass located in the human head. Leadership connections to the brain have been long assumed, given the brain's mediating role in all interactions between people. Emerging knowledge about intelligence, however, presents an opportunity to tighten the brain-leadership connection—an opportunity for leaders to better understand and engage the intelligence of self and others.

A Perceptual Shift That Is Required and Accommodated

Perceptual reflection about leadership is an ongoing requirement, given that leadership is contextually influenced and responsive to changing challenges. The particular nature of social, political, economic, and environmental challenges at the turn of this century certainly makes a case for reflection about how leadership might be rendered yet more effective. The good news is that such reflection is accommodated in a timely fashion by emerging knowledge about the brain, knowledge that cannot be ignored any more than the sun can be ignored as the center of the solar system or germs as agents of contagion. There is unprecedented knowledge about the physiological, social, emotional, constructive, reflective, and dispositional dimensions of human intelligence—knowledge that leaders now have available to use in reconstructing perceptions about behavior that engages the human capacity to achieve.

Breaking Through to a New Theory of Leadership

Breakthroughs in thinking and understanding happen, but they seldom just happen— they most often evolve at the prodding of proactive inquiry. Perkins (2000) speaks to this in his description of a fivefold structure that characterizes the process of breakthrough thinking:

- Breakthrough thinking characteristically requires a long period of searching.
- A typical breakthrough arrives after little or no apparent progress.
- The typical breakthrough begins with a precipitating event.
- When a breakthrough happens, it happens as a cognitive snap—things fall into place rapidly with not much time separating the precipitating event from the solution.

- The breakthrough transforms one's mental or physical world in a generative way—altering both thinking and action.

This fivefold structure is relevant to inquiry about leadership and its relationship to the brain. Humankind consciously values leadership and has sought to understand its critical attributes for many centuries. While many models and theories of leadership have evolved from this long search, it is fair to say that common perception and unifying theory remain elusive. The event of significant advances in knowledge about the human brain and the intelligence it enables, however, precipitates an opportunity for a breakthrough to new understanding about the nature of effective leadership. Accordingly, a cognitive snap that transforms leadership thinking and action may be at hand.

Summary Observations

- It is human nature to figure things out.
- Periodically, human inquiry strikes a vein of significant new knowledge.
- Breakthroughs in knowledge influence perceptual shifts that, in turn, influence change in behavior—that is, significant new knowledge provokes change in how people understand their world and, subsequently, how they behave in it.
- One need not know everything for change in perception and behavior to happen—essential understanding is the key.
- Advancement in knowledge about the human brain and the nature of intelligence is one of many significant developments that are converging at the beginning of the 21st century.
- Leadership attention to breakthrough information about the brain and the nature of intelligence is appropriate. It presents an opportunity for leaders to better understand and engage the intelligence of self and others and, thereby, more effectively influence human responses to the challenges of the 21st century.
- The ultimate implication of emerging knowledge about the brain and intelligence is the prospect for a breakthrough in leadership theory.

Reader Reflection

- How does information influence perception?
- How does perception influence behavior?
- What would be a historical example (other than that of Louis Pasteur) of a breakthrough in information leading to a shift in human understanding and, subsequently, behavior?

- Can you recall an instance in which new information led to a significant shift in your perception and behavior?
- Why might a leader be interested in knowing more about the brain and intelligence?
- Other thoughts and questions?

2

In Search of Intelligence

If your brain were so simple that you could understand it, you would be so simple that you couldn't.

—Anonymous

Chapter Orientation

Beyond the Obvious

Leadership *is* connected to the brain. Given the brain's commanding role in the mediation of all human behavior, this connection is not an option. Whether dancing, playing cards, or selling real estate, the what, why, and how of human behavior are directly connected to the physiological mass that occupies body space above your ears—the brain. The question is not *whether* leadership is connected to the brain; rather, it is a question of *how* leadership is connected to the brain—and how said connections might be optimized.

The Connection Target

Leadership necessarily interacts in some manner with virtually all aspects of brain function and activity. This comprehensive relationship, however, is ultimately defined by a connection between leadership and the intelligence the brain enables. In effect, leadership is more concerned with what the brain does than the brain itself.

Intelligence, then, is *the* leadership-brain connection to be examined. To that end, this chapter initiates a review of emerging knowledge about the nature of human brain capacity for intelligence—a review that will continue into in the following chapter. The content of this chapter will address the following:

- Brain purpose
- The intrigue of intelligence
- The challenge of defining intelligence
- The status and significance of emerging knowledge that is enlightening understanding of human intelligence
- A proposition as to how leaders might get a grip on emerging knowledge, that is, how leaders might explore and organize such knowledge to the advantage of informed and, thereby, more effective leadership behavior

What's a Brain For?

Taking Care of Business

Gazzaniga (1998) observes that evolutionary biologists are guided in their efforts to understand the brain by the essential question posed in the investigation of any biological organ or system: What is this for and why does it do what it does? In the case of the brain, he observes, the flippant answer to the question is sex. The more complete explanation is that the brain's purpose—its primary business if you will—is that of making decisions about how to enhance the reproductive success of its host body. This purpose, of course, is a legacy spawned in the primordial soup, a genetically programmed directive to survive and reproduce. Such a blunt, no-frills description of brain purpose may appear to be unappreciative of the complex and refined operations of the brain, particularly the human brain. Understanding the nature and potential of human intelligence, nevertheless, requires this perspective of original and prevailing brain purpose.

To understand what the brain is for, it is also helpful to reflect on the fact that brains did not exist until they were needed. Early life forms on the planet were brainless . . . as well as heartless, breathless, sightless, and, in many other ways—less. Over the vast span of evolutionary time, however, the biological process of natural selection favored mutations that produced more complex life forms. These more sophisticated organisms generated survival advantages such as cardiovascular, respiratory, and visual systems. The evolution of specialized subsystems within complex organisms subsequently valued biological adaptations that led to the development of brain structures. In effect, as life forms on the planet progressed from simple storefront operations to complex, multidimensional enterprises, centralized management systems were in demand. The brain thus emerged as a biological adaptation in concert with other adaptations like the heart, lungs, and eyes. It evolved from random mutations to centralize management of the integrated elements of organisms and the processing of environmental information.

The business of the brain, then, is the monitoring and adjustment of the internal elements of an organism in concert with the monitoring and processing of information about the organism's external environment. A brain performs this integrated internal-external information processing function to enhance the survival of its host body system. This is the basic business conducted by all brains in all animals, be they reptiles or primates. Many millions of years of performing these basic responsibilities under diverse environmental conditions, however, inevitably produced a brain that became extraordinarily good at the survival business—so good, in fact, that it began to restructure and expand on its basic business.

The Business of Intelligence

Absent disease or other conditions of dysfunction, the human brain admirably attends to the basic survival business of managing the internal elements of its host physiological system. This aspect of what your brain does is so fundamental and well established that it operates mostly beyond your conscious awareness or control. This survival service, however, is not a distinguishing factor in separating the quality of a human brain from the brains of other animals, particularly other primates. The human brain's adeptness in the survival business of acquiring and processing environmental information, on the other hand, is a different story—a story that differentiates human development, experience, and potential. As Pinker (1997) observes, it was the refinement of a capacity to process information that facilitated our ancestors in the resolution of problems associated with a foraging way of life, "in particular, understanding and outmaneuvering objects, animals, plants and other people" (p. 21).

The survival business of the brain has been expanded and reconstructed in humans to a highly evolved capacity for interpreting, organizing, and applying information—the business of intelligence. This capacity to process and use information is represented physiologically in the uniqueness of human brain structure and size. It is a capacity that is demonstrated in the exercise of analysis, conjecture, and imagination. It is compounded in applications to problem solving, decision making, and creativity. Humans survive and thrive by this capacity to acquire and apply knowledge, particularly in the context of new challenges. Simply put—and in reference to an old James Bond movie theme song—nobody does it better.

Intrigue

Intelligence Aware of Itself

Human intelligence is irrepressibly intrigued with itself. This is not a matter of vanity or self-indulgence; it is simply the nature of the phenomenon. On evolving to a point of self-awareness, human intelligence inevitably understands its value to human welfare and wants to know more about its nature and potential. You can test this assessment yourself by answering two simple questions:

1. Given the option, is it generally to the advantage of an individual or a group to have more or less capacity for intelligence in any given situation?

2. If new information becomes available about how human intelligence works and can be used or improved to greater advantage, do you want to know about it?

The fact that you are reading this book pretty well anticipates your response to the second question. Your response to the first question (despite the disposition of your intelligent mind to consider alternatives) is also predictable, *if* you are being honest about what you would want for yourself and those whom you care most about. Furthermore, your responses to both questions were likely executed without any deep conceptual reflection about what intelligence is—the point being, you have an immediate, if not innate, sense of its importance. After all, you know intelligence is a determining force in the quality of human existence because you observe its imprint everywhere you look.

The Tracks of Our Mind

The story of human intelligence surrounds you. You need only to look out from your vantage point of the moment to observe evidence of humankind's extraordinary capacity to acquire and apply knowledge—a capacity that defines and sets the species apart. Looking up from this text while located in your home or another building interior, for example, you will immediately observe artifacts such as furnishings, art works, printed material, appliances, communication technologies, and energy systems. Note that even the most rudimentary exhibit, for instance, a pencil or coffee mug, is the product of complex knowledge acquisition and application. Every human product that meets your eye is representative of integrated applications of accumulated human knowledge in the natural, physical, and social sciences. And such representations are everywhere.

If a window is available, your gaze will predictably fall on a variety of architectural structures, transportation systems, and alterations of landscape. With the advantage of a high-rise location, your vision might observe human engineering of the infrastructure of manufacturing, commercial, recreation, energy, and transportation systems. In a more rural environment, you would likely observe land clearings, irrigation systems, buildings, and equipment dedicated to managed plant growth and animal husbandry. And if, by chance, you look up from this narrative while traveling as a passenger in a human-intelligence-produced car, boat, train, or plane, your observation of the products of human capacity to acquire and apply knowledge will be further magnified in volume and dimension.

The fact of the matter is that you need not look up from these pages to appreciate the evolved status of human intelligence. You are reading and comprehending an arrangement of symbols that comply with evolved human rules for language, printed on material produced by evolved human knowledge of science, and distributed in accordance with evolved human interpretation of economic principles. Better yet, you can simply close your eyes and reflect on any exemplary social, political, economic, technological, or artistic product of human intelligence that comes to mind and, well, . . . your intelligent mind gets the picture.

The artifacts of human intelligence surround us. Whenever you choose to do so, you can see, hear, smell, taste, and feel it. And you are well-advised to periodically pause and to stand in awe of the tracks of human intelligence—tracks that lead from hand-held tools and communal shelters to the harnessing of the power of atoms and the creation of complex social structures. These tracks of our intelligent minds tell us where we have been in our long evolutionary story. They also provide clues about paths to the future, choices to be made, and the requirements of intelligence thereof.

Experiencing the products of intelligence may certify its presence, but it does not explain the phenomenon of intelligence itself. Nor does it address fundamental questions about where it comes from and how it works—questions heretofore difficult, if not impossible, to answer. As a matter of fact, humans developed and exercised extraordinary intelligence long before they knew they had it, much less had a word to describe it. Inevitably, however, human intelligence became aware of itself—and its current hosts are engaged in a vigorous campaign to understand its nature. Indeed, this is a natural progression in the evolution of intelligence itself. Awareness of this extraordinary ability to access, interpret, organize, and apply information has led to intrigue with its potential. There is a sense that there is more to know—that one might go to a next level and do better yet by this talent.

A Definition in Progress

> We may not be able to explain intelligence in all its glory, but we now know some of the elements of an explanation.
>
> —(Calvin, 1996, p. 11)

Common Perceptions

It is highly improbable that a reader of this book would not have a basic conceptualization of what intelligence is. You have heard and read about intelligence through a variety of media over your lifetime, and it is likely that you have engaged in some direct study of the topic in your formal educational experience. It is also safe to assume that you are provoked on many occasions (perhaps while at work or listening to the evening news?) to reflect, discuss, or even write about intelligence as it relates to qualities present or lacking in human behavior. To demonstrate to yourself the understanding your brain has constructed about intelligence, we suggest that you take a minute (literally) to complete the following sentence stem:

Intelligence is _____.

Invariably, this prompt produces a wide range of responses about what individuals understand intelligence to be. There are, however, statements and themes that commonly emerge, some of which are presented here for comparison with your definition:

Intelligence is the ability or capacity to solve problems, organize information and act on it, reason, think, respond to novel situations, figure things out, learn, imagine and create, make judgments and decisions.

Authoritative Interpretations

Perhaps your informal definition of intelligence coalesces around one of the definitions listed above. It is also possible that your intelligent brain has organized a significantly different interpretation. In any case, your personal understanding of intelligence is a good base from which to reference what authoritative sources think it is. For example:

- What you use when you don't know what to do (J. Piaget, 1923/1990).
- A triarchic composition of ability to contextually adapt to environments, experientially cope with novel situations, and componentially process information effectively (R. Sternberg, 1985).
- Guessing well (Barlow, 1987).
- Slipping the bonds of instinct and generating novel solutions to problems (J. Gould & C. Gould, 1994).
- Dimensions of neural efficiency, experiential knowledge and reflective thinking strategies that contribute to intelligent behavior (D. Perkins, 1995).
- A biopsychological potential to process information that can be activated in a cultural setting to solve problems or create products that are of value in a culture (H. Gardner, 1999).

You may find this sampling of expert observations about intelligence to be a bit troubling in its breadth of interpretation. You might even be moved to ask whether anyone really knows what intelligence is. The quick and honest answer to that question is—no. More specifically, humans posses a mental capacity that has evolved to a point of awareness of itself and a disposition and ability to investigate itself but has yet to fully explain itself. You are confronted, then, with this reality of being in the middle of a grand human inquiry about the nature of human intelligence, an inquiry that has been in progress for several thousand years and has no foreseeable end. Some judge it to be the ultimate investigation—intelligence in search of itself. It is an investigation that has progressed remarkably in recent decades, but an investigation, nevertheless, susceptible to developments that flare, muddle, and fizzle.

And the Theory Goes On and On and On

The pursuit of understanding human intelligence has generated a range of theoretical interpretations over time. Theorists, drawing on scientific knowledge of the moment, have variously constructed interpretations that describe intelligence as general, multiple, genetic, fixed, malleable, experiential, neural, modular, triarchic, fluid, and reflective in nature. Such theoretical interpretations, along with hosts of definitional interpretations, are representative of ongoing attempts to get a conceptual handle on the phenomenon of human intelligence.

Alas, intelligence theory will always be a work in progress because the target concept moves with new insights from ongoing research in diverse fields of study. Significant evolution of theory has occurred, however, in recent years. Gardner (1999) is representative of a contemporary perspective of human intelligence that embraces the interplay of genetic and environmental factors with multiple intellectual faculties. His theory of multiple intelligences proposes a spectrum of at least seven facets of human intellectual capacity: verbal, mathematical-logical, spatial, kinesthetic, musical, interpersonal, and intrapersonal. Sternberg (1996) identifies academic, practical, and creative classifications of intelligence. In alignment with these interpretations of a multiplicity of human talents subject to environmental influence, David Perkins (1995) advocates for a "Copernican shift" (p. 5) toward understanding the nature of intelligence as multidimensional and learnable. This new perspective of intelligence as *multidimensional and malleable* draws on recent and emerging research across the biological and social sciences. It represents a departure from the influential perspective of intelligence that emerged from the early 20th-century work of psychometric investigators such as Alfred Binet, H. H. Goddard, and Charles Spearman. That perspective packaged intelligence as a single, genetically endowed and fixed entity that was measurable by assessment instruments that could interpret prospects for life success. Suffice it to say that the new view capitalizes on current knowledge about the human brain to break away from a limited and inhibiting understanding of human intelligence. Indeed, one might observe that a historically puritan perspective of human intelligence has been discounted in favor of a more generous and encompassing contemporary view—one that embraces dimensionality and growth.

A Serviceable Conceptual Orientation

The challenge of defining intelligence, then, is that it must be defined within a context of emerging information from an ongoing investigation of incredible complexity. Subsequently, there is the inevitability of moving through incomplete and conflicting interpretations. In the meantime, what we have to go on is what we have to go on—and go on we must.

Calvin (1996) thinks of intelligence as "the high-end scenery of neurophysiology—the outcome of many aspects of an individual's brain organization that bear on doing something that one has never done before" (p. 11). This is a useful conceptual orientation to intelligence. It speaks to a capacity to organize and use information to advantage—particularly in novel situations. It is a conceptualization that draws from the previously cited developmental psychology interpretation of Piaget and the neuroscience interpretations of Barlow, and Gould and Gould. It is also a general definitional perspective that accommodates current theory about the multiple and malleable nature of intelligence as described by Gardner, Sternberg, Perkins, and others. And when the dust clears at the end of the definitional debates, it is fairly

simple language about the capacity of the human brain to figure things out—
language that is consistent with a straightforward dictionary definition of intelligence: "the capacity to acquire and apply knowledge" (*American Heritage Dictionary*,
2000, p. 910). Thus from myriad definitional explorations, a serviceable conceptualization of intelligence emerges:

Intelligence: *The collective attributes of the brain that contribute to the acquisition and
application of knowledge in diverse and novel situations.*

A Phenomenon of Self and Systems

Intelligence, in one of its most basic senses, is the capacity to solve problems,
meet challenges, or create valued products. In this sense, organizational intelligence represents that capacity as it emerges from the complex interplay
of people and relationships, culture and roles within an organization.

—(Goleman, 1998, p. 297)

In considering definitional perspectives of human intelligence, it is also important
to note that intelligence is a phenomenon that operates within individuals *and* systems.
This is a particularly important perspective for the examination of the relationship between leadership, intelligence, and the achievement of organizational purpose. Simply
put, intelligence occurs within the individual, but it is also exercised within groups as a
collective capacity to acquire and apply knowledge in diverse and novel situations. Subsequently, leadership involves a relationship to the intelligence of the individual (i.e.,
both of self and individual members of the organization) as well as the collective intelligence of the membership of the organization (i.e., the system).

Enlightenment

A Story . . .

While sharing information with a group about his travels across the broad
savannas of Africa, a friend showed photographs of spectacular sunrises
and sunsets. The powerful visual images of the sun rising and setting above
the hauntingly beautiful African landscape evoked a strong response from
the audience, and many comments came forth about the extraordinary displays of color and contrast that had been captured on film. These emotional
musings about solar artistry were interrupted, however, by the photogra-
pher's observation that people tended to be intrigued by the rise or demise of
the sun in unique settings, yet oblivious to the beauty of the same event in
their own backyard—whether that backyard be composed of water, moun-

tains, cornfields, or city landscapes. This comment created a reflective si-
lence in the room. It was, to be sure, not an original insight, but it struck a
chord with our group. It reminded us of a sometime troubling aspect of
human nature—a capacity for overlooking what is readily available to be
seen and appreciated.

Seeing What Is There to Be Seen

Similar to the human proclivity to overlook the presence of everyday beauty is
the possible oblivion of many to the ubiquitous nature of human intelligence. This
pattern is demonstrated by society's intrigue (fed by the mass media) with displays of
prowess and success by the famous and powerful. People are seemingly dazzled with
the brilliance of the scholar, CEO, politician, or artist who excels but are blind to the
intelligence that surrounds and glows within each human being. At what cost does
society sustain such limited vision of where and how intelligence shines? What ex-
cuse does society have for maintaining such a myopic view, given the quantity and
quality of available knowledge about the nature of human intelligence at the beginning of the 21st century?

Ultimately, failure to engage and appreciate contemporary knowledge about
human intelligence is a particularly ironic example of human capacity to overlook
readily available information of consequence. The price of being oblivious to such
knowledge, unfortunately, is to be denied insight into the spectacular architecture
and artistry of that which defines humankind—and the guidance therein for how
best to conduct human affairs.

Sunrise

At the dawn of a new century, light is being cast in dramatic fashion on the nature of human intelligence. Technology-assisted investigations into the physiological
architecture and processes of human anatomy have been particularly effective in further prying the lid off of what has been the "mysterious black box" of the brain. Magnetic resonance imaging (MRI) technologies provide cross-sectional images of the
soft tissues of the living brain. Through functional magnetic resonance imaging
(FMRI), this technology has evolved to a point where it can observe real-time cognitive activity in the brain. Positron emission tomography (PET) is an imaging process
that tracks the consumption of radioactive tainted glucose in the brain to map mental
activity. Electroencephalographic (EEG) and magnetoencephalograhic (MEG)
mappings read faint electrical outputs and magnetic fields generated by the brain's
neural networks, thereby measuring brain wave patterns and activity during specific
events. The technology of spectrometers adds further insight into the workings of the
brain through measurement of the status of essential brain chemicals (i.e.,
neurotransmitters) during different brain states and activities.

Integrated with investigations across many fields of scientific inquiry—such as
evolutionary biology, animal research, and clinical studies of human subjects—

microtechnology-abetted neuroscience has generated an exciting, almost surreal advancement in information about the inner workings of the brain. The information thus revealed by this technological boost to brain research is capturing the attention and imagination of observers well beyond the scientific community. Insight into the collection of organs that enable human intelligence intrigues people. It is, after all, information that sheds original light on the essence of humankind—illuminating how and why we think, feel, learn, and act. People cannot help but be attracted to this dawn of new knowledge. It is real-time revelation about what makes us . . . us, revelation that responds to a long and prevailing human inquiry.

Moving through a significant threshold of knowledge by virtue of accumulated study and technological breakthrough, we are at the dawning of a new age of investigation about our capacity to think and learn and achieve—a period of enlightenment about the human brain that is of a historical magnitude. What has been hidden and mysterious to us is now being revealed—how the brain processes sensory information, constructs meaning and memory, employs emotion, and reflectively applies prior knowledge. What had been suspected or assumed is either verified or challenged by the science now available. The intuitive speculation that "the mind once stretched never returns to its original shape" is now verifiable through microtechnologies that expose the environmentally stimulated construction of dendrite-axon connections between neural cells. That is, the physical stretching of the brain's neural network can now be physically observed. The significance of such direct confirmation of the plasticity of neural networking cannot be overestimated, given that it repudiates the once common perception of human intelligence as fixed by nature and unalterable by nurture.

A Moment to Be Seized

The occasion of a convergence of scientific enlightenment about the nature of human intelligence generates a need for leaders to judge the implications of this new knowledge for appropriate adjustments in leadership practice. If the turn of the 21st century is truly witnessing a *Louis Moment*, that is, a time of breakthrough revelation about the structures and operations of the human brain, the challenge becomes one of how to seize this moment to advantage. A practical first step in seeking such an advantage, we suggest, would be an investigation of current knowledge about human intelligence. If hidden secrets of the human brain are being revealed, a leader should consider the return that might be realized from a small investment of time spent peering into the heretofore black box to see what is there for the seeing. If the information thus obtained proves to be of interest and of some value for guiding leadership behavior, the investment of time will be worthwhile. If, on the other hand, the information proves to be interesting but inconsequential, the leader will have the comfort of having explored and judged the merits of an initial offering of new knowledge. In any case, it is ill advised for a leader to be oblivious to this historical opportunity, an opportunity to engage emerging knowledge that may have the potential to incite a

Copernican revolution in leadership perspective and behavior. It is an opportunity, no less, to become more intelligent about intelligence—in both thought and deed.

Getting a Grip

A Daunting Sea of Knowledge

A standard joke heard at professional gatherings that focus on emerging knowledge about the human brain goes something like this: "You are going to be introduced to a great amount of new and exciting information about the human brain at this conference . . . some of which is undoubtedly true."

Knowledge about the human brain is vast, complex, and constantly adjusting to new revelations from ongoing scientific investigation. This circumstance presents a dilemma. Intriguing new information about the nature of human intelligence is pouring forth from a multitude of sources, yet we are a long way from having the full story. What we think we know today may be significantly altered or even stood on its head by tomorrow's new discovery. The dilemma is that, despite its emergent nature, we are compelled to examine the implications of this information for leadership practice. Accordingly, if this growing and shifting reservoir of knowledge is to productively influence perceptions of effective leadership behavior, it must be organized and interpreted in a practical fashion. It must also be approached from an honest assessment of what is realistic and necessary for a leader to know.

Knowledge to Navigate By

Given that most leaders do not have the time or inclination to pursue a parallel career in neuroscience, a practical approach to constructing personal knowledge about the human brain is to engage interpretations and summaries that distill essential information. More specifically, the recommended strategy is judicious engagement of sources that focus on productive areas of investigation. This approach is similar to the discrimination practiced in the selection of dig sites by paleontologists, anthropologists, and archaeologists. These scientists do not excavate at random in their pursuit of discovery about life in the geological and historical past. Rather, they carefully judge the merits of candidate investigation sites by evidence of prior and potential productivity. Thus we observe the focusing of such investigations in potent discovery areas like the Black Hills region of North America, the Olduvai Gorge of Africa, and river and coastal sites in the Middle East. In like manner, the next chapter will adopt a discriminating approach in introducing the reader to dimensions of the human brain that have been productively investigated and hold promise for yet further revelations about the nature of intelligence.

With a focus on productive information sites, the distillation of essential understanding from a plethora of available resources can proactively attend to the summarization of knowledge from credible experts and translators. Thus a leader will expeditiously organize essential knowledge about the brain through the cultivation of core, heart-of-the-matter information from available sources (see Figure 2.1). Such an approach is compatible with what Gazzaniga (1998) tells us is the brain's natural affinity for acquiring the "gist" of things rather than attending to details.

Let the Distillation Begin

Without a provisional framework, we would be simply swamped with data, knowing neither what we should be looking for nor what it might mean.

—(Mithen, 1996, p. 62)

Organize information about the brain as you will, but organize it you must if you aspire to acquire knowledge that has the potential to inform effective leadership behavior. To that end, the next chapter will model a gist (i.e., general sense of) and essence (i.e., essential qualities of) organization of information about select dimensions of the nature of human intelligence. The dimensions to be considered arise from an orientation to the brain's survival business—a business that operates multiple and malleable facets of intelligence. They are not, to be sure, *the* dimensions of human intelligence. They are, however, representative of rich investigation sites—fertile ground on which to construct personal understanding about the brain. Indeed, it might be useful to think of each dimension as a physical space that you will visit to observe and reflect about an important quality of intelligence—a room with a particular view, as it were, of the nature of intelligence:

- **ℙ** A **physiological** dimension that provides the platform of cells, circuits, and chemicals that enable the acquisition and application of knowledge
- **Ⓢ** A **social** dimension that provokes and refines the acquisition and application of knowledge
- **Ⓔ** An **emotional** dimension that arouses, focuses, and motivates the acquisition and application of knowledge
- **Ⓒ** A **constructive** dimension that discerns and organizes information patterns that underlie the acquisition and application of knowledge
- **Ⓡ** A **reflective** dimension that directs the acquisition and application of knowledge
- **Ⓓ** A **dispositional** dimension that determines the efficiency and effectiveness of the acquisition and application of knowledge.

Summary Observations

- Leadership is intimately connected to the brain by virtue of body physiology and the brain's mediation of all human behavior.

Figure 2.1. Distillation of Essential Knowledge About the Nature of Intelligence

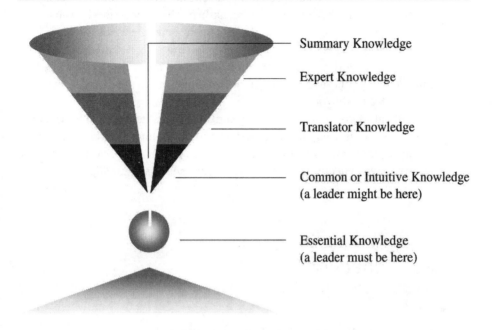

- Summary Knowledge
- Expert Knowledge
- Translator Knowledge
- Common or Intuitive Knowledge (a leader might be here)
- Essential Knowledge (a leader must be here)

- *Expert:*   Knowledge that is original, extensive, refined, or profound
- *Translator:*   Summation and interpretation of expert knowledge
- *Common:*   Knowledge that is known to most people
- *Intuitive:*   Understanding something without reasoning or being taught
- *Summary:*   Knowledge of major points

- The leadership-brain connection is ultimately defined by the intelligence the brain enables.
- The brain's purpose is to manage the survival success of its host organism. Human intelligence emerged from this survival business as a highly refined capacity to interpret, organize, and apply information to a survival advantage.
- When human intelligence evolved to a point where it became aware of itself, it began to investigate itself—it wanted to understand its nature and potential.
- Although it is universally valued and studied, intelligence has yet to be defined due to its extraordinary complexity. A serviceable definition is that intelligence is the collective attributes of the brain that contribute to the acquisition and application of knowledge—particularly in novel situations. This definition might be shortened to *the capacity to acquire and apply knowledge.*
- The nature of human intelligence is multidimensional and malleable.
- Intelligence operates at individual and systems levels.

- By virtue of a historical convergence of new technologies and accumulated knowledge across a wide spectrum of scientific investigation, the beginning of the 21st century is witnessing a breakthrough in understanding about the nature of the human brain and the intelligence it enables.
- To efficiently and effectively seize the opportunity represented in this *Louis Moment* of scientific breakthrough, a leader will advisedly develop essential knowledge about the nature of human intelligence as a means to inform more effective leadership practice.
- A practical approach to constructing personal understanding about the nature of intelligence is to engage sources that summarize information from productive areas of scientific research and theory (i.e., physiological, social, emotional, constructive, reflective, and dispositional dimensions of intelligence).

Reader Reflection

- Intelligence is . . . ?

- Leaders should be knowledgeable about the nature of intelligence because . . . ?

- A good way to organize personal understanding about the nature of intelligence would be to . . . ?

- The benefit of a gist-and-essence understanding of the nature of intelligence is . . . ?

- Other thoughts and questions?

3

Revelations

And here we are, sitting in a hut in the woods,
looking back on a process that has taken three or four
billion years. And in us, this long process has finally
become aware of itself.

—Jostein Gaarder (1996, p. 426)

Chapter Orientation

Getting to Know You

A brain-friendly way to engage information about the nature of human intelligence is to access what your brain already knows about itself. To that end, take a moment to locate a pen or pencil and write down

1. Three or four things you know about your brain
2. One or two questions you might have about your brain

> *Reflection Time*

Gaarder's (1996) Darwinian analysis of the evolution of life on Earth concludes that several billion years after its inception in the primal seas of a young planet, life evolved to an awareness of itself. That is, evolution produced within the human species a capacity whereby life became consciously aware of its relationship to the grand schemes of nature. As you are presently engaging this capacity in a conscious reflection about itself, you might appreciate the magnitude of its evolution. The good news is that it is relatively natural and easy for you to do so.

Your response to the reflection exercise above demonstrates a natural appreciation for the workings of the brain. When you take time to think about it, you realize you know and want to know things about your brain. What you specifically know or want to know is not really that important. What matters is that you are a member of a species that is motivated and able to accumulate such knowledge. The purpose of this chapter, then, is to describe and engage a strategy that builds on that interest—a strategy for extending knowledge and answering questions about your brain and the intelligence it enables.

Getting a Grip on the Multidimensional You

Brains make sense of the world by selectively processing information and constructing useful mental patterns and models. A human brain is subject to this behavior in all circumstances, including an investigation of itself. Accordingly, anyone who aspires to understand the nature of the human brain and the intelligence it enables must embrace two realities:

1. Your brain cannot construct useful patterns or models (i.e., understanding) without first accessing and processing relevant information. That is to say, if you have a thirst for knowledge, you have to go to the river and draw water. In this particular instance, the source to be tapped is the reservoir of information about the human brain.

2. Your brain need not engage all available information to construct useful patterns and models. A river of knowledge most often contains more than what can be productively consumed. Consequently, you need to be selective about where and what to draw from the reservoir of information about the human brain.

With these admonitions in mind, what might a leader do to organize the torrent of emerging knowledge about the human brain? A necessary first step, as suggested in Chapter 2, is to engage sources of interpretive and summary information as available through literature, video, the Internet, seminars, or other mediums (the annotated bibliography presented in Resource B is a place to start). A leader is also well-advised, as a practical consideration for anyone not versed in cognitive and neuroscience, that such inquiry be attentive to established investigation sites. This chapter will model said approach by introducing information from investigations into physiological, social, emotional, constructive, reflective, and dispositional dimensions of human intelligence (see Figure 3.1). In doing so, the construction of a refined knowledge base will be facilitated—a base that will be useful to ideas presented in following chapters. Construction of this knowledge base will also demonstrate a practical means for getting a grip on information about the nature of human intelligence in a manner that aids interpretation of connections to leadership practice—a process that will be described more extensively within a framework presented in Chapter 6.

Figure 3.1. Dimensions of the Nature of Intelligence

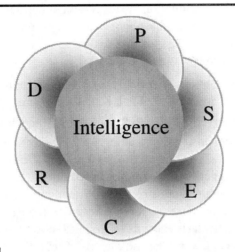

- Physiological
- Social
- Emotional
- Constructive
- Reflective
- Dispositional

Caveats

1. The dimensions of intelligence addressed in this chapter are not *the* dimensions of the nature of human intelligence; rather, they are credible and useful organizers for the construction of a personal knowledge base about significant qualities of the nature of intelligence. As noted in the previous chapter, intelligence has been sliced many ways by many theorists—an inevitability when dealing with an open and complex concept. In response to this circumstance, each dimension of intelligence presented herein was selected on the basis of three criteria:

   - It represents a productive area of scientific investigation that draws on the research and theory of substantial and authoritative sources.
   - Its absence would render human intelligence either inoperable or dysfunctional.
   - It is functionally applicable to the leadership framework that follows in Chapter 6.

2. Chapter sections examine select dimensions of intelligence in a sequence (i.e., physiological, social, emotional, constructive, reflective, dispositional)

by which the dimensions initially considered contribute information relevant to the examination of subsequent dimensions. In any case, if you are already knowledgeable about any content presented within the chapter, you may wish to fast-forward to the *Essence* and *Implications* summaries at the end of that section.

3. The investigations of various dimensions and qualities of the human brain will be up close and personal, with direct reference to *your* brain—because your brain is naturally disposed to be interested in itself.

4. Specific dimensions or qualities of intelligence never operate independently of each other. A dimensional organization of information about the nature of intelligence is employed herein to facilitate your brain's construction of understanding about a complex phenomenon. The multiple dimensions of human intelligence, however, operate as an integrated whole. That integration is particularly evident—as you will soon observe—in your brain's construction of knowledge and exercise of reflective thinking.

The Nature of Human Intelligence: Gist, Essence, and Implications

Nature: The essential characteristics and qualities of a person or thing

—(*American Heritage Dictionary*, 2000, p. 1172)

The information that follows in this chapter about the qualities and characteristics of human intelligence is organized into six sections that address the physiological, social, emotional, constructive, reflective, and dispositional nature of human intelligence. Each section addresses a particular dimension of intelligence through content that describes:

1. The **gist** of the dimension: basic information useful in forming a general sense of the dimension

2. The **essence** of the dimension: a summation of essential qualities of the dimension

3. The leadership **implications** of the dimension: initial observations about ways to align leadership behavior to the dimension

The intent of this format for organizing and processing content, then, is to facilitate your brain in its progressive distillation and construction of personal knowledge about the nature of human intelligence.

Ⓟ The Physiological Nature of Intelligence

Let's Get Physical

The physiological architecture of the human brain is the platform on which human intelligence performs its extraordinary feats of conscious thought. It is also the biological bridge to an extended physiology of subconscious intelligence. Accordingly, construction of personal understanding about the nature of human intelligence is served by an orientation to its physiological underpinnings—a peek, as it were, under the hood.

The Gist of It

First Impressions

Picture yourself lifting the top of your skull, removing your brain, and holding it in your hands (we know you can do this because of your brain's capacity for imagination). You will note that it weighs approximately three pounds and is comparable in size to a large grapefruit or two fists held together palm to palm. This soft biological mass is composed primarily of water (78%), fat, and protein. It is slippery from the protective fluid and thin membrane that buffer it within the hard shell of the cranial skull. There in your hands is the major component of the human central nervous system. Neurally and chemically connected to the entire human physiology, it simultaneously monitors and regulates other body organs and systems, operates movement and communication, and centrally processes environmental information. You are contemplating the collection of biological structures that enables conscious contemplation. With brain in hand, you are gazing on and thinking about that with which you think.

On this initial observation, the human brain thus exposed may appear somewhat inadequate for the important and complex tasks attributed to it. Subsequently, to understand how the brain performs its myriad responsibilities, you will find it useful to examine the components of this special parcel of anatomical real estate. To that end, the geography of the human brain is mapped in a variety of ways by neuroscientists to organize relationships between its physical components and perceived functions. Such mapping describes the physiological terrain of the brain by regions, structures, hemispheres, lobes, areas, cells, and circuits. New technology has recently enhanced such territorial investigation, progressively revealing the operational secrets of specific locations within the brain. Understanding of the holistic operations of this integrated collection of biological structures, however, remains a more difficult puzzle to solve. Nevertheless, mapping the territory is a necessary and valuable approach to composing the big picture of the inner workings of your brain. Your exploration thus proceeds to examination of exterior regions.

Surface Features

Scanning the exterior of your brain, you will observe first and foremost the *cerebrum*, the large forebrain component of the central nervous system that almost completely enfolds other brain structures. A lateral view of this structure is perhaps the most common visual image people have of their brain (see Figure 3.2). The surface of the cerebrum is dominated by the convolutions of its mantle area called the *cerebral cortex*. This outer, gray matter region of the cerebrum is about the thickness of a grapefruit peel (cortex is from Latin for bark or rind). A rich vertical and horizontal networking of neural cells dominates it. The horizontal organization is marked by a six-layer lamination of cells, and the vertical organization features a multitude of columnar structures. It is deeply folded as an evolutionary means to provide maximum surface space and, thereby, maximization of the number of brain cells that can be accommodated within the restricted space dimensions of the human skull. John Dowling (1998) captures the significance of this physiological feature in his observation that the human brain is qualitatively similar to the brains of other animals but quantitatively different. That is, a more highly developed cerebral cortex is the physiological base from which the higher neural functions of humans evolve—such as language, logic, and creativity. If you were to compare the cortex of your brain to that of other highly evolved animals, particularly your primate relatives, you would quickly discern the extreme advantage in size and density of the cortical area of the human brain. The cortex is, indeed, the crowning glory of human brain mass. Most significant, the majority of the neurons housed in your cortex are undedicated, meaning they are not committed to specific survival tasks. Rather, they are abundantly available on demand to be applied to any thinking task that arises. Accordingly, as we shall consider in later sections and chapters, this brain territory is a primary leadership connection target.

Hemispheres

As you further observe the surface of your brain, you will notice deep furrows or fissures within the folds of the cortex. Most noticeable is the prominent enfolding called the medial sulcus, which divides the cerebrum from front to back into two hemispheres (see top view of brain presented in Figure 3.2). The motor areas of the right hemisphere are responsible for movement on the left side of the body, and the left hemisphere is responsible for movement on the right side of the body. The two hemispheres are connected, however, by a thick concentration of neural communication fibers known as the *corpus callosum*. The significance of this connection is that your brain is able to (and does) have each hemisphere assume different processing styles and responsibilities while maintaining a communication bridge that informs and coordinates the activities of one with the other. Again, it appears that this is an evolu-

Figure 3.2. Lateral and Top View of the Human Brain

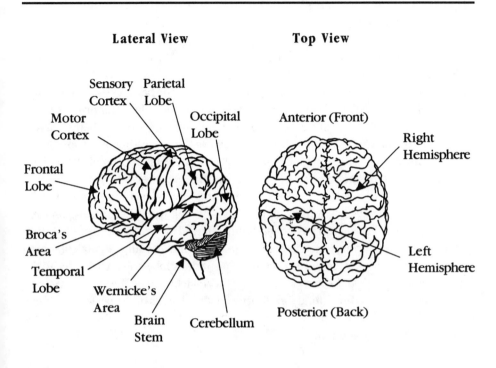

tionary strategy that seeks to maximize the efficiency of available brain resources. While one hemisphere is processing information in parts and sequence, controlling fine motor skills, and recognizing positive emotional states, the other is seeing the larger picture, controlling gross motor skills, and responding to negative emotional states. In effect, your brain determines which hemisphere will do what but insists that the two keep in touch with each other about what they are doing. This differentiation and interplay between hemispheres is made more interesting by the fact that hemisphericity varies in individuals by nature and nurture.

Lobes, Strips, and Areas

Neuroscientists divide each cortical hemisphere of the brain into four lobes (again, reference Figure 3.2). Rotating your brain in your hands, you can locate the area that aligns with your forehead. This area of each hemisphere is called the *frontal lobe*. The foremost portion of this area is the prefrontal lobe, which is associated with critical thinking, problem solving, creativity, and planning—the complex reasoning processes that most distinguish the mental abilities of humankind. Reflective mediation of emotional responses is attributed to an interior region of this area called the *orbitofrontal cortex*. To the lower rear of the frontal lobe in the left hemisphere (reversed to the right hemisphere in 5% of the population) is a portion of cerebral landscape referred to as *Broca's area.* Located in proximity to the primary motor area associated with face, tongue, and jaw movements, this area is concerned with the production of language—another distinguishing human capacity. Immediately behind the frontal lobe in each hemisphere is a strip called the *motor cortex,* which controls voluntary movement in the opposite side of the body.

Rotating your brain 180 degrees, you will observe the back area of each hemisphere called the *occipital lobe.* This area has primary responsibility for processing visual information. The area of the brain above the occipital lobe in each hemisphere is called the *parietal lobe.* Its primary functions involve the processing of sensory information from the opposite side of the body. A strip at the front portion of the parietal lobe adjacent to the motor cortex is the called the *somatosensory cortex,* the area where your brain receives feedback about pain, pressure, temperature, and touch.

With a quarter turn of your brain to either side, you will locate the *temporal lobe* above and around the ear area in each hemisphere. This area assumes a primary responsibility for hearing as well as a role in memory and learning. A particular area at the junction of the left temporal, occipital, and parietal lobes (again, reversed to the right hemisphere in 5% of the population) has been identified as *Wernicke's area.* This site is located between the primary auditory and visual areas of the cortex and is primarily concerned with comprehension of speech as well as the organization of words in speaking, reading, and writing.

Below the Surface, Structures Large and Small

It is helpful at this point in your examination of your brain's physiology to bisect the entire mass front to back along the deep fold of the medial sulcus. This division of your brain into two halves provides what is known as a medial view of the brain, a view that reveals features and structures that are partially or completely hidden beneath the mantel of the cerebral cortex. You now have access to a mapping scheme that organizes the physiological terrain of your brain by regions of the hindbrain, midbrain, and forebrain (see Figure 3.3).

The *hindbrain* emerges from the *spinal cord* (the portion of the central nervous system that is not in the head but, in effect, is an extension of the brain) and is composed of the medulla, pons, and cerebellum. These combined structures are commonly referred to as the *brain stem* and, with the cerebellum, represent older architecture in the evolutionary development of your brain. The brain stem is a communication corridor for ascending sensory and descending neural information between brain and spinal cord connections to the rest of the body. A network of *nuclei* (i.e., clusters of brain cells called neurons) in this stem section form the *reticular formation* to regulate involuntary body motor activity such as heart rate, respiration, blood pressure, and gastrointestinal function in relation to what is happening in and around the body. This regulation operates subconsciously in the brain stem, thus re-

Figure 3.3. Medial View of the Human Brain

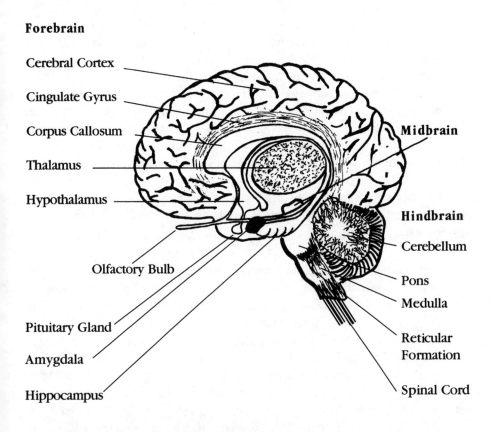

Forebrain

Cerebral Cortex

Cingulate Gyrus

Corpus Callosum   **Midbrain**

Thalamus

Hypothalamus

                                    Hindbrain

                                    Cerebellum

Olfactory Bulb

                                    Pons

                                    Medulla

Pituitary Gland

                                    Reticular

Amygdala   Formation

Hippocampus   Spinal Cord

lieving your conscious brain of constant attention to basic life-support system management. The reticular formation further extends its connections in the brain to form the *reticular activating system* (RAS) that regulates levels of arousal and consciousness in relation to changing conditions in the environment. The RAS performs this function by focusing on relevant stimuli and filtering out trivial sensory information. Nuclei in the brain stem also play a critical role in the production of chemical agents that assume cellular communication and maintenance roles throughout the brain. The *cerebellum* (Latin for *little brain*) is attached to the brain stem below the occipital lobes of the cerebral cortex at the back of the skull. It is associated with movement, balance, and memory of how-to procedures and processes that become automatic—such as riding a bike or multiplication tables. Communication between the cerebellum and cerebral cortex about body movement is mediated by neurons in the brain stem. A relationship is also suspected between the cerebellum and the cognitive activity that occurs in the frontal cortex when movement facilitates thinking and learning—as when you move to write, draw, act out, or verbally express what is in your head.

The *midbrain* is a relatively small area located at the top of the brain stem. This section is also referred to as the midbrain and tectum structure. Its responsibilities are to mediate visual reflexes and to coordinate head and eye movements. In the distant evolutionary past, the midbrain had more extensive responsibility for integrating sensory inputs and controlling motor outputs. As the mammalian brain evolved, however, much of this function was transferred to the cerebral cortex of the forebrain.

You have already observed the exterior of your *forebrain*. It rests on top of the hindbrain and midbrain and is composed of structures that mediate sensation, movement, memory, thinking, and consciousness. The longitudinal view before you, however, provides an interior perspective of the dominating proportion of the forebrain allocated to the folded cerebral cortex. You are also able to observe the arch of hundreds of millions of neural fibers in the corpus callosum that forms a communication bridge between the two cerebral hemispheres. Other structures in the forebrain are also observable:

- The *thalamus* (from Greek for *chamber* or *inner room*) is a walnut-size structure at the bottom of the forebrain in an area called the *diencephalon* just above the brain stem. It functions as a receiving and distribution center that relays incoming sensory and motor information to appropriate areas of the cerebral cortex for further processing, thus informing the brain about what is happening outside of the body and what the body is doing. All sensory information (with the exception of information from the olfactory system, which is directly networked to the cortex) is received and directed to other processing sites by the thalamus.
- Below the thalamus in the diencephalon is the thumbnail-size *hypothalamus*, which relays information about what is happening within the body to other areas of the brain. In interpreting and communicating such information, the hypothalamus serves a primary role in the regulation of basic drives and body states, such as temperature, sexual activity, and appetite. It also interacts with the pituitary gland, to regulate body state, and the medulla area of the brain stem, to control autonomic (subconscious) nervous system regulation of internal organs such as the heart, lungs, and bladder.
- The *pituitary gland* rests beneath the hypothalamus and is regulated by hypothalamic neurons that promote or inhibit the release of pituitary hormones into the bloodstream. Pituitary gland secretions, in turn, engage the endocrine system in the select release of other hormones into the bloodstream to adjust body chemistry in a manner dictated by the hypothalamus.
- The *hippocampus* is not actually observable to a medial view of your brain. If you peel back some layers of the temporal lobe area of the cerebral cortex, however, you will locate a crescent formation that is shaped a bit like a sea-

horse. This structure is associated with indexing of information throughout the brain, thereby enabling learning and the formation of memory.

- The *amygdala* is an almond-size structure that sits at the tip of the hippocampus. It is an area that processes sensory information in a manner that integrates emotion with memory. The amygdala thereby plays a role in initiating reflexive emotional behavior. It also prompts reflective reasoning about appropriate modulation of emotional responses.

Another Way to See It

A medial view of your brain also provides a general perspective of its stem-to-cortex evolutionary progression. This view of the organization of brain structures is particularly helpful to examinations of how and why the brain exercises reason and emotion, as presented in forthcoming chapter sections.

The structures of your brain stem and cerebellum represent features of a brain system that evolved approximately 500 million years ago. These elements of a more primitive central nervous system were all that was required of life forms—such as reptiles—that featured highly programmed regulation of body systems and responses to their environment. If your life experience consists of fixed patterns of feeding, fighting, fleeing, and reproducing, you really do not need much more than a brain stem and a cerebellum. Modern-day reptiles provide ample evidence of the adequacy of such a brain for managing the basics of movement, respiration, and digestion.

The next major stage in brain evolution occurred in mammals that developed new structures around the top of the brain stem—including the thalamus, hippocampus, and amygdala—that enabled more sophisticated processing of information patterns. The development of these mammalian brain structures, commonly referred to as the limbic system (from the Latin *limbus* for *ring*), maintained the services of the reptilian brain structures while adding refined capacity for learning, memory, and emotional response. This brain structure also featured the early development of a primitive cortex that is suspected to have evolved from the information-processing functions of the olfactory lobe.

As the survival needs of some mammals evolved to incorporate more elaborate multisensory information processing, your brain moved on to the next major stage of evolutionary development, leaving other mammals (e.g., dogs, cats, and pigs) far behind in both qualities of complexity and capacity. The major feature of this stage is observed in the development of a large cerebrum covered by a folded and multilayered cortex, a development that was notable in primates—and most dramatic in humans. This modern structure represents approximately 80% of your brain and contains the massive concentration of intricately connected nerve cells that enable conscious and complex reasoning. It is thoroughly integrated, nevertheless, with the structures and operations of the stem and limbic areas. Your brain is the product of progressive evolutionary developments, but you have one brain that incorporates the advantages of all of its evolutionary stages.

Going Micro . . .
Cells, Circuits, and Chemicals

Your exploration of brain features has been very basic to this point. Indeed, your examination has been very similar to that conducted by anyone (e.g., warrior, artist, or surgeon) who historically has had the opportunity and disposition to dismantle a human brain. This general orientation to the physiology of the brain is certainly a necessary and helpful beginning to understanding the physiological platform that enables your intelligence. Left at this stage, however, your investigation is comparable to observing the features of the earth from the vantage point of the moon. You have engaged the big geographical picture of brain structures, functions, and relationships. Now you are invited to move in for a closer look at the landscape. Employing the power of advanced microtechnologies, you will bring into focus the cellular and chemical foundations of human intelligence.

To begin, we suggest that you place the two halves of your brain back together and rotate it 90 degrees. Now slice it vertically from top to bottom into an anterior (front) section and a posterior (rear) section. Putting the anterior section aside, you now have a vertical cross-sectional view of the central posterior brain (see Figure 3.4) to orient your examination of neurons, glial cells, dendrites, axons, myelination, synapse, and neurotransmitters.

Matter Gray and White

Your first observational experience with the microstructure of your brain will note that which is visible to the naked eye. However you slice it, a cross section of the brain immediately reveals a coloration difference between dark and pale areas. The darker areas are commonly referred to as the *gray matter* and the lighter areas are referred to as the *white matter.* Gray matter areas get their dark hue from the concentration of brain cells known as *neurons* in the compact six layers of the cerebral cortex and in concentrated clusters called nuclei in the thalamus, hypothalamus, brain stem, and other areas of the brain. White matter areas draw color from the fatty white substance called *myelin* that coats fibers known as *axons,* which extend from neurons as communication channels to other neurons in the brain, both near and far. Given this visual image and basic background of information, you can see that your brain's cellular organization concentrates neurons in specific sectors (e.g., the cerebral cortex) and then massively connects those sectors by axonal networks (e.g., the corpus callosum). An impression, thereby, emerges of a system of interconnected systems. Different sectors have specialized capacities, but these sectors are intricately coordinated in communication and function.

The Neural Landscape

Your investigation of your brain must now rely on technological revelations about cellular structure and activity beyond the scope of the human eye. It is this mi-

Figure 3.4. Vertical Cross-Sectional View of the Central Posterior Brain

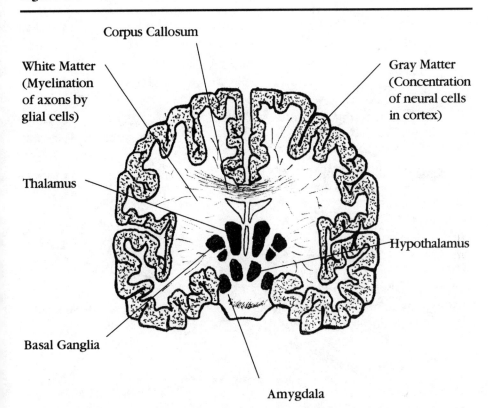

croscopic examination of gray and white matter that explains how your larger brain structures perform their magic.

The neuron is the principle cellular unit of the central nervous system (i.e., the brain). These cells are the units that receive, integrate, and transmit electrochemical signals in neural networks that produce body movement and mental activity. Indeed, all human behavior is the result of communication among neural cells. The three main components of a neural cell that collectively serve this information-processing responsibility are the *cell body*, an output fiber called the *axon*, and multiple input fibers called *dendrites* (see Figure 3.5). It works like this:

- Dendrite input fibers receive *neurotransmitter* (i.e., chemical) information from other neurons.

- The information received triggers electric energy in the dendrite that is then interpreted by the cell body to be either excitatory or inhibitory.

- Inhibitory input will cause the cell to rest.

Figure 3.5. Electrochemical Communication Between Neural Cells

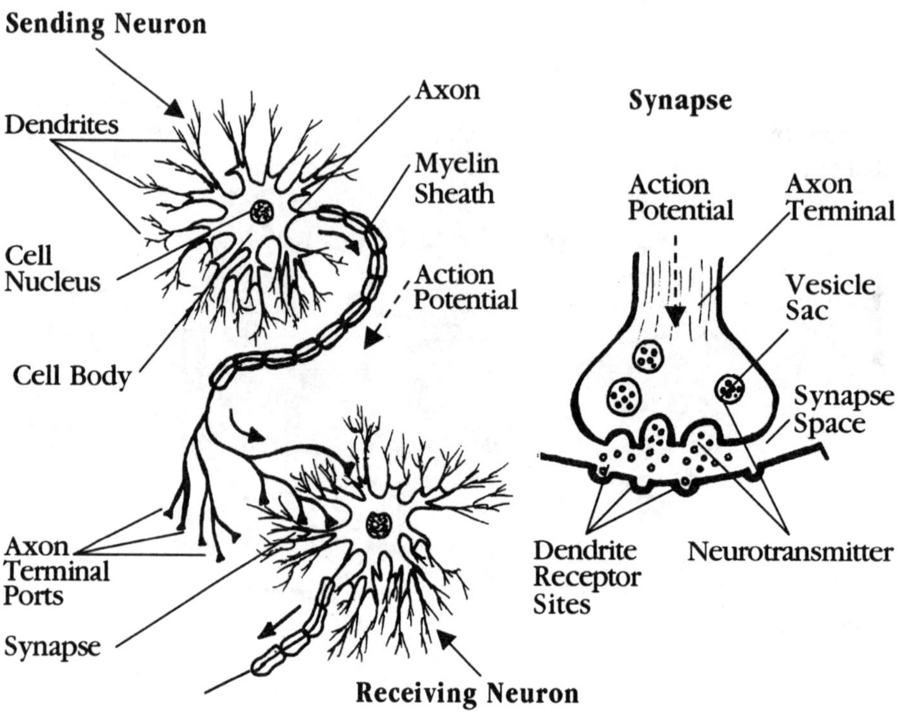

- Excitatory input will drive the cell body to generate an action potential (i.e., an electrical impulse that results from the interaction of positively and negatively charged ions of sodium, potassium, calcium, and chloride across the cell membrane).
- The axon conducts the electrical impulse as a stimulant to the release of neurotransmitters stored in vesicle sacs in its terminal ports.
- The neurotransmitters float into a *synapse*, a small space between the axon and a dendrite extension from another neuron (again, see Figure 3.5).
- Receptors on a dendrite receive the neurotransmitters, and the process is thus initiated in another neuron.

Simply stated, neurons are your brain's communication agents. These agents talk to one another through exchanges of electrochemical codes. You can visualize the process by looking at your right hand and arm. The palm of your hand represents the body cell of a neuron. Your fingers and thumb represent the dendrite extensions. When the dendrites receive a chemically coded message from a synapse interaction with another neuron (wiggle your fingers), that code may generate the firing of an electrical impulse (arch the palm of your hand), which is then conducted by the axon to its terminal ports (follow with your eyes the movement of the impulse from the palm of your hand to the tip of your elbow), where the stimulation causes the release of select chemicals into a synapse space between the axon terminal and a dendrite of another neuron (wiggle the fingers of your left hand next to your right elbow). Thus the conversation continues from neuron to neuron.

While this process may be simply visualized, it is much more difficult to comprehend in its full complexity and capacity. The human brain has a communication community of an estimated 100 billion neurons, which are concentrated in layers in the cerebral cortex and nuclei clusters in other brain structures, such as the thalamus, hypothalamus, hippocampus, amygdala, and brain stem. These neurons utilize nerve fibers and additional neurons in the spinal cord and hormone transmissions in the blood stream to communicate with and manage the entire body system. Consider further that approximately 30,000 neurons can fit on the head of a pin and that a single neuron may utilize hundreds of dendritic branches to communicate with tens of thousands of other neurons (Picture yourself having an ongoing conference call conversation with as many people!), each of which is linked to a like number of other neurons within a collective network that approximates a quadrillion (that's right, a million billion) neural connections. And all of this action takes place at a very fast pace with action impulses traveling down axons at speeds of up to 220 miles per hour—which may not seem extraordinarily fast until the distance covered is considered. With that perspective, the word instantaneous may come to mind (just as these words come to mind the instant you read them). If you put this statistical information together with reference to the complex body management and thinking tasks performed by the neural community within a human skull, a picture should begin to emerge of the awesome power of the neural engine that drives human intelligence.

The Supporting Cellular Cast

The work of neurons is supported by an estimated one trillion *glial cells.* More formally referred to as interneurons or neuroglia, glial (from Greek for "glue") cells provide the physical structure for the movement and organization of neurons in your brain. They also deliver nutrition and other maintenance services to neurons and form insulating *myelin* shields (i.e., white matter) around the axons of neurons. The myelination process is particularly important because the production of this fatty coating both protects and enhances the efficiency of communication signals between neurons throughout your brain. A useful mental picture, then, is that of a ten-to-one ratio between the supporting glial cell cast and the neural cell "stars" that produce mental activity and body movement. Glial cells provide the behind-the-scenes support that enables neural networks that sizzle and dazzle with capacity for processing and acting on information.

Messengers

Neurons are the communication agents of the brain, but neurotransmitters are the chemical messengers employed to do the actual communication footwork. Many different chemicals are in and around the cellular structures of your brain, perhaps as many as 100 different compounds. The word neurotransmitter is itself a general term that describes an array of chemicals that carry information in your brain. Neurotransmitters are generated and stored in neurons and, in response to excitatory stimulation, are released to be received by other neurons. It is by the interpretation of these chemically coded transmissions of information that neurons "talk" to each other and collectively direct human behavior.

The major types of neurotransmitters are *amino acids*, derivatives of amino acids called *amines*, and constructions of amino acids called *neuropeptides*. Amino acid neurotransmitters such as *glutamate, glycine, aspartate,* and *gamma-amino butyric acid (GABA)* directly carry rapid inhibitory and excitatory messages between neurons, thus performing essential on-off roles in neural communication. Amines are often called *neuromodulators* because they generally act at the synapse to modulate the reception of the amino acid neurotransmitters at the target neuron. Common amine neurotransmitters include the following:

- *Epinephrine.* Also known as adrenaline, epinephrine is produced and active in your brain as well as a hormone in the adrenal glands above the kidneys (a hormone is a chemical, usually a peptide or steroid, that is generated and released into the bloodstream from one part of the body to influence a physiological effect in other parts of the body). In both its neurotransmitter and hormone roles, epinephrine functions as a messenger that engages your brain in the communication of a stress response throughout the body.
- *Norepinephrine.* Also known as noradrenaline, norepinephrine is similar in composition and function to epinephrine. It is also produced as a hormone in the adrenal glands. Norepinephrine is the neurotransmitter most involved in the arousal of alertness and the fight-or-flight response that stimulates the eyes, heart, lungs, and release of energy to muscles while inhibiting the activity of the digestive and reproduction systems.
- *Dopamine.* Involved in the communication of body movement and positive moods or pleasure, imbalances of dopamine are associated with Parkinson's disease and schizophrenia.
- *Seratonin.* Associated with relaxation and the regulation of mood and sleep, depletion of seratonin has been linked to depression. Antidepressant drugs are designed to reduce the absorption and prolong the activity of seratonin in synapses.
- *Acetylcholine.* Although it is not truly an amine, acetylcholine is often associated with that group of neurotransmitters because of its capacity to modulate as well as directly excite or inhibit neural communications. It is associated primarily with muscular movement and memory formation.

Neuropeptides are neurotransmitters composed of chains of amino acids that are produced and active in your brain primarily as neuromodulators. Peptides are also produced elsewhere in your body where they perform a hormonal role, particularly in the stomach as a part of the biological mechanism of "gut instinct." Representative neuropeptide neurotransmitters are *endorphins* (your brain's natural opiates) that are associated with pain reduction and feelings of pleasure and euphoria.

A Work in Progress

A mind once stretched never returns to its original shape.

—(Anonymous)

Your examination of microlevel brain architecture and activity reveals the fundamental physiological exercise of your intelligence. It is at this level that the communication of electrochemically encoded information within a massively integrated community of billions of neurons is observed. This is the process that manages and directs all human behavior. It is a phenomenon of neural information processing that likely challenges your conscious brain's comprehension of its own complexity and potential. You may be understandably awestruck by the information-processing marvel in your hand, a biological mass that makes the most sophisticated computer technology look primitive in comparison. Indeed, you might reflect, it is the very information-processing capacity of the human brain that conceives and creates the information-processing capacity of computer technology.

But the news about human information-processing capacity gets even better if you observe brain cellular activity over time. Such observation reveals an extended development schedule, one that is literally lifelong. To observe the developmental experience of the human brain, you will once again utilize the visual enhancement advantages of microtechnology. This time, however, you will also reference time-lapsed video footage of the biological history of your brain's development.

Your historical investigation begins with the observation of your *neurogenesis* (i.e., development of your nervous system) in your mother's womb. About three weeks after your conception, mesoderm cells formed a flat structure called the *neural plate* on the backside of your embryo formation. In about a week's time, this plate folded inward to seal at the top and ends, thus forming a *neural tube.* The neural tube then became the structure that developed into your central nervous system. The anterior region evolved into your forebrain, midbrain, and hindbrain, and the posterior region became your spinal cord.

Viewing the film record of your prenatal brain development, you will be predictably impressed with both the quantity and quality of construction activity. You observe brain cells being generated at a rate of hundreds of thousands per minute during the remainder of your gestation period, producing an abundance of neurons that exceeds your eventual needs. These neurons then migrate to organized layers and clusters of the interconnected structures of your brain according to the genetic blueprint of the human genome you inherited through your parents. This migration is facilitated by *radial glia* (a type of glial cell) that provide scaffolding systems by which neurons find their way to the layers of the cortex and other predetermined locations. As your neurons collect at their designated stations, they begin to form synaptic connections and test initial communication networks by spontaneously firing electrical impulses. During this process your developing brain generates many more neurons and connections than will survive to the time of your birth. The apparent reason for this prolific production and networking of cells is to ensure the eventual success of neural communication systems. Accordingly, neurons that fail to migrate to the right location or establish proficient synaptical connections are pruned away to make way for the cellular networks that prove to be most advantageous to your brain's survival mission.

As you follow your brain's progress into the seventh month of development, you will note that the generation of neurons is complete and that neural pruning is under way long before you are born. You will also observe the development of convolutions in the cortical region as your brain begins to engage the structures and networks associated with sensory organs and the processing of environmental information. This brain development is what prepared you to come into the world hardwired to recognize sounds and shapes and other sensory patterns. As a matter of fact, you began to utilize this cortical region to organize and distinguish patterns of sensory information (the initiation of your human capacity to learn!) while still in the womb. Accordingly, you were familiar with various environmental patterns—such as your mother's voice—on your arrival into the world.

Now, to realize and appreciate a most important characteristic of human brain development, fast-forward the video record of your brain's cellular activity from birth to adolescence. What you will observe from this quick graphic survey of the youth of your brain is that it continually engages in the generation, restructuring, and pruning of neural networks. Your brain does this as a result of genetic directions for the timely construction of communication channels that serve developmental events in your life—such as mastery of visual and auditory acuity, bipedal mobility, and language. There is also, however, a determining element of environmental influence in this precocious networking activity. The basic rule at work here is that networks that are stimulated and productive are networks that are promoted and supported. A neuron will initially commit to associations with other neurons if there is either genetic direction or environmental stimulation to do so. Lacking sufficient exercise of electrochemical interaction, however, a neuron will either seek other neural relationships or simply die. Thus, neural networks associated with your ability to move, see, hear, talk, read, write, and problem solve are genetically installed in your brain and then extensively refined or diminished by their opportunities for environmental experience.

As you continue your video review, you will observe surges of neural network expansion, restructuring, and pruning during strategic periods of your childhood and adolescent development. These surges mirror progressive developmental stages, such as mastery of motor skills, language, and abstract thinking. An important point to make, however, is that modification of neural networking is *always* occurring in your brain, to a greater or lesser extent, throughout its development to a mature adult brain at about 16 years of age. Referencing time-sequenced atomic microscope imaging, you will notice a collective effect of this genetically induced and environmentally nurtured development. Specifically, you will see the extensive bifurcation (branching) of dendrites and myelination of axons extending from the neurons that originated in the womb many years earlier. This growth of "bushy" dendrites increases the mass of gray matter, and the myelinated sheathing of axons increases the mass of white matter. Together, the addition of this gray and white matter contributes to the significant weight increase that occurs in a human brain between birth (approximately one pound) and maturity (approximately three pounds).

This brain maturation process is exceedingly long in humans, reflecting biological commitment and adaptation to the qualities of the adult product. Simply put, by allowing for progressive and ongoing modification of neural networking over a prolonged period of time, nature produces an extraordinary physiological capacity for information processing. And here is the kicker—the really good news and a most salient reference point about adult brains—this trait of neural modifiability, often called *plasticity*, will continue throughout your lifetime.

In effect, the human brain is never complete. Studies conducted by Diamond, Krech, and Rosenzweig (1964), Greenough and Black (1992), and others have firmly established the positive effect of environmental enrichment on dendritic branching, synapse formation, and axon myelination in animals of all ages. Investigations of the effects of aging on the mental acuity of human subjects by Schaie and Willis (1986) and Snowdon (2001) are representative studies that draw the same conclusion— capacity to learn and, thereby, maintain and reconfigure neural networks throughout the life span is strongly correlated with the richness of environmental experience. Specific enrichment factors for humans include level of education, physical activity that enhances blood flow and oxygenation, professional and cultural activities that introduce novelty and challenge, perception of accomplishment and making a difference, and hanging out with smart people. Thus the physiological base of human intelligence is factory installed, but it is a base that is perpetually under construction.

All in all, it is a pretty good deal. You are given a genetic endowment of more neurons than you need plus the capacity to continually capitalize on and refine what you are given. A good deal, that is, if you take advantage of it. And you need to apply environmental stimulation to that end because it is not only a matter of using it or losing it, it is a matter of using and continually adjusting your neural architecture to ongoing advantage.

Maintaining the System

Stepping back from your technologically enhanced review of the cellular nature of your brain, you are once again observing a three-pound biological mass resting in the palm of your hand. As you move to replace it in its cranial nest, however, you might engage in one more reflection about its physiological circumstance, the quite obvious observation that your brain is connected to your body. A more specific observation is that your brain has a reciprocal arrangement with your body. The brain's business is the survival and welfare of its host body, and the brain is in turn dependent on the body for its own welfare. But ultimately, it is your brain that has the responsibility to make conscious decisions about these mutual welfare issues, and a wise brain takes good care of that which cares for it.

Your brain consumes approximately 20% of your body supply of energy in the process of operating and maintaining its neural networks. This is a demanding energy requirement for a biological system that represents only 2% of your body weight. This energy is obtained primarily from the flow of blood through the carotid artery, which supplies the brain with high levels of oxygen as well as nutrients like glucose, protein, and trace elements. Due to its high percentage of water composition, your brain also requires extensive and regular hydration. Other physiological welfare requirements of human brains include regular schedules of exposure to light (preferably natural) and opportunities to rest.

Your body serves the multiple welfare needs of your brain. The body provides nutrients and environmental activities that affect the brain, either directly or indirectly. So what should your brain communicate to its body about its welfare needs? Well, that topic can be exhaustively pursued through the review of related literature about diet, exercise, mental health, and the like. But a quick and serviceable response to the question is: Mom was right! That is to say, common cultural knowledge about healthy living practices—as commonly communicated by mothers to their children—is very much attuned to what is good for optimizing the brain-body relationship:

- Eat balanced meals of fruits, vegetables (particularly leafy greens and beans), fish, lean meats, whole grains, nuts, eggs, and dairy products that provide the proteins, unsaturated fats, minerals, and complex carbohydrates that nurture brain health and operation.
- Drink plenty of water, 8 to 12 glasses per day.
- Exercise daily and change body position often to enhance blood oxygenation and flow.
- Get a good night's sleep, and try to take brief naps during the day.
- Get out into the fresh air and natural light as much as possible.
- Breathe deep and laugh often.
- Take a daily multivitamin pill.
- Avoid excessive sugar, alcohol, caffeine, fast food, and artificial flavorings and additives.
- Tobacco and other drugs? What would Mom say?

Commonsense care of your body system has probably always been a matter of concern to you. As you replace the top of your skull and put your brain back into normal operation, however, you might now have a more refined perspective of what is at stake.

Attention to your physical welfare is not only a matter of a healthy body, it is very much a matter of a healthy mind.

Essence

The human brain is often in awe of the wonders of nature it encounters. You have undoubtedly found yourself in a position to experience this feeling—perhaps while observing the birth of a child, the beauty of a wilderness environment, or the infinity of stars in a clear night sky. The very brain that observes and ponders such wonders, however, has reason to stand in awe of itself. It is, after all, "the most complex structure, natural or artificial, on earth" (Green, Neinemann, & Gusella, 1998, p. 427).

- Your brain is composed of a three-pound collection of physiological structures that interactively regulate and operate all human behavior.
- The physiological evolution of your brain progressed from a base of structures for regulating body systems to structures that enable consciousness, emotional response, and reflective reasoning.
- Areas of your brain are associated with specific functions, but all areas work as an integrated system that constantly cross-references information.
- The fundamental base of your brain operations occurs at the cellular level through interneural communications. It is the transfer of electrochemically coded information between billions of neurons that enables all human behavior.
- Neural communication in the human brain is facilitated by networks of synapse exchange sites between dendrite and axon fibers that emanate from the body of neural cells. It is at these sites that electric impulses from neural cells cause axons to release neurotransmitters (chemicals) to the dendrite receptor sites of other neurons. Given that each one of an estimated 100 billion neurons may have thousands of dendritic branches available to receive neurotransmitter communications, the capacity of the human brain to process information approaches infinity.
- Some neural networks in the human brain are genetically dedicated to regulatory operations (e.g., respiration, body temperature) and, once established, are not altered over the life span. Other networks are genetically generated and environmentally reinforced for the operation of specific functions such as vision, movement, and language. The defining characteristic of the human brain, however, is the extensive expanse of neural circuitry that is undedicated and environmentally responsive. Concentrated in the cerebral cortex gray matter area of the brain, these neural networks exercise a capacity for plasticity over the life span. They are responsive to novel situations and, thereby, continually construct networks that accommodate new understanding and skills. They also enable the sophisticated mental activities of projec-

tion, creativity, and problem solving. Most important, this capacity for generating environmentally stimulated neural networks establishes the physiological base of intelligence modifiability—that is, human intelligence is not fixed but malleable by quality and quantity of environmental experience.

- Each human brain, absent significant developmental miscues or physical trauma, is a powerful physiological system for information processing. Every individual human brain, however, is rendered unique by its particular life experience.

- The human brain is connected to the entire physiology of the human body. It is a system of physiological systems within a physiological system. Accordingly, brain capacity for intelligence is affected by the care and nurture of its host system.

Implications

Whether a leader finds information about brain physiology to be interesting or a bit tedious, the question remains: What does this have to do with leadership—that is, what's the connection? A process that facilitates reflection about such connections is elaborated on in Chapters 4 through 7. The pump is primed here, however, with preliminary observations about how the physiological underpinnings of human intelligence might inform leadership behavior. (*Note:* Your active participation in this reflection is invited and encouraged.)

- *If* human intelligence is enabled by a brain physiology of incredible complexity, capacity, and environmental responsiveness, *then* leaders who ignore or abuse the biology of intelligence do so at the peril of their organizations and selves.

- *If* the quality of nutrition, hydration, movement, rest, oxygenation, and natural light received by the brain affects the optimal exercise of intelligence, *then* productive leadership connections to the complex thinking capacity of the brain require attention to the supporting physiological system of the body.

- *If* everything that a human brain experiences through its sensory mechanisms affects electrochemical exchanges and modulations within a network of a quadrillion synapses between the axons and dendrites of 100 billion neurons, *then* everything a leader does in interactions with associates has a physical effect on the flow of electrochemical energy and information within and between the brains of associates and the brain of the leader.

- *If* neural networking in the cortex of the brain is malleable by environmental experience, and its plasticity in learning continues throughout the life span, *then* leadership behavior influences environmental experiences that either stimulate or diminish neural development in the brains of associates—in effect, a leader unavoidably assumes responsibility for the cultivation of dendritic growth and synaptic connections in brains that are perpetual works in progress.

- *If* the human brain is organized into structures and spheres that assume responsibility for specific functions while operating as a comprehensive and highly integrated system, *then* a leader who is knowledgeable about basic brain structures and functions will have an orientation to the effect of his or her behavior on the brains of associates (e.g., is the behavior connecting with the emotional centers of the brain? . . . the neuron-rich gray matter of the cortex? . . . the regulatory services of the brain stem?).

- *If* _____,

  then _____.

- *If* _____,

  then _____.

⑤ The Social Nature of Intelligence

Now this is the Law of the Jungle—
As old and true as the sky;
And the Wolf that shall keep it may prosper,
But the Wolf that shall break it must die.
As the creeper that girdles the tree trunk,
The law runneth forward and back—
For the strength of the Pack is the Wolf,
And the strength of the Wolf is in the Pack.

—(Rudyard Kipling (born 1865, died 1936)
1968, p. 69)

Getting to Know You and Me and We

The human brain evolved from a long and rich history of social experience. Indeed, scientists are inclined to attribute its unique qualities of size, architecture, consciousness, and capacity for language and cognition to social roots. The physiological architecture of the human brain is the platform on which your intelligence performs, but social experience is an influential architect and operator of that platform. Accordingly, understanding the social nature of your brain—why and how it is social—is essential to understanding the intelligent mind it enables.

The Gist of It

Social: *Living together in organized groups or similar close aggregates. Inclined to seek out or enjoy the company of others. Of, relating to, or occupied with matters affecting human welfare*

(American Heritage Dictionary, 2000, p. 1649)

System: *A group of interconnecting, interrelated, or interdependent elements forming a complex whole*

(American Heritage Dictionary, 2000, p. 1757)

Nature's Way

For as much as individuals must be able to fight or flee, they need sociability. It is necessary for human survival. Children who are not held or given love when young may grow up disturbed, scared or dangerous. Adults who isolate themselves from the world are more likely to die at comparatively young ages. We have a central dependency on others. We are designed for group living. If we can begin to understand how the brain affects social functioning, we will have even more success as social creatures in the future.

—(Ratey, 2001, p. 335)

To understand why your brain is social, you need to start at the beginning—literally—with the subatomic particles spawned at the origin of the universe that organized into atomic structures, which in turn organized as the basic molecules present in the gas cloud of the protoearth. These basic molecules organized into more complex chemical compositions as the earth formed its solid mass and cooled to a temperature that supported liquid water. Taking advantage of this condition approximately 3.5 billion years ago, webs of interacting molecules complex enough to exhibit qualities associated with life (i.e., the ability to metabolize, reproduce, and evolve) culminated in the organization of cellular life forms. Nature thus demonstrated from the very beginning a dispositional pattern of organizing simple structures into complex and evolving systems. This pattern prevailed in creating a "world of stunning complexity where molecules join in a metabolic dance to form cells, cells interact with cells to form organisms, and organisms interact with organisms to form ecosystems, economies and societies" (Kauffman, 1995, p. vii). Thus the human brain is first and foremost the product of nature's dominating propensity to organize parts into systems—be they atoms or galaxies. Your brain exhibits this character as the most complex cellular and molecular system on earth, a system that is disposed to interact with like brain systems to organize and interact in a vast array of social systems—from families and teams to governments and religions.

Selfish gene theory provides further interpretation as to why the human brain is, in its biological essence, social. This theory proposes that individual life forms consistently do things that benefit the survival of their genes. Accordingly, individual cells and organisms engage in altruistic and cooperative behavior as the means to improve the chances that their common genetic code will survive, replicate, and participate in natural selection. Thus genes direct host cells in the organization of host organisms that range from relatively simple bacteria to the mass and complexity of whales. Repetition of this pattern is then observed as the organisms formed by societies of cells in turn organize societies of like organisms. Exemplars of such cooperative societies include ants, termites, bees, wolves, dolphins, and, of course, humans and their primate relatives.

Behind the biological development and operation of complex systems, then, is the principle that genes are selfish and cooperation works. To that end, genes form chromosomes, chromosomes form genomes, genomes form cells, cells form complex cells, complex cells form bodies, and bodies form colonies (Ridley, 1996). The human brain, from this theoretical perspective, is, thereby, both produced and directed by societies of genes dedicated to the construction of organic and social systems that serve their purposes of replication and participation in natural selection. This phenomenon becomes most interesting, of course, when genes evolve to a point where they create a host organism that becomes aware of the process—that is, a human organism (like yourself) that masters an advanced capacity for learning as the ultimate means to survive in unpredictable environments. At this stage, the organism's capacity for processing information, subjectively simulating alternatives, and predicting outcomes culminates in consciousness. Humans, thereby, realize the power to rebel against the dictates of their genes (Dawkins, 1991).

Four billion years, however, is just a long preface to the story of the social nature of human intelligence. If cooperation is woven into the genetic structure of all living things, what is special about the social nature of humans? That is the exciting part of the story, and the pace picks up as we fast-forward to mere millions of years ago when your ancestors began to realize the benefits of living in social relationships with like organisms . . . and one thing led to another.

The Experience

I sense that stepping into the light is also a powerful metaphor for consciousness, for the birth of the knowing mind, for the simple and yet momentous coming of the sense of self in the world of the mental.

—(Damasio, 1999, p. 3)

Over 50 million years ago your ancient primate ancestors had generated relatively large brain size by virtue of a propensity for good cost-benefit calculations and associative learning in pursuit of food sources (Mithen, 1996). They also benefited from the obvious advantages of living in social colonies. There was extended vigilance and combined defense against enemies as well as the calculated probability that predators would harvest slower and more immediately accessible members of the group rather than oneself. Collective numbers of eyes, ears, noses, and limbs enhanced the scavenging and foraging of food. Variables of group size and proximity favored mating opportunities. All of these circumstances enhanced prospects for survival, reproduction, and the natural selection of advantageous physiological adaptations.

Beyond the immediate advantages of cooperative group living was the subtle and determining effect of social interaction on the nature and nurture of the future human brain. In effect, the social context of existence became the cauldron in which human intelligence coalesced. You can best understand this by using that very intelligence to reflect on what your ancestor's social existence would provide, require, and reward.

Specifically, it was important to be attuned to the other members of the group if one were to take advantage of early warnings or communication of other important information. This need encouraged the development of refined sensory processing of visual and auditory information aligned to the body and vocal signals of associates. The name of the game was (and still is) that those who could best discern from verbal or nonverbal information what other members were doing, or were likely to do, had a survival edge. This skill in the interpretation of communication cues became an important means for establishing relationships and hierarchies among members of a group and, thereby, enhanced cooperative efforts at surveillance, food gathering, and problem solving. It also promoted capacity for memory of individuals, events, relationships, geography, and food sources. Ultimately, it placed a high premium on being attuned to the emotional status of others as a variable in anticipating behavior and opportunities therein.

The acquisition of emotional acuity was a pivotal development in the evolution of primates. It emerged from the refinement of social-observation skills over many millions of years to produce a sense of empathy and sympathy for the experiences of others. Siegel (1999) proposes that having this ability to "mind read" enabled rapid detection of the emotional state of another. In essence, your ancestors developed the neural ability to perceive and then feel what another member of the group was experiencing—they could *get into the head* of another and calculate options of reciprocity, cooperation, alliances, and deception. Most importantly, in the process of developing this capacity, *they became aware of self as separate from the other.* The operative term here is *aware,* as in consciousness. Social experience, thereby, moved beyond the promotion of brain capacity for organizing and processing environmental information to the prompting of a brain that was aware of its awareness. Thus informed, the selective pressure for what Humphrey (1976) termed social intelligence was refined in the brains of advanced primates and early humans through hypothesis building and testing about the behaviors of others. By the time your modern human ancestor arrived on the scene approximately 100 thousand years ago, this neural ability to infer, predict, and plan had become a defining species quality.

If the circumstance of social existence promoted mental capacity to anticipate behaviors and events, the infinite observation of what the other guy was doing also encouraged mimicking of behavior and associative learning. Most notably, approximately 2.5 million years ago, a human ancestor put together the neural patterns required for tool making. This entry into tool technology was subsequently observed, mimicked, and refined by the advantage of social proximity. The social opportunity to observe a particular tool application (e.g., the ballistic breaking of animal bones with a stone hand axe) also promoted associative adaptations of that technology (e.g., the ballistic projection of a stone missile in the direction of an enemy or food source). Similarly, social observation and interaction facilitated brain organization of information about the natural environment, such as geographic markers and distribution of resources, habits of animals, and rhythms of seasons and plant growth.

This social aspect of learning is a constant in human experience and clearly evident in every instance of significant achievement. Advances in technology, mathematics, humanities, fine arts, and the natural and social sciences are never the products of lone genius. The contributions of individuals are to be noted and respected, but no individual human mind is untainted by the minds of others. The landing of a space vehicle on the moon, the discovery of a cure for disease, or the production of a work of art are all accomplishments of a human society of mind. Direct contributors to a specific technological, scientific, or cultural product deserve due credit for their culminating interpretation and refinement of information gleaned from other minds. But where is the mind that could or would profess an absence of neural bridging to the ideas and experiences of others?

Thus leading minds in contemporary fields, such as computer technology and AIDS research, are engaging in the same social learning practices as those employed by human ancestors investigating hand tools and food sources—they observe what others are doing and then proceed to mimic and adapt what they observe. A discriminating advantage in contemporary social learning, of course, is the benefit of access to a greater range of other minds through the vehicle of recorded language.

Language is another product (many would say *the* product) of your ancestors' social experience. Dunbar (1993) proposes that this capacity first emerged as a social language within the intimacy of communal life. You can imagine the composition of meaningful sound patterns over millions of years that communicated information in the social proximity of grooming (e.g., "That feels good!"), tool making (e.g., "No! Hold it this way!"), and foraging (e.g., "This is a good place to search."). Progressively, repetitive vocal signaling patterns associated with specific activities promoted neural networks that were adept at recognizing and producing arrangements of sounds (e.g., Broca's area and Wernike's area). Strings of sounds formed words, strings of words formed sentences, and syntax enabled an infinity of sentence constructions. Thus the neurological way was paved for the expeditious communication of information and ideas between brains—as well as the capacity for a brain to talk reflectively to itself.

A picture emerges of a social shaping of the modern human brain that was prolonged and profound. It is important to note, however, that whereas this experience was linear in the general terms of social acuity leading to a level of consciousness that facilitated mental capacity for technology, natural history, and language, there was also a nonlinear element to the experience. It was not simply a matter of one thing leading to another; rather, it was a matter of many developments influencing one another at the prodding of a social existence. For example, among the many collateral developments during this long history of social experience, your ancestors were enticed by food sources to spend less time in trees and to master bipedalism. This evolutionary event encouraged brain growth of the neural circuitry required for two-footed balance and sophisticated hand dexterity (e.g., as in the use of tools). Adaptation to upright posture also provided an elevated perspective for visual scanning of the landscape and reduced body exposure to the sun. Both of these effects enhanced scavenging opportunities for food, notably meat, when four-legged competitors where disadvantaged. Scavenging, in turn, further promoted social communication to coordinate division of labor in hunter-gatherer groups. Success in the acquisition of meat provided a means to survive in temperate climates and the rich protein diet that a brain growing in size and complexity required. It also accommodated a longer life span and prolonged child development—and the further social learning and development opportunities thereof.

The pieces of evidence about the human brain's long history of social experience are many but are incomplete and yet to be definitively assembled. Archaeologist Steven Mithen (1996) surmises a sequential and modular development of social, technical, natural history, and language intelligence. These specialized intelligences eventually coalesced in a "cognitive fluidity" that integrated the contributions of each module. He proposes that this transition from a "Swiss army knife" modularity to a harmonization of mental abilities was provoked by language and facilitated by consciousness. In effect, the advancement of language ability allowed the conscious brain to share with itself and others what the various modules knew and were able to do. This breaking down of mental modular walls, Mithen concludes, enabled the imagination and creativity associated with the origin of art and religion during a "cultural explosion" in human development 60 to 30 thousand years ago (1996, pp. 194-195).

Neurologist Antonio Damasio (1999) reinforces the perspective that conscious awareness of self and surroundings was a critical turning point that opened human evolution to the creation of technology, science, art, conscience, religion, and social and political organization. The appearance of consciousness in humans heralds the dawn of individual forethought, of "minded" organisms capable of shaping their environmental responses by mental awareness and concern for self. More compellingly, he observes, the neural underpinnings of consciousness enabled knowledge of emotional states such as sorrow or joy, suffering or pleasure, embarrassment or pride. He concludes that consciousness provided the key to a life examined, the beginner's permit for knowing about and acting on the biological urge for self-preservation—an awareness that, at its most complex level, leads to concern for other selves and improvement of the art of life.

Theoretical neurophysiologist William Calvin (1996) arranges the pieces of the puzzle in somewhat similar fashion in his conjecture of a quantum leap in cleverness during human evolution. He acknowledges many contributing variables within a social context, including multiple opportunities to observe and mimic, respond to novel situations, and develop sensory templates appropriate to a versatile diet. Calvin speculates, however, that human intelligence received a critical boost from the refinement of a core brain specialization, such as that associated with language. Specifically, the human brain developed a facility and passion for stringing things together. In the case of language it was sounds to words to sentences. But, as Calvin points out, improvement of multifunctional brain mechanisms that serve one critical function (i.e., language) might have had the effect of aiding other functions. Thus the neural mechanisms associated with the who, what, where, when, why, and how rules of language syntax might have been borrowed for other uses—such as the stringing of pieces and patterns of information together in the mental processes of planning, logic, and the creative shaping of ideas prior to acting.

This big picture of human social experience will continue to come into focus through ongoing investigation and debate by scholars in many fields of study. And while many important details are yet to be resolved, the prominent influence of social experience on the nature of human intelligence is beyond dispute. The neural networks forged by that evolutionary experience speak for themselves—literally.

The Result

Relationship experiences have a dominant influence on the brain because the circuits responsible for social perception are the same as, or tightly linked to, those that integrate the important functions controlling the creation of meaning, the regulation of body states, the modulation of emotion, the organization of memory, and the capacity for interpersonal communication. Interpersonal experience thus plays a special organizing role in determining the development of brain structure early in life and the ongoing emergence of brain function throughout the life span.

—(Siegel, 1999, p. 21)

The social heritage of your brain's evolutionary experience is displayed in its physiological size and organization, emotional acuity, capacity to create and manipulate mental templates, and disposition to "figure things out." It is a dynamic society of cells and molecules, a biological system both formed by, and open to, environmental influence. Specifically:

- ***The human brain is endowed with highly evolved neural mechanisms for social interaction.*** Capacity for semantic and syntactic language communication is a most obvious and significant example of evolved neural mechanisms for social interaction. But the human brain has refined acuity for other communication vehicles as well, such as voice inflection and body language. For example, humans and other primates are the only animals that have muscle endings in their facial skin. This quality is connected to neural networks that direct and interpret an extensive repertoire of facial expressions. Accordingly, your brain is always qualifying the verbal messages directed by or to you by accompanying visual and auditory information about the face and tone that delivers it. Refined social instincts are also facilitated by your sensory capacities for smell, taste, and touch. Much of this sensory processing of social information occurs at a subconscious level, but you become consciously aware of it as you revel in the aroma, feel the tension, taste the fear, read between the lines, and experience "gut feelings" in your interactions with other people.

- ***The evolution of human consciousness generated a legacy of neural networking that accommodates meaning, memory, emotion, and reflection.*** An enriched social existence in diverse habitats valued the construction of mental templates that organized useful environmental information from extensive sensory stimuli. It was important to be able to store and retrieve who, what, where, when, why, and how information. Most notably, cerebral space expanded to serve the reflective manipulation of information involved in calculation, planning, and imagination. These neural networks in the frontal lobes and other cortical and subcortical areas also evolved to mediate the awareness and management of emotions. Collectively, with reference to the definitions of *social* and *system* at the beginning of this section, a community of neural networks emerged—a system of socially inspired communication channels that shared information and expertise for a common survival purpose. Thus your brain is wired with an extensive and highly integrated capacity to learn, remember, reason, and manage emotions to good effect—a capacity that is most effectively actualized in a context similar to the social environment that engineered it.

- ***The social nature of the human brain requires social unfolding of its potential.*** The idea that ontogeny (the developmental stages of an individual organism) recapitulates phylogeny (the evolutionary stages of a species) is a concept that is often used—and debated—in biological inquiry. In general application, it is a concept that is useful to the understanding of the social nature of human intelligence. Specifically, you know from prior examination of brain physiology that the fundamental work of the human brain occurs through the flow of electrochemically encoded information at the neural cell level. You also know that the formation and growth of neural networks is both genetically and environmentally directed. In the case of the evolutionary development of your human brain (its phylogeny), the social experience of your ancestors over time favored the development of specific neural networks. These networks progressively influenced the genetic adaptations that recently served as the blueprint for the construction and operation of your individual brain. But the developmental experience of your brain during your lifetime (its ontogeny) requires relationships with its environment, particularly interpersonal relationships, to realize it potential. Your brain requires a social unfolding of its genetic program. In effect, "human connections shape the neural connections from which the mind emerges" (Siegel, 1999, p. 2).

- ***The human brain is experience expectant and experience dependent.*** The experience expectations of the human brain are most readily observed in the genetically generated excess of neural networks that occur at various times in development from birth through adolescence. It is as if nature constructs networks with the expectation that they will eventually have something to do (much like a communications company constructing a cable grid in anticipation of future subscribers). And that is, indeed, what nature is doing. Neurons are created in abundance and placed in prescribed locations with dendritic and axonal extensions at the ready. Some of these networks are engaged and dedicated to subconscious regulation of body systems (e.g., cardiovascular) by a genetic program that remains constant throughout the life span. Other networks, however, "expect" stimulation as cues for their engagement and refinement of operation. Experiencing such stimulation, these preliminary networks are extended, reinforced, and pruned to greater efficiency. Early childhood examples of this process are the requirements for environmental stimulation of networks that are ready and willing to do sight, hearing, language, and various motor skills. These are critical use-it-or-lose-it—and please-don't-abuse-it—requirements that are commonly obliged in normal human environments.

William Greenough (Greenough, Black, & Wallace, 1987) proposes that the experience-expectant mechanisms of the human brain represent an aspect of plasticity that takes advantage of the commonalties of human environments to fine-tune fundamental neural networks. A related feature, he advises, is experience-dependent plasticity. Whereas your experience-expectant brain exercises a "sculpting" effect in pruning and refining neural networks, your experience-dependent brain exercises an influence on the growth and strengthening of new neural networks. This plasticity is what allows your brain to learn from its unique experience in specific environments. In other words, this is the brain's mechanism for creating networks from experience that *is not* expected—an important quality given that a human brain must acquire and adjust knowledge across its life span in whatever cultural or environmental circumstances it happens to find itself. Notably, the experience-expectant and experience-dependent requirements of your brain are not limited to your childhood development. You will recall that brain development is a lifelong event, that neural networks are constantly being refined and adjusted at the bidding of environmental experience. What is a matter of development in the child becomes a matter of refinement and maintenance in the adult.

At any age, interpersonal interaction is important to the effective engagement, refinement, or creation of neural networks associated with your senses, movement, thinking, emotions, and use of language. The sensory and cognitive stimulation you received through prolonged interpersonal relationships with your parents or other adults was absolutely critical to the development of your adult brain and its intelligence capacity. But your adult brain continues to respond to social intimacies of touch, voice, facial expression, and shared thoughts. In fact, direct social interaction with other humans is the primary means by which you develop, maintain, and adjust your emotional and cognitive competencies throughout your lifetime (supplemented, as we shall discuss in the following section, by various indirect mediums for interpersonal interaction). Interaction with the physical environment is also necessary and important to the experience expectation and dependency of your brain, but social interaction is the foil that most effectively sharpens your exotic neural circuitry. Simply put, social interaction is what your brain expects and depends on—no less than your lungs expect and depend on oxygen.

- ***The human brain seeks ways to expand its opportunities to interact with other brains.*** Social influences on human evolution produced the big neural breakthrough of a capacity for complex verbal language. This endowment was of tremendous value to the communication of information in early human communities and a defining factor in the further advancement of human intelligence. But this evolutionary gift was applied to even greater effect when your ancestors invented written language about 5,000 years ago. In effect, the human brain that evolved the capacity for verbal language came to appreciate this advantage so much that it created a means to transfer it to graphic form, thereby extending its reach and power. By this development, human communication moved beyond direct face-to-face interaction to an expanded society of minds—a society that included the recorded knowledge and ideas of brains that were distant in space and time. This communication innovation also demonstrated the human brain's capacity and disposition to take charge of its experience dependency. To that end, by creating written records of ideas and knowledge, the brain enriched its prospects for the stimulation of new learning and neural growth.

  The invention of written language has been followed by other initiatives to affect the scale and quality of human interactions. Such initiative is demonstrated in the communication technologies of printing, photography, radio, cinema, television, and—most recently—the Internet. These communication vehicles, augmented by the invention of transportation technologies and a wide variety of art forms, have continually expanded the means by which humans have access to one another's minds.

  Thus it is the nature of your brain to continually search for means by which it can be more social. This nurture is demonstrated by the progressive development of mediums for social interaction—from language to global computer Internet systems. It is a nature that arises from the survival mission of the brain. There is safety and survival in social membership. That survival advantage is enhanced by social interactions that network the collective knowledge of all members—whether they be present, distant, or deceased.

- ***Social experience actualizes human intelligence.*** Your brain was designed by nature to interact with other human brains. Social interaction in your childhood was the essential vehicle by which you constructed meaning for your physical and biological world, sense of self, and moral and cultural orientation. In adult life, interaction with the brains of others—whether through direct face-to-face encounters or indirect mediums of print and audiovisual technology—continues to be the primary means by which you exercise and refine your intellectual capacities. You engage the knowledge and ideas of others through observation, conversation, dialogue, debate, reading, writing, and artistic representations. Social interaction, whether direct or indirect, creates a flow of energy and information within and between the neural networks of individuals. Such interaction stimulates emotional attention, pattern recognition, cognitive dissonance, and reflective reasoning. It physically affects electrochemical activity in participating brains and, in response to a quantity and quality of stimulation, stimulates neural network growth and rewiring. It is how you refine your emotional being, resolve your beliefs, and think your best thoughts.

Essence

We live in towns, work in teams, and our lives are spider works of connections—linking us to relatives, colleagues, companions, friends, superiors, inferiors. We are, misanthropes notwithstanding, unable to live without each other . . . . We are far more dependent on other members of our species than any other species of ape or monkey. We are more like ants or termites that live as slaves to their societies. We define virtue almost exclusively as prosocial behavior.

–(Ridley, 1996, p. 6)

- Human orientation to social systems is not only in the brain, it is in the genes. Nature's propensity to organize complex, interactive systems is exhibited at all levels of scale throughout the universe. The genetic organization of molecules and cells into an organism is representative of this natural disposition. Thus a human organism is composed and maintained as a system of interactive molecular and cellular relationships.
- The human brain is disposed by nature to replicate the pattern of its own interactive molecular and cellular organization by establishing interactive relationships with other brains. The pattern of colonies of interactive neurons forming brains is replicated in colonies of interactive brains forming social systems.
- Social existence is a survival strategy that is common to animals. It has also been a strong environmental influence on the evolution of intelligence. Intelligence effects from millions of years of social experience are readily observable in many species, for example, the capacity of rats, dolphins, dogs, and chimpanzees to learn and solve problems (not to mention the adeptness of squirrels in outwitting human efforts to protect bird feeders!). But the social experience of human evolution was unique in the influence of collateral developments—such as bipedalism, scavenging efficiency, division and coordination of group labor, diversification of diet, adaptation to temperate cli-

mates, extension of life span, and prolonged juvenile development. Thus the social existence of early humans both encouraged and responded to the emergence of highly successful survival strategies. This mix of evolutionary developments accentuated human social experience and, ultimately, generated a larger brain structure with both new and refined neural capacities.

- The exact progression of social influence on the evolution of human intelligence is not known. The collective evidence to date, however, suggests a general scenario in which social proximity stimulated expansion of neural capacity for constructing and storing patterns of information. This expanded capacity for the meaning of patterns facilitated neural awareness of the emotional states and behaviors of others, which eventually prompted a conscious neural awareness of self. Awareness of self, that is, consciousness, in turn encouraged the development of neural networks that enabled language and reflective reasoning. In any case, this progression would have been synergistic in nature as different neural advancements (e.g., capacities for language and reflective reasoning) interacted with each other and were, thereby, stimulated to further development.

- Human intelligence is endowed by eons of social evolution with unparalleled neural capacity for meaning, memory, emotion, language, and complex reasoning. The unfolding of this endowment, however, is expectant of and dependent on the same social experience that constructed it. Accordingly, social interaction is a critical attribute of the environmental experience of a brain. It is a primary means by which neural circuitry is activated and reinforced. Most important, interpersonal relationships are foils by which neural networks are maintained and refined.

- An overarching human need and disposition is to connect and interact in a society of mind. This need is so ingrained that technological mediums—for example, print, radio, television, and computer networks—have been invented by the human brain to extend social interaction beyond face-to-face encounters. Whether direct or indirect, social interaction engages a flow of energy and information through a collective intelligence. It is through interpersonal neural networking that ideas are generated, critiqued, and refined—and human potential to think and learn is realized. It is this networking that generates art, philosophy, and moral perspective. Most important, communities of mind emerge from such networking to solve difficult problems, create better systems, and invent new technologies.

Implications

- *If* it is nature's propensity to organize complex, interactive systems at all levels of scale throughout the universe, *then* it is most natural for a human brain to organize interactive relationships with other brains.

- **If** social interaction is a survival strategy that has advanced the development of intelligence advantages throughout human evolution, **then** a leader might conclude that social interaction likely remains a force in the advancement of intelligence capacity during the present stage of human evolution and activity.
- **If** human intelligence capacities are environmentally expectant of and dependent on a social unfolding of their potential, **then** leaders are in a position to influence the quality of social experience.
- **If** human intelligence can be directed to both competitive and cooperative ends, **then** social interactions between humans always occur in a moral context.
- **If** human intelligence has invented mediums that expand opportunities by which human brains can establish interactive relationships, **then** a leader is in a position to facilitate access to and engagement of such mediums.
- **If** social interaction is the foil by which human intelligence is actualized in its capacity for constructing meaning and memory, awareness of emotional states, and exercise of language and complex reasoning, **then** a leader is in a position to create opportunities for the interneural networking of the members of an organization.
- **If** _____,
  then _____.

Ⓔ The Emotional Nature of Intelligence

While conscious control over emotions is weak, emotions can flood consciousness. This is so because the wiring of the brain at this point in our evolutionary history is such that connections from the emotional systems to the cognitive systems are stronger than connections from the cognitive systems to the emotional systems.

—(LeDoux, 1996, p. 19)

This Emotional Life

The human brain is awash in emotion, and the proof is in the behavior. Consider, if you will, the joke attributed to investigators of the emotional attributes of humans: "Look at the things people do—they get married, go on family vacations, and buy lottery tickets, none of which they would do if they were completely rational." Jokes aside, investigations into the emotional nature of the human brain constitute an area of research that has been most productive and revealing. Insights about the emotional operations of the brain are particularly significant to understanding how humans learn and achieve.

The Gist of It

Feel the Power

As a means to initiate your examination of the emotional nature of human intelligence, please pick up a pen and write down what immediately comes to mind when completing the following sentence stem:

One of the happiest moments of my life to date was when _____

_____.

Now, put this book down, close your eyes, and for one full minute revisit the particular moment of happiness you have identified.

| Reflection Time |

Memories of joyous moments will vary, of course, according to individual life experience. One person may revisit a childhood adventure, first love, or professional triumph. Another might recall a particular act of kindness, the birth of a child, or the excitement of travel to an exotic environment. There will be a consistency among all human brains that entertain strong memories, however, in that all such recollections will invoke emotion related to the event held in mental focus. That is, your brain recalls not only the event but also associated emotional states. In fact, in spending a few minutes revisiting a memorable moment of happiness, you experienced this phenomenon—to a greater or lesser degree—in one or more of a wide range of possible expressions. Perhaps you experienced a sense of calm or pleasure, change in body temperature or posture, alteration of facial expression—a slight upward turn of your lips?

There is also the possibility that your recollection of a happy event was not entirely pleasant. In remembering something good that happened, your brain may have activated neural networks that associate sadness with the happiness remembered. That is, your mental images expanded from the initial reconstruction of a joyful event to reflection about related events that have subsequently transpired—perhaps the loss of youth, opportunity, or loved ones. Most assuredly, if you were to reflect on a particularly unpleasant life experience, you would also evoke the emotional status associated with that recollection, perhaps along the order of feeling anxious, chilled, restricted in breathing, tightness in the stomach, and tension in the face.

The point to be made is, whatever the memory, some sense of mental and body state—whether subtle or strong—will be associated with the meaningful experience recalled. What you sense or feel during such a recollection is the effect of emotion associated with the event remembered. You are similarly aware of emotion charged states in your body and mind during some events as they happen or are anticipated. For example, you are likely aware of changes in your mind and body when you observe a red light flashing in the rear view mirror of your car, sway to the music of a slow dance, answer an unexpected late-night phone call, forecast an exotic vacation trip, or contemplate a major financial investment. Thus in its multiple forms, the pervasive and enduring power of emotion in your brain and body is occasionally revealed to you. The question then arises, what exactly is the nature of this powerful influence on your mind and body?

What Are Emotions?

Emotions have mostly been studied psychologically in modern times. Such efforts have provided insights, to be sure, but they also have a couple of drawbacks. One is that, in effect, everybody knows what an emotion is, but no one seems to be able to define it. The other is that there are as many theories of emotion as there are workers in the field. But studies of the brain can provide new insights into how a psychological process like emotion might work and are a valuable approach.

–(LeDoux, 1999, p. 124)

On becoming aware of a phenomenon, humans find it natural to attach a name to it as a precursor to figuring out exactly what it is and how it works. Thus human intrigue about a collection of forces experienced in mind, body, and behavior led to the identification of a phenomenon labeled *emotion* (*bodily humors* was an earlier label popular in the Middle Ages). This label reflects the common definitional interpretations of the effect of the phenomenon: agitation of the passions or sensibilities, often involving physiological changes; any strong feeling, as of joy, sorrow, reverence, hate, or love arising subjectively rather than through conscious mental effort (from Old French *esmovoir*—to excite; Latin, *emovere*—to move out, stir up, act; impulse to act).

Over the centuries, awareness of the phenomenon of emotion prompted ongoing theoretical and clinical investigations into its nature. Such studies have collectively contributed many insights about the role of emotion in humans and other animal organisms. Most recently, however, inquiry into the nature of emotion has benefited substantially from applications of new neuroscience technologies in combination with clinical studies. Accordingly, science is beginning to reveal the biological underpinnings of emotion. This new information, while not yet definitive, significantly advances understanding of the role of emotion in human intelligence and behavior. In effect, scientists are beginning to "see" emotion in the form of neural and chemical processes—emotion in action at a cellular and molecular level. From this vantage point, refined interpretations about the nature of emotion are emerging.

- Emotions are complicated collections of patterned chemical and neural responses that regulate an organism in a manner that is advantageous to its survival (Damasio, 1999, p. 51).

- An emotion is a given mental state that is mediated by a specific neural system as a response to particular assessments of internal and external information, which, in turn, give rise to measurable physiological states as well as observable behaviors (LeDoux, 1999, p. 125).

- Emotions represent dynamic processes created within the socially influenced, value-appraising processes of the brain that ready the brain and body for action (Siegel, 1999, pp. 123-124).

So, what are emotions? Generally speaking, *emotions are biological processes that regulate mind and body responses to subjective evaluations of internal and external information.* This simple interpretation aligns well with the emotions you know so well when you feel them and see them, such as fear, anger, happiness, sadness, surprise, and disgust—processes that, when activated, trigger immediate transitions in your mind and body.

Feeling Emotion

It is important to understand emotion as a subconscious process that becomes known to the conscious brain through its effect on mind and body states. As will be commented on further in later sections, emotion operates as an unconscious arousal system that, if sufficiently active, may escalate to a point that activates conscious feelings—what Damasio (1999) refers to as "the feeling of that emotion and knowing that we have a feeling of that emotion" (p. 8). Perception of this process is critical, because it establishes the reflexive nature of emotion. Such perception also establishes the relation of emotion to other dimensions of intelligence. Specifically, refinement in brain capacity to feel transitions in body states is thought to have been a critical factor in the evolution of a mental awareness of self and, thereby, capacity for conscious reflection and construction of knowledge. What is most important to be aware of at this point in your examination of emotion, however, is the distinction between emotion and feelings—two words that are sometimes used synonymously. A feeling is generated by emotion and is something that you become aware of and can do something about. Emotion, on the other hand, will do what emotion will do, and you will not be aware of it until its work becomes manifest in the form of a feeling.

Emotion Abounds

There are many manifestations of emotional processes in human organisms, but the aforementioned primary emotions (i.e., fear, anger, happiness, sadness, surprise, and disgust—sometimes called categorical emotions) are universally observed across all cultures (Ekman, 1984). Variations and combinations of these primary emotions are also observed and organized by scholars into secondary classifications. For example, variations in fear would be anxiety, concern, or nervousness. Similarly, happiness might be modified to mental and physiological states associated with pride, rapture, or whimsy.

To get a better sense of the range and subtleties of human emotions, you might make a quick reference to a specific event, such as a recent political election. Based on personal voting activity in relation to the election outcome, a particular citizen (yourself for example) might experience any number or combination of emotional responses as the final vote counts are announced—perhaps satisfaction, terror, relief, concern, embarrassment, guilt, despair, joy, consternation, amusement, panic, amazement, wonder, or indifference. But whatever the nuance, the emotion experienced is a biologically determined process that is directed by a select ensemble of subcortical brain devices that regulate and represent body states (Damasio, 1999). Moreover, it matters not whether the stimulation comes from an election result, hazardous weather, or winning the lottery, emotions are in the business of affecting transitions in body and mind states as induced by mental or sensory information. As such, emotions are bioregulatory responses that attend to the basic and subtle requirements of human survival—which is, of course, the reason that emotion is in the brain.

Why Be Emotional?

Survival depends on finding and incorporating sources of energy and on preventing all sorts of situations that threaten the integrity of living tissues.

—(Damasio, 1999, p. 23)

What would your life be like if you were not emotional? Think about that for a minute. What would it be like if you were not susceptible to fear, anger, happiness, sadness, surprise, disgust, or any of the infinite blendings of primary emotions? Would your life be better or worse if you were completely unemotional?

Your reflection on the above question might have led to the quick conclusion that life would be pretty boring if you were never happy or if there were no surprises. You might also have flirted with the allure of a life without fear or anger. As you may have already surmised, however, the answer to the question as posed is that, without emotion, you would not have a life—literally—because emotion is an integral element of survival in animal organisms.

The brain's business, you will recall, is survival, and emotion is a frontline player in the survival business of animal organisms. Emotions are processes that affect transitions in mental and body states. The transitions they affect happen for a reason: to prepare for and support action that is of survival value. In effect, emotions provide your mind and body with the means to attend to, evaluate, and act on information that warrants attention, evaluation, and action.

The key word here is *evaluate*. The human emotional processes that emerged from eons of evolutionary history rapidly assess the merits of internal and external information to determine the need for specific preparations of mind and body for action. Consider the following example:

While walking down the sidewalk of a heavily traveled thoroughfare, your brain is informed by sensory information (i.e., visual and auditory patterns) of the presence of a large truck weaving erratically in your direction and about to jump the curb. This information is instantaneously made available to neural circuits associated with the emotion of fear. Given a genetic and experiential understanding of the nature of large objects aggressively moving in the direction of its host organism, these circuits assess the implications of the given information for your welfare and determine that a full engagement of a fear response is in order. Subsequently, in a matter of milliseconds, a transition in your mental and body state occurs that prepares you for what you must do to survive, that is, flee the path of the oncoming truck.

It is important to note that all mind and body activity in this fictitious scenario occurred at a subconscious level. The processes associated with the emotional state of fear are engrained within your neural networks and brain mechanisms. These processes constantly assess incoming information for indications of a need for their services. On determining such a need, they immediately trigger the mind-body state they are responsible for. Again, this occurs without consultation with the conscious you. Only after you have escaped the danger do you become aware of what your emotional processes have been up to. It is at that point that you begin to *feel* the adjustments that emotional processes associated with fear have directed within your body—the accelerated rush of blood pumping through your heart, the tightness in your stomach, and the trembling of your limbs.

Why be emotional? It is the means by which you judge what is good and what is bad as measured against your survival interests. In some instances such judgment is primitively basic and instant. A truck moving directly at you at high speed is bad; therefore, you respond with fear. The offering of a large increase in salary and benefits is good; therefore, you respond with happiness.

The benefit of basic emotional processes should become even more obvious when you rerun the runaway truck scenario from a perspective of the hypothetical *emotionless* you. Without emotional processes in place that evaluate incoming information and efficiently engage appropriate response mechanisms, you would be indifferent to the truck because you have no means to judge its relationship to your welfare. And if, by chance, you are tempted to make the argument that, absent all emotion, you would still be in a position to engage your rational thinking skills to determine how to deal with the truck, be forewarned—without emotion there can be no rational thought. The reason that this is so, as will be discussed further in a following section, is that rational thought requires valuation of all manner of information, including options and possibilities that are generated thereof. The reason that this is known to be so is that humans who suffer injury to areas of the brain associated with emotional processes are impaired in their capacity for rational thinking.

Even if it were possible to be unemotionally rational (and it is not), by the time you consciously gather together the relevant pieces of information and consider your options, the truck has been and gone—and you likely with it. This is another advantage of emotion. Emotional processing of information from stimulus to action is infinitely more efficient than cognitive processing of information from stimulus to action. Just as your brain has circuits that unconsciously regulate the autonomic system's operation of basic body survival activities (like breathing and blood circulation), it also has neural circuits that subjectively screen information for patterns that immediately and subconsciously induce prescribed mind-body responses.

Emotional processing, however, is not limited to the organization of rapid responses to basic survival needs. Human emotion covers a wide range of refined responses to events and interests. Most commonly, emotion is also engaged by humans through the reflective processing of mental patterns associated with past, current, and future events. In this manner, emotions are employed more subtly and gradually to affect mind-body states and behaviors. This circumstance sheds further light on why emotion is necessary to human survival. Specifically, humans cannot pursue all goals at once. Pinker (1997) puts it this way: "If an animal is both hungry and thirsty, it should not stand halfway between a berry bush and a lake" (p. 373). That is, an animal must commit itself to one goal at a time, and the goals have to be matched with the best opportunities for achieving them. Emotions, then, are mechanisms that help the brain make decisions and establish priorities—whether they be matters of career options, personal relationships, or selecting a brand of toothpaste. Thus ongoing screening of internal and external information brings forward all manner of emotional assessments that "chart the course of moment-to-moment actions as well as set the sails toward long-term achievements" (LeDoux, 1996, p. 19).

To summarize to this point, emotions are not things that you can pick up, kick around, and describe as being larger or smaller than a bread box. Rather, emotions are best understood as complicated collections of neural and chemical processes that regulate a wide range of mind and body states. They perform their regulatory tasks through subjective evaluations of internal and external information that both determine and initiate mind-body responses. As such, emotions are critical contributors to your brain's survival business. Given this assessment of the importance of emotion, your brain's emotional centers might be interested in an examination of how humans are emotional.

How Are Humans Emotional?

The evidence suggests that the emotions of all normal members of our species are played on the same keyboard.

—(Pinker, 1997, p. 365)

To establish a reality reference for your subsequent examination of how humans are emotional, you are again asked to access your personal emotional experience. This time, however, the activity will expand on the scope of human emotion and require deeper reflection about the process and effect of emotion as you once experienced it. Specifically, you will reflect about what occurred in your mind, body, and behavior during specific events—that is, you will describe *how* you were emotional in specific contexts.

This activity will take only a few minutes to complete and you will have choices as to what to reflect about within three categories. Please be advised that writing is an important component of this exercise because (as will be elaborated on in following sections on the constructive and reflective nature of your brain) it will enhance your neural reconstruction of specific events and associated emotional experiences.

But first a warning: A range of emotional experiences are purposely solicited in this exercise, some of which will likely resurface strong feelings. That is, some recollections will predictably evoke feelings of happiness and joy and others will likely evoke feelings of sadness and discomfort. You will be conducting this exercise in the comfort of private reflection, and you are afforded choice in what life experiences you will recall. Nevertheless, you may be revisiting some difficult-to-bear memories. So, to paraphrase the famous Bette Davis line, hang on, it's going to be a bumpy emotional ride.

This is what you are requested to do:

A. Write brief descriptions of events in your life that correspond to given categories.

B. Write brief descriptions of what was occurring in your mind, body, and behavior during the described events.

Example:

A. Description of the event: A visit to a memorial site.

In 1973, I spent a summer working on a kibbutz near the Gaza Strip in southeastern Israel. I was there to gather information relative to the completion of my master's thesis. Working on the kibbutz provided room and board during my stay. It also provided opportunities for traveling throughout the country on nonworking days. On one occasion, I traveled to Har Hazikaron to visit Yad Vashem, the national monument to victims of the Nazi Holocaust. I recall that the buildings were located within a forest that had been planted in memory of John F. Kennedy. Inside, there were many exhibits depicting the transportation, imprisonment, and killing of millions of Jews, Gypsies and other victims of Nazi racism. At the center of the memorial building was a large area of marble flooring bordered by a low railing. Visitors stood at the railing and looked down on slabs of dark marble set in the lighter colored floor. Each slab was engraved with the name of a concentration camp—names like Treblinka, Dachau, and Auschwitz. I think there were about 20 names in all. An eternal flame flickered at the center of the floor. I remember that it was very quiet, that people were crying softly, . . . and that some visitors had numbers tattooed on their arms.

B. Description of what was occuring in mind, body, and behavior:

I remember being attentive and somber when going through the exhibits surrounding the memorial. As a history teacher, I had a good background of information about World War II and the holocaust, but my mind was nevertheless captured by the graphic representations of the multimedia displays. When I arrived at the marble memorial surrounding the eternal flame, however, I was suddenly overwhelmed—by the physical memorial to millions of lives subjected to unimaginable injustice, the crying of grieving people, and the presence of survivors. I felt a heaviness in the air and a constriction in my throat and chest. I think I may have stopped breathing for a moment. My jaw clenched and my eyes watered. I bent over, placed my hands on my knees, and breathed deeply. I felt both great anger and sadness. My mind was trying to comprehend the magnitude of the inhumanity and suffering . . . and searching for answers to why and how such atrocities happen.

Now it is your turn. Remember, you have choices as to what to recall and write about in different categories. You may decide to respond to more than one suggested prompt, but it is important that you complete a written response to at least one prompt in each category. (*Note:* The physical organization of information into a written response is adequately served by notes jotted down on any available piece of paper.)

Category One: *An event that evoked fear, sadness, disgust, or anger*

Prompts: an event that involved a visit to a memorial, the death of a loved one, failure to achieve a goal, a life-threatening experience, observation of great cruelty, witnessing a natural disaster, an encounter with human tragedy, other

A. Description of the event:

> *Writing Time*

B. Description of what was occurring in mind, body, and behavior:

> *Writing Time*

Category Two: *An event that evoked joy or inspiration*

Prompts: an event that involved observation of courage, personal achievement, artistic expression, moral victory, friendship, the beauty of nature, family events, human triumph over adversity, displays of compassion, other

A.   Description of the event:

> *Writing Time*

B.   Description of what was occurring in mind, body, and behavior:

> *Writing Time*

Category Three: *An event that required an important decision*

Prompts: an event that involved a relationship, children, a moral dilemma, educational options, career choices, travel opportunities, property, financial investment, other

A.   Description of the event:

> *Writing Time*

B.   Description of what was occurring in mind, body, and behavior:

> *Writing Time*

Given the events that you have revisited and described above, how are you emotional? What happens in your mind, body, and behavior during events that evoke stress or pleasure? Do you laugh, cry, run, perspire, fret, tremble, focus, smile, freeze, frown, scream, stammer, or squeak? And what about events in your life that require major decisions? Do you experience emotional effects in mind, body, and behavior in those situations also?

You probably have a pretty good feel for how you are emotional if you did, indeed, complete the prescribed reflection activity. That is, once again, the point to make. You feel the effect of emotional processes associated with events and are able to describe their influence on mind, body, and behavior. But why do your emotional responses vary according to events, and how are these responses generated? In other words, what are the inner workings of how you are emotional? To answer these questions, we turn to the biology that underlies emotion.

The Basic Picture: Ready, Fire, Aim

In a typical emotion, then, certain regions of the brain, which are part of a largely preset neural system related to emotions, send commands to other regions of the brain and to most everywhere in the body proper. The commands are sent via two routes. One route is the bloodstream, where the commands are sent in the form of chemical molecules that act on receptors in the cells that constitute body tissues. The other route consists of neuron pathways and the commands along this route take the form of electrochemical signals that act on other neurons or on muscular fibers or on organs (such as the adrenal gland) which in turn can release chemicals of their own into the bloodstream. The result of these coordinated chemical and neural commands is a global change in the state of the organism.

—(Damasio, 1999, p. 67)

Emotion is about motion and everything that the word implies—movement, change, action—within body and mind. It is a process, like digestion or respiration, rather than a thing, like an elbow or nose. It is a process that assesses the survival merits of information moving within and about an organism to determine advantageous movement in mind and body states that, in turn, direct movement in behavior. The basic process, then, in every instance of emotional experience (such as those described by you in the above exercise)—whether stressful, pleasant or decisive—is as follows:

1. Neural networks in various regions of your brain (e.g., in the amygdala and brain stem) comprise *emotion centers* that are committed to the regulation of mind and body responses to particular configurations of internal and external information. You might want to think of these neural centers as sentries that monitor information brought forth for their inspection by your senses and body movement through the thalamus and the olfactory lobe.

2. On detecting an information pattern that it judges to be of importance to its particular responsibilities (e.g., assessing for information that suggests danger, opportunity, or novelty), an emotion center informs other parts of the brain of its discovery and concern.

3. Thus alerted, some neural networks initiate prescribed transitions in mind and body states appropriate to the nature of the information received. These transitions occur through electrochemical communications in neural networks and chemical releases into the bloodstream to enable action or behavior judged by your brain to be in your best interest (e.g., fight, flee, focus).

4. Subsequently, other neural networks become aware of the transitions that are occurring in body and mind—they *feel* the emotional response.

5. Finally, the prefrontal cortex and other cortical areas become informed of the emotional arousal, response, and feeling that have arisen subconsciously

in your brain. Thus after your brain has reflexively reacted to important sensory information, you are presented with an opportunity to consciously reflect about what is happening and what you want to do about it. It is as if your subconscious brain is reporting to your conscious brain about events that have occurred.

An important point about the sequence just described is that emotion dictates an act-first, think-later response to information. Whether the action is as extreme as physical aggression or as mild as a focusing of attention, emotion is very much in the driver's seat in determining what you will attend to and how you will initially respond to that which captures your attention. In a classic fear response, for example, neural clusters in the amygdala scan sensory information for patterns that suggest the possibility of danger. On detecting such a pattern, the amygdala sounds an alert to other brain centers. The informed neural networks act on the alert by releasing hormones, increasing heart rate and blood pressure, slowing breathing, mobilizing muscle groups, shutting down systems unnecessary to the moment (e.g., digestion), and referencing the hippocampus and other memory systems to retrieve information that may be valuable to the matter at hand. Importantly, sensory information that is presented to the amygdala is also communicated to the cortex. The amygdala, however, receives the information milliseconds before the cortical areas and, if said information is judged by the amygdala to warrant an alarm, the brain is, in effect, hijacked to serve an emotional priority (LeDoux, 1996)—that is, the reflective capacities of your cortex are put on hold while your brain attends to first things first. This phenomenon is, once again, born of the survival imperative that drives your brain. Eventually, your powers of rational thinking are brought to bear on what the amygdala and other emotional mechanisms have already acted on, but only after your brain has reflexively taken steps to ensure that you will be around to do some thinking. The advantages of this arrangement between the reflexive and reflective qualities of you brain are obvious when you reflect that it was important for your early ancestors to refrain from engaging in observations about the comparative qualities and habits of approaching carnivores until after the safety of a perch in a tall tree afforded security for such reflection. In such instances, an attend-react-then-think approach would seem necessary for participation in the gene pool. What might not be as obvious is that this arrangement for attending, responses, and incorporating reflection is at work in your brain in all instances of life experience— be they large or small, dramatic or mundane.

Some other information worth considering about the basic nature of the emotion in your brain is as follows:

- **In the beginning, it was all about body.** Before there were brains, there were bodies without brains. Accordingly, as Pert (1997) describes, there was a body chemical nervous system before there was a central nervous system that incorporated electrochemical communications. That original body system remains in operation. It is a system that evaluates and responds to information by means of parasynaptic transmissions (i.e., transmissions that are second-ary or parallel to synaptic exchanges of chemicals in neural circuitry) of li-gands (i.e., neurotransmitters, hormones, peptides) through extracellular fluids to receptor molecules on cells throughout the body. This chemical com-munication system is the means to affect adjustments in body states as di-rected by information processed directly in the body or communicated by the brain. This is an important point. As the brain evolved and assumed its system management and decision-making responsibilities, it incorporated the exist-ing body communication system. Thus the brain informs and affects the body, and the body informs and affects the brain. You truly do have a mind-body. This is part of the explanation for gut instinct. Your stomach acquires and acts on information and informs your brain accordingly. Likewise, your brain acquires and acts on information that becomes known to the stomach. This two-way-street arrangement is observed when an upset stomach trips emo-tional centers in the brain and when emotional alerts in the brain initiate physical responses in the stomach. What happens to the body happens to the brain and vice versa—and always with emotional markers.

- **The nose knows.** The olfactory lobe is suspected of having played a pivotal role in the evolution of higher brain structures. Specifically, the ability to de-tect, organize, and recall a wide range of scents became a very valuable sur-vival skill. It was a means to determine what was good or bad to eat, be near, or do. As the mammalian brain evolved at the prodding of mobility in rich expe-riential environments, there was more to smell and, subsequently, decipher and organize as important information patterns. Such environmental stimu-lation is thought to have encouraged the beginnings of complex information-processing and memory systems, including the development of a cortex. As mammals became more multisensorily adept, this brain development was accelerated. It is helpful to remember, therefore, that the sophisticated infor-mation and memory systems in your brain originate from a survival need to judge what is good for you and what is bad for you—an emotional orientation that remains deeply invested in all the information processing you engage in.

- **Emotion is everywhere.** Damasio (1999, p. 61) advises that there is no single site for the processing of emotions. There are, however, discrete systems asso-ciated with different emotional patterns. Thus, different sites induce different emotions, such as the association of sadness with the ventromedial prefrontal cortex, hypothalamus, and brainstem and the amygdala's involvement with fear and anger. LeDoux (1996, p. 16) agrees with this assessment, stating that emotion is not something that the brain has or does, rather that it is some-thing a number of neural systems are involved with. Accordingly, there is no single brain system dedicated to emotion; the emotional system you use to defend against danger is different from the one you engage to procreate.

- **Like an individual neuron, emotion considers the source.** Neurons fire their chemical messages based on the quality and quantity of electrochemical information that they receive from other neurons. This pattern is observable in emotion as a relevant network does not sound an alert unless sufficiently encouraged by sensory information that such attention is warranted. This explains why you are not constantly emotional in every possible way.

- *A strong emotion is designed to be a sprinter, not a distance runner.* The primary job of emotion is to alert other brain-body systems about the need for their services. Monitoring sensory information is a relatively low-key function of emotion, similar to the low expenditure of energy required of sentinels standing watch at their posts. On detecting an information pattern of concern, however, emotional networks adopt a more energy-consuming posture— they literally light up with the electrochemical flow of information that alerts and enacts transitions in mind and body. A problem arises, therefore, when emotional networks are overengaged or sustained in use. It is equivalent to the problem that arises from running a car engine at top speed for a sustained period of time—such stress can damage the components of the system. In the case of emotion, neural networks are subject to damage from the extended presence of associated chemicals, such as the cortosol secretions involved in a fear response. Having performed its initial arousal service, however, an emotion network needs to adopt a lower-level maintenance role and attend to further monitoring of incoming sensory information. This is modeled in nature by the grazing animals of the African savanna that quickly revert to normal feeding and social behaviors after the emotional surge associated with escape from the attack of a predator.

The Complex Picture:
The Fine Art of Emotion

There is nothing simple about emotion or any other quality of human intelligence. Beyond the marvel of the basic character and function of emotion in mind and body, however, is the nature of its relationship to the complex thinking capacities of the brain:

- *Emotion is the arbiter between lower and higher brain structures.* As Sylwester (2000) describes it, sensory information patterns activate emotional systems that activate brain attention and, most important, your capacity to construct understanding, solve problems, and make decisions. Emotion is in partnership with the cortex, then, not to resolve but to involve. From systems located primarily in the lower and older areas of the brain, emotion initiates a process that informs the prefrontal cortex about what it should be thinking about. The cortex, in response, acts to understand what has been brought to its attention and to generate behaviors that will relieve the concerns therein.
- *Emotion flows uphill.* More neural communications flow from emotion systems to complex reasoning systems than from complex reasoning systems

to emotion systems. The good news about this arrangement is that the prefrontal cortex is provided with many challenges that both require and sharpen its reflective, problem-solving, and decision-making capacities. The thinking cortex is also afforded many opportunities by this directional flow of information to refine its capacity for emotional intelligence, that is, to manage emotion in a manner that contributes to your welfare and quality of life.

- *Emotion can be turned on by the thought of you.* From your experience with several exercises earlier in this section, you are already aware of your ability to engage emotion at will by conscious reflection. The significance of this ability is that you are not completely at the mercy of your emotions, that your cortex can manage and adjust your emotional state by its conscious actions. If you can turn it on, you have some leverage on turning it down or otherwise tuning it to your advantage.

- *Too much of a good thing co-opts the work of the best and brightest.* Intense or sustained surges of emotion initiate processes that highjack the brain to a basic survival focus. In such instances, the services of the analytic and creative thinking areas of the prefrontal cortex are compromised. When emotionally overwhelmed, your brain experiences difficulty in attending, learning, remembering, or making decisions. As Goleman (1995) relates, "Stress makes people stupid" (p. 149).

- *Emotion moves beyond the passion of the moment.* While less-evolved life forms have a more restricted range of responses to environmental stimuli, a larger and complex human neocortex enables a more expansive and nimble repertoire of emotional assessment and behavioral response (Goleman, 1995, p. 12). Thus human emotion systems are capable of influencing refined and subtle regulation of mind and body states as well as full-blown alarm exercises. This refined capacity for assessing the merits of environmental information is also the means by which emotion initiates and sustains human passion for art, philosophy, and other applications of complex reasoning.

A Popular Dance Partner

Emotion does not dance alone on the multidimensional stage of intelligence. The physiological platform of intelligence is saturated with the webs and chemicals of emotion systems, and the healthy functioning of such systems is dependent on the healthy maintenance of brain physiology. Social experience is a primary source of influence on emotional systems. You feel emotion well up inside you as you approach a podium, visit a gravesite, attend a wedding, cross the finish line, or engage in office politics. It is in the constructive and reflective dimensions of your intelligence, however, that a particularly intimate dance of knowledge acquisition and application is engaged at the valuation lead of emotion. You only construct understanding and reflect about that which is judged to be worth knowing and thinking about. Similarly, emotion prods and reinforces disposition to develop and habitually exercise productive thinking skills. Thus emotion moves—step for step—with other qualities of intelligence across the comprehensive landscape of human learning and achievement.

Essence

We are about as effective at stopping an emotion as we are at preventing a sneeze.

—(Damasio, 1999, p. 49)

- Emotion is an evolutionary survival mechanism in life forms that move and, therefore, have need to quickly screen, judge, and react to a vast array of environmental information.
- Emotion is an endowment that has been highly refined in humans by the influence of rich environmental experience born of social existence and high mobility over a long evolutionary period.
- Emotion is a means for arousing attention and focusing capacity for constructing understanding and resolving problems and decisions.
- How it works: Sensory information is processed by the thalamus to emotional centers connected to memory sites in the amygdala, hippocampus, and other brain areas that, if sufficiently excited, activate the endocrine system and otherwise alter mind and body states that may generate feelings that inform the prefrontal cortex that there is something worth thinking about.
- The purpose of emotion is to ensure that the organism reflexively acts first, and then reflectively thinks later.
- Emotion is designed for limited engagement and may endanger if sustained over time due to the adverse effect of associated chemical releases.
- Humans are aware of and able to mediate emotional responses. This capacity has been referred to as emotional intelligence.
- Emotion is intimately involved with all other dimensions of the nature of human intelligence.
- Emotion is an old and proven survival system that is still very much in charge of human behavior. Accordingly, it is not productive to try to stop emotion—one might just as well try to stop a cat from hunting mice. It is important to understand this relationship between emotion as a subconscious arousal system and the feeling of the consequences of the activation of such a system (e.g., fear). There is little that can be easily done to alter the subconscious spontaneity of an emotional response—tears and laughter come not at the bidding of conscious will. Conscious awareness of an emotional effect, however, is the gateway to reflection about how to manage the power of emotion to advantage.

Implications

- *If* the brain is emotional, ***then*** a leader should not perceive or behave as if it were otherwise.
- *If* emotion is the means by which humans attend, make judgments, and are motivated, ***then*** the development of a common vision of meaningful purpose is important to tapping emotional commitment and passion in individuals and organizations.
- *If* the intelligence capacity of the human brain is challenge motivated and threat inhibited, ***then*** the art of leadership is the creation of productive levels of goal tension.
- *If* emotion is intimately integrated with other dimensions of the nature of intelligence, ***then*** use it to advantage in arousing and motivating the construction of knowledge and the reflective resolution of problems.
- *If* _____,
  then _____.
- *If* _____,
  then _____.
- *If* _____,
  then _____.

C The Constructive Nature of Intelligence

The brain detects, constructs, and elaborates patterns as a basic, built-in, natural function. It does not have to be taught or motivated to do so, any more than the heart needs to be instructed or coaxed to pump blood.

—(Hart, 1983, p. 60)

Genius

In common use, the term *genius* distinguishes individuals who, among the masses, demonstrate great natural ability—exceptional mental ability in particular. Genius is also a term, however, for describing the definitive ability of a particular group.

To further construct your personal understanding of the genius of human intelligence, revisit for a moment the occasion of your birth. You will likely not recall the details, but, assuming a normal process, you were resting comfortably in an environment that adequately satisfied your needs for warmth and nutrition. Then things changed dramatically. Following some minutes or hours of pushing and pulling (depending, in part, on how accommodating you were to the process), you were thrust into a completely different environment. Cold air assailed your naked skin and shocked your untested lungs. Bright light pierced your still-closed eyelids. And the noise! Chaotic sounds swirled around your tender auditory sensing system. Indeed, the combined stress from temperature, light, and noise was most likely overwhelming—causing you to cry out in distress.

Now fast-forward a few years to your first day of school. Many things have changed since that chaotic, disorienting moment of your entry into human society. Most notably, you have mastered the basics of a defining human skill—language. Specifically, you have established semantic mastery of a vocabulary approximating 5,000 words. You have also become adept in the syntactical arrangement of sounds, words, phrases, and sentences that underlies language communication. Thus you are able to verbally communicate easily and profusely with peers and adults as you enter the classroom—a matter that quickly becomes a classroom management issue for your teacher.

This mastery of verbal language is both impressive and important. After all, it represents a skill base that enables both formal and informal learning throughout your lifetime. What is most impressive, however, is that you mastered this sophisticated skill *without the benefit of formal language instruction!* The question then arises, how did you master the complexities of verbal language between birth and age five?

| Reflection Time |

Your reflection about your mastery of language skills will predictably credit opportunities to observe, mimic, and interact with peers, siblings, and adults. Social exposure to modeling, trial and error, and feedback is, of course, a factor common to all human learning. Beneath this social framework, however, beats a more fundamental rhythm of learning. To better understand this, return once more to your prenatal experience.

You might not recall, but can trust in the fact, that your womb experience involved exposure to many sounds—more specifically, sound patterns. From the very earliest emergence of your sensory and cortical structures, you were exposed to the thump-thump of beating hearts (yours, mom's, and any sibling who might have been with you at the time), the whoosh of blood through veins and air through lungs and, yes, the distinct vibration patterns of your mother's voice. How did you master the basics of language? The human brain is committed, as you are already aware, to the discernment and organization of information patterns that serve its survival instincts. To that end, your brain was neurally prepared and primed for pattern recognition in the womb. That is, you did not arrive in this world quite as helpless as it might have seemed at the time. You were armed with a neural predisposition to detect and connect information patterns. Your early discernment of patterns, such as that of a heartbeat, then connected to the rhythmic sounds emitted by hovering adults and other environmental sources. These patterns, in turn, prompted early monosyllabic and polysyllabic trials, possibly "Momma" or "Dadda." Thus, one pattern connected to another and another . . . until that day you walked through the schoolhouse door empowered to communicate and learn with teachers and peers.

This, then, is a foundational quality of the genius of the human species—an extraordinary capacity to perceive and endlessly construct useful connections between information patterns. It is a capacity that underlies human cognition—the process by which knowledge is acquired. It is also the foundation for all the proficiency and achievement cognition engenders, be it a child's mastery of language or a physicist's formulation of $E = mc^2$.

The Gist of It

A Lean, Mean, Pattern-Making Machine

As soon as the infant can see, it recognizes faces, and we now know that this skill is hardwired into our brains. Those infants who, a million years ago, were unable to recognize a face smiled back less, were less likely to win the hearts of their parents, and less likely to prosper. These days, nearly every infant is quick to identify a human face, and to respond with a gooney grin.

—(Sagan, 1996, p. 45)

Every healthy human brain possesses genius for detecting and organizing patterns that are useful to the determination of advantageous behavior. There is, to be sure, individual genius within this specieswide genius, but every human is adept at pattern discrimination and construction—to a degree that challenges the comprehension of the very intelligence that is operating it.

Consider once again the example of your early mastery of verbal language. Such accomplishment is impressive enough as a pattern discernment process that your brain engaged in to perceive relationships within and between sound, semantics, and syntax. The process becomes more impressive, however, as one further considers all that your brain was doing to put the pieces of language together. After all, words and phrases were not coming from one source. There were different voices, pitches, inflections, accents, and a host of other language propensities from many sources that assailed your young brain. There also were all kinds of other auditory events (e.g., bells, whistles, hammers, horns, barking dogs, instrumental music, the hum of a car engine) vying for your pattern discernment attention. Accordingly, Smith (1990) advises that an aspiring infant linguist is doing much more than merely mimicking or copying sounds in a passive or mechanical sense. Rather, the infant is engaging in a complex process of analysis that ultimately synthesizes important patterns and rules for language. This analysis and synthesis is all the more impressive given that it occurs primarily at a subconscious level—at the same time the infant is similarly mastering complex patterns associated with capacities such as sight, movement, and social relationships.

Patterns represent the currency of intelligence in the business of survival. Your brain is designed to construct a wealth of meaning from internal and external sensory information. It does so by detecting patterns that can be assigned meaning in relation to patterns previously established in neural networks. The brain employs this process to organize information important to survival. For example, it is of survival importance for an infant to recognize the faces of primary caregivers, master communication skills, comprehend physical objects, and acclimate to cultural norms. The pattern detection and construction apparatus of the brain is the means by which a child achieves such needs. It is this same process that constructs conceptual and procedural understanding throughout the life span—whether it is understanding about economic principles, a new technology, or a recipe for preparing chicken curry. This, then, is the purpose of brain information processing, the acquisition and integration of highly organized and interconnected information patterns—commonly referred to as knowledge.

The Power of Patterns

> The process of learning is the extraction of patterns from confusion—not from clarity and simplicity.
>
> —(Hart, 1983, p. 75)

Knowledge is power—power to survive born of constructed understanding about objects, people, events, processes, and abstract concepts. Such constructions arise from your brain's incessant detection and integration of information patterns. The following exercise illustrates the process:

Task: Memorize information about new symbols for the numbers 1 to 10.

Step One: Within 60 seconds, and using only visual observation (i.e., without the aid of pencil, paper, or other props), commit to memory new symbols for the numbers 1 to 10 as presented in Figure 3.6.

Step Two: After the 60-second time period has expired, hide the above information from your view and attempt to write familiar number sequences (e.g., your street or apartment number, phone number, social security number) using the new number symbols as you are able to remember them.

Figure 3.6. Alternative Number Symbols Exercise

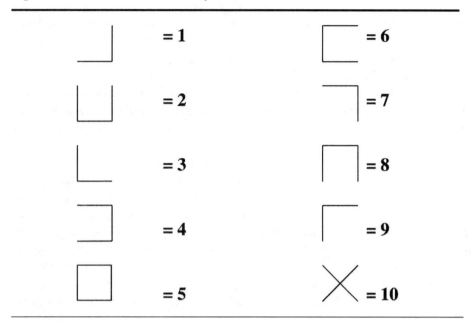

You may have completed the above task with little difficulty—which would certainly reflect brain capacity to organize new information within a short period of time. Most people experience some frustration with this task, however, given the strangeness of the proposed new symbols and the limited time span in which to learn it. Therein lies an important insight about a basic principle of knowledge construction. When confronted by new information that does not immediately connect to existing neural networks, your brain (given sufficient motivation and time) searches further for relationships to established patterns. Ultimately, it will construct a pattern that incorporates the new with the familiar. Perhaps you were aware of your brain doing this as it recognized a similarity between the shape of the traditional number 7 and the proposed new symbol. If such a connection does not occur, however, your brain is stymied, confused, or simply oblivious. The new information does not have meaning because the informational pieces have not been put together in a recognizable or useful pattern. To your brain, such disconnected information takes on the qualities of a stranger passing by (i.e., I do not know this person, this person means little to me) or not recalling something about familiar people (e.g., their names, where and when you were with them, what you did together). Thus your brain is either oblivious or frustrated until information pieces are put together in such a manner that a pattern is either recognized or created.

To more fully appreciate this proclivity for seeking and connecting patterns, take a moment to reference Figure 3.7. If your brain has not already arrived at this connection, you will gain a greater sense of its pattern connection and construction bias. That is, mastery of the alternative number symbol system is almost instantaneous when a familiar pattern establishes a relationship with the new information. Thus, an established neural pattern (i.e., the tic-tac-toe grid) serves as a framework that facilitates the neural organization of a new pattern (i.e., a new number symbol system).

Be assured that you have an infinity of intricately constructed information patterns established within your neural networks. Indeed, some patterns were genetically installed in your brain, such as neural networks dedicated to the recognition of geometric shapes, numbers, and the sounds for all the languages in the world—a necessity, given that you did not know where you were going to be born and what language you were going to learn! Most of the information patterns that you hold in your brain, however, are the constructions you have been putting together throughout your life experience, in response to environmental stimuli. Such constructions represent, among other things, all that you know about people, history, literature, geography, operating a business, driving a car, and chocolate cake. These information patterns represent your knowledge, your personal understanding of the world you live in. It is vast knowledge that extends well beyond your conscious awareness. It is so profound and integrated that it is capable of generating patterns of information that do not exist (as you shall experience it a bit later in this section). Furthermore, given the experience of tomorrow, your knowledge then will be greater than that of today.

Given the powerful constructive nature of the brain in the detection and organization of information, it is worthwhile to reflect about how humans came to possess this capacity.

The Legacy of Mobility:
The Rich Get Richer

You do not need a brain if you are not going anywhere.

—(Sylwester, 2000, p. 41)

With locomotion, whether by foot, fin, wing, or other means, comes adjustment in the quantity and quality of life experience. It's a simple equation: Mobility expands the potential environmental experience of an organism, which, in turn, engenders more opportunity to detect and construct information patterns. The rule, it would appear, is that those who wander have greater opportunity—and need—to ponder.

Sylwester (2000) accents mobility as a defining property of human experience and a central reason for a having a brain. Plants, he points out, do not have brains because their immobility renders a brain unnecessary to the information processing required for survival interaction with their environment. In fact, ignorance is a blessing on an immobile organism unable to escape forces that might approach with consumption or other forms of assault in mind. What purpose would it serve to detect and construct information patterns that cannot be responded to?

Figure 3.7. Graphic Reference for Alternative Number Symbols Exercise

1	2	3
4	5	6
7	8	9	X = 10

Mobile organisms, on the other hand, have options, and options require decisions, and decisions require information—good information. In deciding to go here or there and do this or that, an organism that moves of its own volition must constantly reference its survival interest in relation to current, prior, and anticipated experience—which places a high premium on the detection, construction, and elaboration of information patterns. This circumstance is amplified by environmental circumstances that promote mobility as a means to acquire food, safe harbor, and reproduction opportunities.

Calvin (1996) is among those who observe a correlation between varied diet, mobility, and mental versatility. Omnivores (e.g., octopuses, rats, and primates) exemplify this correlation in the construction of an extensive repertoire of sensory templates and movement options that correspond to their need to identify a wide range of environmental sounds, smells, tastes, textures, and images. The advantage that occurs from the construction of such an extensive library of patterns is that the organism has more pattern templates to reference and manipulate when confronted by novel information. This phenomenon is amplified further in organisms (e.g., humans) that have evolved as omnivores in diverse climates. A temperate climate is particularly provocative to the construction of mental templates that interpret patterns of changing food sources and shelter needs within cyclical seasons.

At a basic level, the effect of mobility on pattern construction can, once again, be observed in early child development. Diamond and Hopson (1998) describe the brain development that is observed in children as they begin to crawl. They note, in particular, the dramatic increase in neural activity and networking that occurs as a child employs the four-point mobility system of crawling to expand its environmental reach and experience. The dramatic increase in sensory stimulation that results from such exploration provides a richness of data from which the baby detects and connects patterns, thus feeding the construction of personal knowledge about objects, people, language, and how things work.

The same phenomenon of knowledge acquisition and integration abetted by mobility is represented in the historic experience of humans as the most mobile life forms on the planet. Early evolutionary development of oppositional thumbs and bipedalism enabled climbing of trees and mountains as well as roaming of broad savannas and deserts. Hand dexterity also contributed to the development of basic tool technologies that enhanced excavation and cultivation of the earth, hunting of large animals, and construction of clothing and shelter—all of which made it possible to explore and survive in all geographic regions and climates on earth. The development of transportation systems and strategies has also played a role in the success of human mobility. From the domestication of animals and the invention of the wheel, humankind moved on to trains, planes, and automobiles. More recently, human travel has moved to the depths of sea and space. The effect of this mobility experience is the same as that on a crawling infant. In the case of vast historic time, however, the effect is observed as a compounded influence of the interface between mobility, experience, and the acquisition of knowledge. Over time, as humans moved through diverse environments and encountered an infinity of new and novel experiences, they provoked natural selection for brain capacity that was increasingly adept at detecting, organizing, storing, and retrieving information patterns important to survival. In effect, more movement generated more experience, which generated more neural networking. Thus humans have historically expanded their capacity to acquire and integrate knowledge through the aggressive exercise of their capacity to move to new experiences—and the pattern rich, thereby, have progressively become richer in both accumulated knowledge and capacity to generate more.

In the 21st century, humans still move in and out of multiple and varied environments, thus feeding the brain the raw material of experience that it needs to construct knowledge that serves advantageous behavior. Movement to new experience in this current time, however, is very much facilitated by technological developments, such as personal computers, the Internet, and other communication media. These technological developments in themselves represent new information patterns for the human brain to entertain and interpret—to construct meaning that will influence decisions about the next moves. Fortunately, the neural construction crew that has brought humanity to this point in time is up to the task.

Taking Care of Business:
Subcontractors

The ancient Greeks surmised that the stuff of the universe was made up of tiny "uncuttable" ingredients that they called atoms. Just as the enormous number of words in an alphabetic language is built from the wealth of combinations of a small number of letters, they guessed that the vast range of material objects might also result from combinations of a small number of distinct, elementary building blocks. It was a prescient guess. More than 2,000 years later we still believe it to be true, although the identity of the most fundamental units has gone through numerous revisions.

—(Greene, 1999, p. 7)

The basic rule that guides your brain's pattern construction activity is that *things unknown become known when connected to things known.* Accordingly, when your brain confronts information that is unfamiliar, its task is to establish a relationship to familiar patterns as a base on which to construct new understanding. This process is observed in the construction of a vast vocabulary from a limited number of letters in an alphabet. It also reflects nature's disposition to generate great diversity from different combinations of limited elements—as observed in the wide range of physical and biological constructions that emerge from the basic building blocks of atomic and subatomic elements. Thus the human brain is endlessly interpreting the infinite array of patterns that nature puts together from basic information elements such as shape, sound, taste, smell, pressure, temperature, and movement.

Given the extent and complexity of the task, the brain's knowledge construction business is not attributable to a particular neural site, physiological structure, or dimension of intelligence. The acquisition and integration of important information patterns is the business of the entire brain. Accordingly, the physiological, social, emotional, reflective, and dispositional dimensions of intelligence collectively contribute to the constructive dimension of intelligence—a dimension that detects, connects, stores, and retrieves blocks of knowledge that serve the intelligence business of making sense of what is encountered and deciding what to do about it (see Figure 3.8). In effect, the aforementioned dimensions of intelligence are subcontractors that collaborate in the knowledge construction business—a knowledge construction firm, you might say. Notably, not all of the subcontractors are on the job at the same time, but they all contribute in some manner to constructions that matter.

Physiological Construction

Imagine, if you would, a very small person moving among a thick maze of electrical cords and outlets in your head, incessantly connecting plugs to sockets to form circuits and networks that become increasingly more interconnected and complex. This simple visualization provides a basic perspective of *the construction site* for knowledge acquisition—construction that occurs at the cellular level of your brain through processes that involve:

- **Using sense to make sense.** The initial key to knowledge construction is direct and multiple sensory input. In fact, the more direct and multisensory the experience, the more effective the construction. The explanation for this is fairly simple—the greater the intimacy and range of sensory information, the more pieces of the puzzle the brain has to work with in constructing meaning. The brain conducts this construction activity by directing sensory input through the brain stem to the thalamus, which distributes it to other brain sites for further processing. Virtually every part of the brain is involved in this processing, but different sites have different interests. For example, the amygdala screens information for patterns of emotional interest, the cerebellum is interested in patterns affecting procedural and automatic exercises of

Figure 3.8. The Multidimensional Nature of the Construction of Knowledge

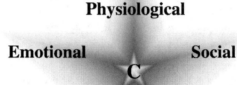

Physiological

Emotional

Social

C

Reflective   Dispositional

Multiple dimensions of human intelligence collectively contribute to a constructive brain capacity for organizing, storing, and retrieving useful information patterns:

1. The physiology of the brain provides the construction site on which information is sensed, organized, stored, and retrieved in neural networks that are continuously refined by experience.

2. Social interaction, either direct or indirect, is the primary source of rich environmental experiences that nurture brain discernment of meaningful information patterns.

3. Emotion arouses the brain to what is worth understanding.

4. Reflection refines existing information patterns and uses them to organize complex and original constructions.

5. Disposition determines the quantity and quality of brain investment in information construction.

---

body or mind, and the hippocampus analyzes and indexes patterns related to words, facts, and places. Information is also processed in primary and associated cortices (e.g., visual, auditory, motor) where additional pattern connections are examined and constructed. Analysis of the merits and potential of information patterns in the frontal lobe cortex is particularly important to such examination and construction. It is in this area that your brain is *consciously* exploring relationships between prior knowledge and new information.

- ***Neurons firing and wiring together.*** Neurons that are stimulated by sensory input form alliances that acknowledge useful information patterns (Hebb, 1949). When an established neural alliance detects a recognizable information pattern, it will respond to that pattern in some manner (e.g., initiate a standard behavior, seek more information, share the information with other neurons). If the information is new, the established neural networks will attempt to connect it to existing patterns and, thereby, form new alliances. The importance of this phenomenon is that alliances of neurons are formed, normed, and renormed by both quantity and quality of sensory input. Your brain is continually undergoing a synaptic sculpting process as neural affiliations grow and divorce at the influence of environmental experience. This is the working of plasticity in your brain, the means by which you continually reinforce and reconstruct your knowledge in response to a continually changing environment.

- ***Memorable patterns.*** An information pattern constructed is a pattern remembered—if it is constructed well. The basic workings of memory are the same as those of knowledge construction. Information that is attended to and processed by your brain stimulates the formation of neural networks that are responsive to that information. If such neural alliances are well constructed by a quality and quantity of input, the information pattern thus organized can be recalled. Furthermore, the more frequently the pattern is recalled, the more often the relevant neurons access the blood, glial cell, and chemical resources that support that neural alliance. In this fashion, a network becomes more strongly established—and memorable. It is, in effect, a *the more you use it, the better you build it, and the less likely you are to lose it* process of both constructing knowledge and the ability to access said knowledge.

Social Construction

The human brain constructs its understanding of its environment the old-fashioned way—it earns it. That is to say, given its original base of genetically installed information patterns, each human brain is left to its own experience and initiative to make sense of the world. Interaction with the physical environment is, of course, a primary and continuing source of experience that feeds the brain's construction of knowledge. The most important variable in human knowledge construction, however, is social interaction. In effect, if the physiological nature of the brain is the construction site for knowledge, the social nature of the brain is *the major supplier of material and labor* for the construction process.

A simple way to test the importance of social interaction to human construction of understanding is to reflect about what you have learned in your lifetime that did not involve such interaction in some way. How did you learn about language, cooking, mathematics, etiquette, philosophy, charity, music, ethics, science, juggling, geography, racism, loyalty, poverty, love, or growing roses? The nature of exceptional human capacity to construct knowledge is born of long evolutionary experience in social communities. This is not to say that you do not learn when physically alone through individual engagement of environmental stimuli. In such moments, however, you are most likely reviewing or preparing knowledge that has a social origin or target through a social medium of some sort—such as a conversation, book, lecture, film, report, meeting, or work of art. Furthermore, the more significant the knowledge construction, the more likely that it is the product of teamwork. Even such an apparent construction of singular insight as Einstein's $E = mc^2$ was a construction born of extensive interaction between the knowledge of an individual and the knowledge of others.

As examined in a prior section of this chapter, social interaction is the environmental experience that the developmental unfolding of your brain most expects and depends on. Your brain particularly expects opportunities to construct valuable information patterns through observing, mimicking, playing, listening, debating, and other social interactions. In fact, the quantity and quality of knowledge patterns organized by your brain depends on the quantity and quality of social experience it encounters. Again, the importance of such interaction cannot be overestimated. It is the most effective means available not only to construct understanding but also by which cognitive dissonance is generated and established information patterns are challenged and refined.

The importance of social interaction in the construction of neural patterns has also been reinforced by research into the phenomenon of "mirror neurons" in which coalitions of neural networks are developed and reinforced by "sympathy" firings that mentally reflect or perhaps simulate the actions of others (Motluk, 2001). In this social manner, the brain constructs and rehearses patterns that aid language, procedures, empathy, and anticipation of actions.

Vygotsky (1978) is among the many cognitive theorists who have concluded that strong and lasting knowledge constructions are the product of highly interactive social experience. Indeed, this theoretical position is supported by research on the positive achievement effects of cooperative learning for children and adults as reported by Slavin (1990) and others. Such findings reinforce common perceptions, such as "two heads are better than one," "no one of us is as smart as all of us," and "you never learn anything so well as when you teach it to others." In fact, appreciation for the influence of social experience on learning engenders a perception of a community of mind, one that is collectively constructing a shared human knowledge base though synapses that bridge the physical space between individual brains.

Emotional Construction

Emotion decides what the brain will attend to. In effect, the role of emotion in the construction of knowledge is that of *the comptroller of the construction schedule*—that is, the construction supervisor that decides what, where, and when construction will take place. This is an essential element of knowledge construction. As good as it is at physiological and social processing of information, your brain cannot attend to and process everything. Accordingly, emotional networks screen and prioritize brain attention to information judged to have potential for some degree of survival advantage.

Emotion also influences the organization, storage, and retrieval of information patterns by the association of emotional context to the construction experience (e.g., pleasure, fear, excitement, anger, fun, sadness). More specifically, the construction of knowledge is enhanced by challenge and inhibited by threat (Caine & Caine, 1991). For example, stress states raise the level of the hormone cortisol in your body, which has an adverse effect on information indexing by your hippocampus. In the other direction, the periodic release of noradrenaline in response to challenges you judge to be achievable helps to focus and sustain knowledge construction. In the best-case scenario, the establishment of a clear goal or purpose is a means to both arouse and sustain brain passion for knowledge construction.

Reflective Construction

There is knowledge construction . . . and then there is knowledge construction. That is, knowledge is inevitably constructed, torn down, and reconstructed in your brain. The role of reflection in the knowledge construction business is that of *the architect* responsible for envisioning the merits and potential of information patterns. Such reflection occurs in the frontal lobes as the brain consciously mulls over information that is arriving from sensory inputs of the moment in relationship to information accessed from existing neural networks. Thus, reflection is the means for refining and extending existing knowledge. It also designs and directs the construction of original ideas from the creative interplay of the brain's wealth of diverse information.

Basically, reflection is a frontal-lobe-directed examination of information patterns in the process of forming hypotheses, making predictions, conducting experiments, and formulating theories about how things work or might work. It is a continuous process of explaining and exploring relationships between patterns. Notably, organized information patterns are the building blocks for reflective thinking and learning, which, in turn, provide stimulus for the construction of more patterns.

Dispositional Construction

As will be described in a following section, dispositions are inclinations or tendencies of behavior that are born of both genetic programming and environmental experience. The dispositional nature of intelligence is revealed in the disparate manners in which individuals and groups exercise their capacity to acquire and apply knowledge. More simply put, dispositional intelligence is a matter of habits of mind—the tendencies and inclinations that characterize one's thinking.

Dispositional intelligence might be thought of as *the financier* that determines the investment to be made in knowledge construction and, thereby, the likely return to be realized from such investment. For example, one might be disposed to maintain a healthy physiological brain state, seek out social stimulation, and learn and engage in reflective thinking strategies—or one might be disposed to abuse the physiology of the brain, withdraw from human contact, and think about things as little as possible. The point is, humans have considerable power to shape the dispositions that habitually direct their behavior. Importantly, a broad disposition to proactively cultivate and exercise intelligence is an important influence on the construction of knowledge—and, when specifically aligned with the exercise of reflective intelligence, it is a means to govern the double bind of your brain's proclivity for such construction.

Governing the Double Bind

We are constantly thinking about what the world is like, and what it is likely to be like, and even about worlds that are most unlikely. Our explanations about the world constantly change as a consequence of our experience and in the process we collect—construct might be a better word—*knowledge* or *information.*

— (Smith, 1990, p. 13)

Your brain is very good at constructing organized information patterns, that is, knowledge. According to Perkins (1995), it is a pattern machine that becomes attuned through experience to familiar and useful patterns in the world—and adept at replaying such patterns efficiently and reflexively. This is easily illustrated though a simple exercise. To that end, take a moment to read the following paragraph:

Scenario: *Emily was playing with her friends when she heard the ice cream truck coming down the street. She remembered her birthday money and ran into the house.*

Question: What is Emily going to do?

Reflection Time

If your mental response to the above question entertained the thought that Emily was going to purchase ice cream with her birthday money, that is understandable—from a brain-as-pattern-machine perspective. Review of the paragraph, of course, reveals that there is no narrative information that supports such a conclusion. All you know for sure is that Emily heard the ice cream truck, remembered her birthday money, and went into the house. Might the truck be a refrigerated semitrailer rig delivering its cargo to a Wal-Mart? Might such a truck rumble by an outdoor café where 25-year-old Emily is playing bridge with Bubba, Bruno, and Boris when she remembers the $5,000 birthday check she received the day before from her wealthy Aunt Ruth, causing her to run into her neighbor's house to call the local Harley-Davidson dealership to order that red Sportster motorcycle she's had her eye on? No? Well, the point, of course, is that each scenario is as likely as any other from the information given. What your constructive brain most likely did, however, was infer an outcome from patterns of information that it is familiar with and that have served it well in the past.

A capacity for inference is, of course, a desirable quality of the reflective nature of intelligence—as will be examined in the next section. Perkins (1995) advises that there is an evolutionary double bind in the constructive works here, however, in that your intellectual strength carries some baggage in the form of an inherent weakness. That is, the effectiveness and efficiency of the constructive nature of your intelligence is subject to bias toward patterns that work well most of the time. There are at least two dangers associated with this circumstance. One is that inappropriate applications of ingrained patterns might be made to novel situations that require new understanding and original responses. Another is that your brain is very capable of constructing a deficient (i.e., wrong, inaccurate, misinformed) information pattern based on limited or prejudiced experience. Fortunately, there are reflective and dispositional dimensions to the nature of your intelligence, dimensions that provide governance for the double bind of your brain's pattern-making proclivity—when exercised effectively. The final sections of this chapter address these two dimensions.

Essence

In essence, the quality of information to which one is exposed and the amount of information one acquires is reflected throughout one's lifetime in the structure of the brain.

—(Bransford, Brown, & Cocking, 2000, p. 118)

- To survive, organisms must recognize and remember information patterns.
- The more mobile the organism, the higher the premium on pattern recognition.
- The human brain is a lean, mean, pattern-making machine in residence within the most mobile organism on earth.
- The organization of neural-network alliances and the dynamic manipulation of arithmetic variables enable human brain capacity for constructing meaning and memory.
- Capacity to detect, organize, and store information patterns is genetically installed in the human brain during prenatal development, for example, neural networks dedicated to lines, shapes, colors, sounds, taste, smell, and so forth.
- The human brain constructs patterns from sensory input stimulated by environmental experience. Accordingly, brain capacity for constructing meaning and memory from useful informational patterns (e.g., sounds, shapes, sequences) is expectant of and dependent on environmental experience.
- The richer the sensory experience, the richer the construction of meaning and memory.

- Emotion is a critical element of experience enrichment in the construction of meaning and memory.
- Social interaction is a primary means for providing an emotional context and other information enrichment in environmental experience.
- The construction of strings of patterns of information into ever more complex relationships is the cognitive process that underlies the most sophisticated work of the human brain, for example, language, abstraction, logic, metaphor, imagination, and so forth.
- Capacity to construct useful mental models presents a double bind when openness to alternative patterns is ignored or resisted.

Implications

The learning process, by which patterns are sorted out so that increasingly more sense is made of a complex world, goes on incessantly, and each individual, in a purely individual way, gathers features and clues that gradually mount up. Progressively, the pattern is grasped more sharply and greater discrimination becomes possible.

−(Hart, 1983, p. 77)

- *If* the human brain is a lean, mean, pattern-making machine that physically connects new information patterns to established patterns in neural networks, *then* leaders would be wise to forego extensive efforts to instruct in favor of providing opportunities for individuals to construct personal knowledge.
- *If* mobility has been an important variable in expanding the environmental experience and, thereby, knowledge construction opportunities of the human species, *then* leaders should facilitate the movement of organization members to stimulating environmental sites, for example, groups, conferences, workshops, job changes, the Internet, certification programs, travel, and so forth.
- *If* the human brain is designed to discern meaningful patterns through direct and active experience with information, *then* a leader should provide opportunity for the members of an organization to write, speak, draw, and otherwise manipulate information they need to understand.
- *If* social interaction is a primary source for engaging emotion and other information-enriched experiences that aid the construction of knowledge, *then* a leader should arrange frequent opportunities for structured social interaction between members of the organization as they process information relevant to their responsibilities and organizational purpose.
- *If* humans are subject to becoming comfortable with familiar patterns at the risk of remaining oblivious to other more advantageous patterns, *then* a leader might contemplate strategies that would challenge existing knowledge

and promote contemplation of other patterns and connections from new information sources.

- **If** _____,
  then _____.
- **If** _____,
  then _____.

ⓡ The Reflective Nature of Intelligence

No technology has received more attention from natural selection, more refinement via natural selection, than intelligence. Everywhere around us is evidence of the tendency of intelligence to grow through evolution. The most spectacular example, with all due modesty, is us.

—(Robert Wright, 2000. p. 280)

Imagine

Reflect: *To throw or bend back; form an image of; to think or consider seriously*

—(*American Heritage Dictionary*, 2000, p. 1467)

To orient your reflection about the uniqueness of the reflective nature of human intelligence, you may wish to access a nearby mirror (if a mirror is not immediately available to you, however, it is not a problem, just *imagine* your use of a mirror). Looking into the mirror (real or imagined), you will recognize the arrangement of image patterns that your brain has neurally constructed to represent your face and, if it's a full-size mirror, your body. Turning slightly to the right or left, you will observe different perspectives of yourself. Similarly, tipping your head forward or backward, smiling or frowning or any other manipulation of posture or facial muscle will affect what is reflected back to your sensory vision (it's what makes the difference in those driving-license mug shots).

Thus far in this exercise, your intelligence has been employing its physiological and constructive qualities to register recognition of familiar sensory information patterns as well as to connect new information that is worthy of attention—perhaps the status of your hair, weight, muscle tone, or a new wrinkle or suspicious blemish (which, of course, engages the emotional nature of your intelligence). You are able to see much more in the mirror reflection, however, should you elect to do so. Picture what your hair looked like 10 years ago and what it might look like 10 years into the future. How about your weight and muscle tone? Is there anything that you have done in the last 10 years that has contributed to your present condition? Is there anything that you might have done differently? What about the future? What are your options? Is there anything you can do to influence these factors in the next 10 years?

You might note that at this point in the exercise, you are seeing things in your mind that are not in the mirror. That is, your reflection has moved from observation of a present reality to envisioning what has been and what might be and what has made or will make a difference to either. This experience exemplifies how humans re-create, explain, and forecast everything, be it as simple as your a reflection about the effects of diet and exercise or as profound as John Lennon (1971) poetically imagining that the "world will be as one." Your brain constructs its understanding of things the way it thinks they are, but it also has the capacity to reconstruct how and why they were as well as to project how and why they might be. In the very big picture of survival as a species, this capacity has made a defining difference in what it means to be human. It is a difference that is observed in the exercise of analytic and creative activities such as decision making, problem solving, questioning, experimentation, invention, forecasting, comparison, abstraction, and inductive and deductive thinking. It is a capacity to see and debate answers to questions of why and how and what if—within the confines of one's own mind: to imagine.

The Gist of It

An Executive Function

The frontal lobes perform the most advanced and complex functions in all of the brain, the so-called executive functions. They are linked to intentionality, purposefulness, and complex decision making. They reach significant development only in humans; arguably, they make us human . . . . The frontal lobes are to the brain what a conductor is to an orchestra, a general is to an army, the chief executive officer is to a corporation. They coordinate and lead other neural structures in concerted action. The frontal lobes are the brain's command post.

—(Goldberg, 2001, p. 2)

Goldberg observes that the evolution of a cortical principle of brain organization enabled far greater complexity and connectivity of information processing than would be accommodated by a modular principle of brain organization. In effect, the brain developed a truly "dynamic topology" (2001, p. 218) as the cortex evolved. Such explosive development in capacity, however, required the emergence of a mechanism for managing it to effect. Enter the frontal lobes of the brain.

It is useful to reference the physiological evolution of the brain when investigating its reflective capacities because the physiology helps to explain the reflective process. Specifically, the frontal lobes of the brain represent an evolutionary development that met the need for "coordinating and constraining the activities of a vast array of neural structures at any given time and over time" (2001, p. 218). You might say that, just as the brain evolved a means to coordinate the components of increasingly complex organisms, the frontal lobes evolved to coordinate the components of an increasingly complex brain. To that end, the frontal lobes are globally connected to the rest of the brain so that they might access and configure information in the manner required of any specific circumstance. The frontal lobes also have the capacity to constrain, redirect, or remediate actions initiated in other brain areas.

The frontal lobes, then, represent the area of the neural landscape that humans depend on to maximize brain capacity to resolve, create, and project. As such, the frontal lobes are "truly the organ of civilization" (2001, p. 24), the physiological area capable of lighting up intelligence capacity within individuals and organizations.

Vive la Différence

We certainly have a passion for stringing things together in structured ways, ones that go far beyond the sequences produced by other animals. Besides words into sentences, we combine notes into melodies, steps into dances, and elaborate narratives into games with procedural rules. Might structured strings be a core facility of the brain, useful for language, story-telling, planning ahead, games, and ethics? Might natural selection for any of these abilities augment the common neural machinery, so that improved grammar incidentally serves to expand plan-ahead activities?

—(Calvin, 1996, p. 95)

If information patterns are the currency of intelligence, reflection is the compounding of returns on the original investment in their construction. That is, reflection is the ultimate stringing together of patterns of information through serious consideration—a conscious bending back—of constructed knowledge to proactively explore further configurations, implications, and applications thereof. In effect, the reflective qualities of your brain engage in examination of how that which is mentally constructed might best be invested—exploited might be a better word—to the advantage of survival interests.

Calvin (1996) advises that the neural mechanisms that enable the stringing together of meaningless phonemes to form meaningful words is the same mechanism that underlies the stringing together of words into sentences, concepts, and narrative stories. Ultimately, this stringing together of patterns is exhibited in the unique human capacity to string together mental narratives about events, issues, possible actions, and probable effects—that is, the capacity to analyze, plan, and predict. This capacity emerged, as previously reviewed in a prior chapter section, from the strong influence of social experience that marked human evolution. A culminating effect of such experience was enhanced brain physiology for the construction of information templates. This base of neural capacity for extensive experiential knowledge served the evolution of conscious empathy for the experience of others, which in turn enabled mental narratives strung along the lines of "why" and "how" and "what if." It is simple narratives such as these that eventually lead to the more complex narratives that accompany the invention of religion, art, philosophy, and scientific inquiry—ultimate expressions of human desire to explain and influence their environment.

Capacity for conscious reflection, then, is *the* distinguishing dimension of human intelligence—a dimension that is differentiated from the construction of knowledge by its physiological complexity, social unfolding, emotional refinement, and constructive capacity. It is, Damasio (1999) advises, how we know of ourselves in the past and future as well as the present.

The Mirrors of Your Mind

The game of social plot and counter-plot cannot be played merely on the basis of accumulated knowledge. . . . It asks for a level of intelligence that is, I submit, unparalleled in any other sphere of living.

—(Humphrey, 1983, p. 21)

With reference to definitions presented in Chapter 2, reflection is a term that many would immediately associate with intelligence. Indeed, mental images of Rodin's *The Thinker* might come to mind when one contemplates the defining nature of intelligence. Intelligence, from such a perspective, is the capacity to reflectively contemplate, to think deeply with fist to chin and elbow to knee in quest of answers to challenging problems and issues of human existence. Such capacity, however, does stand on its own. As in the case of the construction of knowledge, your capacity for reflective manipulation of information patterns is intimately enmeshed with the collective qualities of other dimensions of intelligence.

Returning for a moment to the mirror exercise presented at the beginning of this section, the reflective nature of intelligence can be interpreted as the conscious bending back of information patterns to discern potential relationships of peril or promise. This bending back and replaying of information occurs on a massive level in the cortex and subcortical regions during reflective thought. In effect, your brain performs as a house of mirrors as it plays the light of new and established information among an infinity of neural networks to create and explore different perspectives. That is to say, your reflective brain is not content to stare into the mirror and accept what is immediately revealed. Rather, in its reflective mode, your brain is moving information at will to generate alternative images.

Reflective intelligence, then, is about enhancing the perception potential of information by organizing alternative poses from multiple information sources. Such reflection might be envisioned as a laser light show occurring within your brain, involving electrochemical messages flashing between trillions of synapses in incredibly complex arrangements of incoming, recalled, and reconstructed information patterns—the physical reality of brainstorming. Evidence of this neural activity is visibly observed in chess players planning 12 moves out, scientists planning a landing on the moon, and coaches planning for the big game. It is also observable in the creativity and problem solving of artists, politicians, and entrepreneurs. The same process is at work in evaluating a personal relationship, planning a vacation, or pondering a career move. Most of all, it is a process that unifies the multidimensional nature of your intelligence in the act of meaningful real-world thinking and learning. It is such thinking, Senge (1990) observes, that "gets to the heart of what it means to be human" (p. 14)—to recreate ourselves, reperceive the world and our relationship to it, extend our capacity to create, and be part of the generative processes of life.

A Unifying Intelligence

The prefrontal cortex plays the central role in forming goals and objectives and then devising plans of action required to attain these goals. It selects the cognitive skills required to implement the plans, coordinates these skills, and applies them in a correct order. Finally, the prefrontal cortex is responsible for evaluating our actions as success or failure relative to our intentions.

—(Goldberg, 2001, p. 24)

It is possible, of course, for you to reflect about anything, including your navel. Your reflective intelligence is usually reserved for more interesting and challenging situations, however, such as making decisions or resolving problems that are of consequence to you and others in the context of work, home, or play. Such employment of reflection naturally draws together other dimensions of knowledge acquisition and application (see Figure 3.9).

- **Physiological.** Conscious reflection about concepts, events, and options lights up your brain—literally. Functional magnetic resonance imaging (FMRI) scans of your brain while it is engaged in problem solving or other reflective exercises will detect extensive electrochemical activity as neural networks are activated in cross-referencing of available information patterns. This is particularly evident in the cortex, the crowning glory of human brain evolution, the neural field within which "brainstorming" physically occurs. Such neural communication is most dramatic when the reflective task is novel to your brain, thus placing greater demands on the working memory functions of the prefrontal lobe as well as access to undedicated neural space in various associative cortices that accommodate the storage, retrieval, and continual sculpting of information patterns.
- **Social.** Reflection seeks out interaction with the knowledge of other brains, either through direct or extended means. Such interaction is an essential source of dissonance and options for your brain's reflective efforts. Social experience is the great provocateur of reflection, the foil that challenges and refines existing patterns in the quest for the better pattern. It is an element of

Figure 3.9. The Unifying Influence of Reflection on Multiple Dimensions of Intelligence

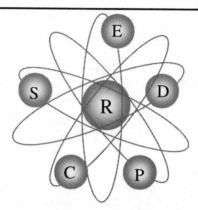

A meaningful problem-solving, decision-making, or other challenging reflection task requires:

1. **P**hysiological engagement of the brain's comprehensive network of cells, circuits, and chemicals
2. **S**ocial acquisition and refinement of information
3. **E**motional arousal
4. **C**onstruction of relevant information patterns
5. **D**isposition to exercise productive thinking strategies

reflection born of highly social communities, one that supplies new information and encourages the asking of who, what, where, when, why, and how.

- **Emotional.** Reflective intelligence is not engaged unless the emotional centers of the brain have judged a situation or circumstance worthy of your brain's conscious attention. Once engaged, however, reflective pursuit of an answer, solution, or original product or idea is itself an influence on your emotions. In effect, confrontation with a meaningful, real-world challenge both arouses and fans the passions of the mind, thus engaging reflective focus and perseverance. The danger that lurks, however, is that the reflection challenge is of a magnitude that overwhelms or intimidates, thus stimulating an emotional decision to withdraw.
- **Constructive.** Reflection about a meaningful problem or other challenging task provides your brain with the greatest motivation and opportunity to construct knowledge. One cannot reflect about alternatives and options without relevant information. Accordingly, information must either be retrieved from existing neural networks or new patterns of understanding must be constructed. The building blocks of knowledge must be available for your reflec-

tive intelligence to play with if it is to compose its virtuoso performances of thought and deed.
- **Dispositional.** Habits are formed, not born. The exercise of reflective intelligence requires a disposition to analyze, create, and resolve. The establishment and refinement of such disposition, moreover, is the product of reflective thinking experience. To that end, to cultivate productive dispositions toward the effective exercise of reflective thinking strategies, the old adage applies—practice, practice, practice.

Intelligence Most Conscious

To conjure up an internal representation of the future, the brain must have the ability to take certain elements of prior experiences and reconfigure them in a way that in its totality does not correspond to any actual past experience. To accomplish this, the organism must go beyond the mere ability to *form* internal representations, the models of the world outside.

It must acquire the ability to *manipulate* and *transform* these models . . . the organism must go beyond the ability to see the world *through* mental representation; it must acquire the ability to work *with* mental representations.

—(Goldberg, 2001, p. 25)

Human intelligence is made distinct by a unique capacity for mental visioning and rehearsal of behavior options prior to action. This specific capacity for the reflective review and manipulation of information is of particular survival advantage when confronted by novel environmental challenges—when guessing well is, indeed, the game, and pressure is on your brain.

If the genius of human intelligence rests on an extraordinary capacity to construct useful information patterns, then reflection is the exhibition of virtuosity in the application of that genius. This is observed in the fact that the resolutions of problems or tasks are often the products of mentally massaging existing information. A brief exercise illustrates this point:

1. Extend your right arm in front of you at chest level with the palm of your hand facing down and make a fist.
2. Think of a controversial issue that is currently being hotly debated in the nation, your community, your home, or your place of work.
3. Identify the pro and con positions of the issue you have identified (e.g., for or against a large tax cut, for or against physician-assisted suicide, for or against drilling for oil in wilderness areas, for or against the pending school referendum).
4. Indicate your position (i.e., for or against) by extending the thumb of your extended fist up or down. You may think about this for a moment, but you must take a thumbs-up or thumbs-down position on the issue.

5. Put your arm down, grab a pen, and jot down your rationale, that is, your reasons for your position on the issue.
6. Now write down what you believe advocates of the position opposite yours would write as their rationale for their position.
7. Question: What was happening in your brain as you completed steps 1-6?

$$\boxed{\textit{Reflection Time}}$$

The above exercise becomes more stimulating of the reflective circuitry in your prefrontal cortex, as well as its interaction with the rest of your brain, if you have access to someone who advocates for an opposing position. You would be able, thereby, to compare what you anticipated about each other's reasoning to each one's actual arguments. You might also be prompted to reflect further about evidence and opinions that support or detract from either position—you might even change your position. What you should be aware of, in any case, is that your neural circuitry was able to do the following:

- Access existing information that has been stored throughout your brain by prior information constructions
- Articulate a position on the issue that you reconstructed in your mind
- Articulate a second perspective about the same issue
- And . . . given the seventh step in the exercise, you were also able to analyze what your brain was doing as it was doing it.

As simple as this exercise was, then, it reveals the essence of the reflective difference in your brain compared to brains of other life forms—the capacity to replay information sequences and patterns in your head at will; to think 12 steps out on a chess board or in career planning; or to construct deeper understanding of an issue, process, or concept. This is what your brain does when it is performing at the high end of its evolutionary endowment. It is the quality of human intelligence that draws on all other dimensions of mental capacity to orchestrate the phenomenal success of the species. It is also the quality that will determine future success. Incredibly, as will be observed in the following section, the effective exercise of this powerful capacity for analytic and creative thinking is optional, at the disposition of those who are blessed with it.

Essence

- The human capacity to reflectively review and endlessly reconfigure relationships within and between established patterns of information represents the essence of human intelligence. It is this capacity to apply information to the processes of complex reasoning (e.g., abstraction, classification, deduction, prediction, invention) that defines human effectiveness in guessing well. Ultimately, it is the intelligence variable that enabled human invention of art, religion, and scientific inquiry.

- The reflective nature of human intelligence emerged from the social evolution of brain capacity for information patterning, emotional awareness, and language. These developments promoted neural networking in the prefrontal cortex that enabled conscious reflection about events and options. In effect, the human brain developed the capacity to conduct a conscious conversation within itself—thus the stringing together of information patterns into words and sentences was paralleled by the stringing together of information patterns into abstractions and hypotheses.

- Reflective reasoning is observed at the neural level in the outer layers of the prefrontal lobe of the cortex. Microtechnology can further locate specific complex reasoning processes, such as problem solving, in the lateral prefrontal cortex. But reflective reasoning is intimately connected to the entire neural system.

- The reflective nature of human intelligence is dependent on physiological health, social interaction (direct and indirect), emotional tension (versus stress), construction of a knowledge base, and disposition to engage in thinking strategies.

- Reflective reasoning is the business—the biological niche—of humans. The exotic exercise of divergence, imagination, improvisation, and foresight in thought and subsequent action has been the key to human versatility and survival success. Specifically, it is a means to govern the double bind of neural pattern construction, thus maintaining a capacity to continually entertain new ideas and processes. It is also the means by which humanity aspires to consciously manage the dictates of its genetic heritage.

Implications

- *If* the reflective reasoning capacity of the human brain is centered in the prefrontal cortex, *then* leaders should "go for the gray" by structuring opportunities for the regular exercise of analytic and creative thinking strategies.

- *If* reflective thinking is a catalyst for the integrated operation of multiple dimensions of human intelligence, *then* a leader might most effectively advance the collective intelligence of the organization through the regular involvement of the membership in meaningful problem-solving and decision-making activities.

- *If* the reflective nature of human intelligence invented such things as art, religion, and scientific inquiry, *then* it is reasonable to assume that it will be the determining variable in whatever future humanity will have.

- *If* _____,
  then _____.

D The Dispositional Nature of Intelligence

If it ain't in your heart, it ain't in your horn.

—(Attributed to legendary saxophonist Charles "Charlie" Parker)

Dispositions Fair and Foul

Think about a friend, colleague, or family member whom you hold in high esteem. What do you appreciate most about that person? Similarly, what qualities do you admire and appreciate in people whom you know less well—for example, people you encounter in the process of conducting your work, shopping, engaging professional services, or while dining out?

Reflection Time

Attributes that you admire in the people who cross your path—whether through lasting relationships or brief encounters—are, of course, almost limitless in their possibilities. It is predictable, however, that qualities of being positive, proactive, kind, productive, creative, friendly, organized, sincere, open-minded, modest, conscientious, resilient, fun loving, considerate, confident, dedicated, responsible, or compassionate are representative of what might come to mind while envisioning an admirable person. Opposing perceptions are also easily accessed. That is, unfavorable attributes will readily emerge when reflecting on a close relationship or passing encounter with an individual held in low esteem. Take another minute to test this out. How would you describe the qualities of a person whom you find to be less than admirable in some way?

Reflection Time

Again, the range of attributes that could be used to describe undesirable qualities in people is endless—but terms such as negative, reactive, cruel, lazy, unimaginative, cold, disorganized, insincere, closed minded, conceited, inattentive, morose, dull, rude, indecisive, uncommitted, irresponsible, or insensitive might come to mind.

What of yourself? What attributes—be they admirable or unfavorable—come to mind when you contemplate your personal qualities? The test for this reflection is to assess how you might commonly respond in given situations. For example, how would you respond to the following:

- Another driver cutting you off in heavy traffic?
- Criticism from a colleague of an idea that you have proposed?

- The announcement of a major restructuring of your organization?
- An innovative idea that proposes a radical change in an existing policy or practice?
- A news report describing a social injustice committed against an individual or group of people?
- Winning the lottery?
- Responsibility for organizing an investment portfolio, family vacation, political campaign, construction project, wedding, or other major planning activity?
- A decline in market share for your organization due to new competition?
- A problem that has not been resolved after several efforts to find a solution?
- Training requirements for learning how to use a new technology?

How do you see yourself responding to the above situations? Would others see you in the same light? Would you resist the allure of road rage, persist in the face of a daunting problem, be open to critical review from a colleague? What do your projected responses reveal about your admirable qualities as a human being—or qualities you would judge to be less than admirable?

Refection Time

What might be concluded from these exercises? It should be clear that humans adopt and exhibit characteristic behavior patterns. It should also be clear that you know what you appreciate and do not appreciate about other people—just as they know what they appreciate and do not appreciate about you. Indeed, humans determine defining qualities of self and others through valuation of behaviors habitually demonstrated in social contexts. That is, individuals in human communities come to know one another by their characteristic behaviors. Such distinctions would not be possible, of course, if individuals were not inclined to habitual behavior—behavior that reveals dispositions of mind and character.

The Gist of It

Disposition: A habitual inclination; a tendency

—(*American Heritage Dictionary*, 2000, p. 522)

The Disposition of Disposition

Dispositions shape our lives. They are proclivities that lead us in one direction rather than another within the freedom of action that we have.

—(Perkins, 1995, p. 275)

There are many levels and facets of human disposition that invite investigation. It is the proclivity of human intelligence to engage and cultivate itself, however, that is of particular interest to this narrative. Specifically, how are qualities of mind and character arranged as tendencies and inclinations that affect the exercise of intelligence? The answer to this question, predictably, is that it is a matter of brain nature and nurture.

Dispositions evolve from the electrochemical compositions, allocations, and interactions that mediate all human behavior. That is, dispositions are ultimately the product of electrochemical activity within the neural networks of the brain. Accordingly, at birth, an infant has genetically established neural circuits that are disposed to engage particular behavior patterns in particular situations. Some of these dispositions are so universally demonstrated—for example, crying when hungry or otherwise physically distressed—that they are hardly distinguishable among infants. As every parent of more than one child well knows, however, individual infants almost immediately demonstrate dispositions that mark their unique character as human beings. Thus infants are evaluated as being more or less irritable, anxious, or easygoing by the habitual behaviors they exhibit. Parents, teachers, and other observers of child development will also note that initial dispositional exhibitions may strengthen, diminish, or otherwise change over time due to the influence of environmental experience.

The bottom line is that some dispositions are factory installed in the brain by virtue of the genetic endowment of the human species as passed on from parent to child. This inheritance accesses the common dispositional attributes of the human species as evolved over millions of years of natural selection. Some of these dispositions are immediately evident while others become more apparent at later developmental stages. Gopnik, Meltzoff, and Kuhl (1999) speak to such inherited species attributes when they describe children's natural interest and behavior in making sense of the people, objects, and language that they encounter as analogous to the disposition and behavior of scientists. That is, children naturally seek to construct understanding by forming hypotheses; making predictions; conducting experiments; and formulating theories about how people, things, and language work. Disposition that is originally installed, however, is also immediately and continually influenced (commencing in the womb) by the specific environmental experience of the individual. Thus human disposition is disposed by both nature and nurture—as are all other qualities of human organisms. The challenge and potential, of course, lies in the nurture.

Why Dispositions?

Humans are prepared by their biology to form friendships, fall in love, cope with fear, and try, continually, to move toward their prized goals, despite early experiences that might make these attainments hard to accomplish. These urges are remarkably difficult to subdue.

—(Kagan, 1998, p. 109)

Returning once again to the primary business of the human brain, dispositions can be interpreted as habitual patterns of behavior that the brain at some level—consciously, or subconsciously, disposed by nature or nurture or a combination thereof—judges to be of survival value. This does not mean that a particular behavioral pattern is, indeed, a good one; it just means the brain at some level believes that it is somehow useful to behave in a certain manner (e.g., to be habitually positive or negative, open- or closed minded, timid or adventurous, trusting or suspicious, active or lethargic). The discernment of such patterns is consistent with the basic information-processing operations of the brain that determine patterns useful to the guidance of advantageous behavior—whether determining patterns pertinent to object recognition, feeding, communication, or any other survival advantage. The discernment of dispositions is, in effect, the organization of behavior patterns at a broad level—patterns that are established and exhibited as habits, tendencies, or inclinations. Such patterns reflect the brain's decision that it is of value to adopt a tendency to behave in a certain manner. Importantly, at a conscious level, the discernment of preferred dispositional patterns engages the physiological, social, emotional, constructive, and reflective dimensions of human intelligence. That is, the physiological platform enables the construction and reflective adjustment of dispositional survival patterns that unfold within the context of social and emotional experience.

Kagan (1998) speaks to the nature and nurture of human disposition in his analysis of transitions that occur in initial exhibitions of high- and low-reactivity temperaments by infants. He speculates that infants inherit different neurochemistries in brain structures that mediate avoidance reactions to novelty. Subsequent developmental stages combined with nurturing environmental experiences, however, assert an altering influence on the initial high-reactivity dispositions of many infants. This effect is most dramatically demonstrated by the resiliency of war orphans who, by virtue of nurturing adult care, progress from anxious and subdued dispositional states to normal psychological profiles.

So it is with humans over the life span. Dispositions—by other names loosely and variously referred to as habits, tendencies, inclinations, attitudes, personality, character, or temperament—are rooted in genetic blueprints but malleable by experience. The malleability of disposition is observable in the adolescent that breaks or reverses an established dispositional pattern as well as the adult who is dispositionally transformed by significant changes in professional or personal circumstances. Dispositions bloom and sour at the experience of new schools, jobs, challenges, interpersonal relationships, and other significant life experiences—as well as the cumulative effect of more subtle everyday experiences. They are also affected, as will be discussed shortly, by conscious reflection about dispositional status and what actions might engender the attainment of preferred states.

Why dispositions? It is nature's way to organize and adapt patterns. Dispositions are habitual behavior patterns that are observable in every arena of human activity. They serve as behavior templates that affect hygiene, exercise, diet, interpersonal relations, work, and virtually any other activity that presents an option as to how to act. In fact, it is difficult to imagine human existence without the element of habitual behavior. Life would be considerably more difficult to manage on a moment-to-moment basis if one had to continually pause to reflect about each and every behavior option. The establishment of habitual behavior patterns relieves the brain of such mundane preoccupation with how to act in every instance (e.g., to be positive or negative, open-minded or closed minded, etc.). The trick, of course, is to establish productive dispositions that generally guide advantageous behavior over the wide range of human activity, thus freeing the reflective powers of the brain for more momentous tasks.

The advantage of a productive disposition (and, conversely, the disadvantage of a detrimental disposition), then, is that it provides ready propensity for behavior by which humans might more efficiently and effectively conduct their survival business. Nowhere is this more significant than in the human disposition to engage and exercise intelligent behavior.

Disposition of Mind

A disposition is a propensity to act in a certain way. Viewing intelligence dispositionally says that intelligence is expressed as characteristic patterns of intellectual behavior in everyday situations.

—(Tishman, 2000, p. 43)

All forms of human disposition matter, whether they are genetically ingrained or experientially cultivated. Disposition to consciously exercise the multiple dimensions of human intelligence, however, is of particular importance. In effect, it is the nature of human intelligence to adopt habitual patterns for the engagement of its diverse and powerful properties. Significantly, it is disposition to consciously engage intelligence that holds sway over all other possible human dispositions—good or bad. Furthermore, such disposition might be exercised on both broad and specific levels of engagement.

Broad Disposition to Engage
and Cultivate Intelligence

Humans are gifted by nature with an unsurpassed intelligence capacity. This capacity is available on demand for use and development as individuals and organizations choose to engage it. There lies the rub. Capacity does not equate with effective utilization or realization of potential. Natural capacity to walk, talk, or create visual images does not automatically evolve to ballet, opera, or the Mona Lisa. Likewise, human capacity for intelligence does not automatically translate into intelligent behavior. Humans are, indeed, genetically disposed to exercise physiological, social, emotional, constructive, and reflective dimensions of intelligence. There is no choice in this matter. It is human nature to acquire, organize, and apply information in such multidimensional fashion. It is as natural as breathing. Human intelligence must be consciously and regularly exercised, however, if it is to realize its potential. Accordingly, disposition to consciously exercise intelligence is key to maximizing intelligence. And what would such disposition look like if applied broadly to different dimensions of the nature of human intelligence? It might advisably involve the following:

- Disposition to consciously engage the *physiological* nature of intelligence: Humans are biologically endowed with extraordinary brain capacity for monitoring and processing information. This capacity arises from a physiological platform of malleable circuits, cells, and chemicals that are intimately integrated with the entire physiology of the host organism.

  A disposition to consciously exercise the physiological dimension of intelligence to optimum effect might be expressed through characteristic propensities for physical exercise, healthy diet, water consumption, fresh air, natural light, and stimulating environments and experiences.

- Disposition to consciously engage the *social* nature of intelligence: Humans both expect and depend on a social unfolding of intelligence capacity.

  A disposition to consciously exercise the social dimension of intelligence to optimum effect might be expressed through characteristic propensities for seeking and structuring social opportunities for collaboration and the sharing and challenging of ideas.

- Disposition to consciously engage the *emotional* nature of intelligence: Human emotions arouse mind and body to advantageous response states and actions.

  A disposition to consciously exercise the emotional dimension of intelligence to optimum effect might be expressed through characteristic propensities for metamood (thinking about the state and management of one's emotional state), emotional intelligence (awareness and reflective mediation of emotion in a manner that contributes to the quality of one's life), proactive management of detrimental stress factors (e.g., cultivation of a balance of exercise, healthy diet, social activity, and work), and orientation to meaningful professional and personal purpose.

- Disposition to consciously engage the *constructive* nature of intelligence: The human brain is preeminently designed for the discernment, organization, and storing of useful information patterns from the richness of environmental experience.

  A disposition to consciously exercise the constructive dimension of intelligence to optimum effect might be expressed through characteristic propensities for direct experience with information through writing, speaking, drawing, enactment, assembly, experimentation, demonstration, or other means for constructing personal understanding.

- Disposition to consciously engage the *reflective* nature of intelligence: Humans represent the only species with evolved capacity to reflectively assess objectives, obstacles, and options.

  A disposition to consciously exercise the reflective dimension of intelligence to optimum effect might be expressed through characteristic propensities for engaging specific thinking strategies (e.g., problem solving, analysis of perspective, metaphor, lateral thinking, etc.).

- Disposition to consciously engage the *dispositional* nature of intelligence: Every healthy human brain is genetically disposed to the physiological, social, emotional, constructive, and reflective exercise of intelligence. Beyond basic biological and psychological prescriptions, however, human disposition in the exercise of intelligence is malleable by environmental influence and conscious reflection about advantageous options.

  A disposition to consciously exercise the dispositional dimension of intelligence to optimum effect might be expressed through characteristic propensities for metacognition (thinking about one's thinking) as it pertains to physiological, social, emotional, constructive, and reflective dimensions.

Specific Disposition to Think

Beyond a broad disposition to engage and cultivate intelligence lies the opportunity to employ specific strategies that maximize the phenomenon. This perception is reflected in a wide range of research about effective thinking, the findings of which point to specific qualities and behaviors of effective thinkers. Notably, scholars in this arena argue for the distinction between human capacity for intelligence and specific thinking strategies that take full advantage of said capacity. They also acknowledge the importance of thinking disposition, that is, the disposition to both learn and, subsequently, apply thinking skills.

Perkins (1995) advises that a thinking disposition is a tendency, habit, or commitment toward thinking in a certain way, for example, the disposition to be open-minded, the disposition to think in an imaginative and adventurous way, or the disposition to seek out evidence. Perkins further points out that, while the cultivation of intelligence certainly involves skill development (e.g., in problem-solving, decision-making, or creative-thinking strategies), the disposition to employ such skills needs attention also. That is, people can become reasonably skilled at an activity like swimming or selling or thinking without being especially disposed to engage in it. Examples of the skills dispositions of effective thinkers, as identified by Perkins and others, follow.

- Paul (1990) proposes seven interdependent traits of mind that are important to critical thinking: intellectual humility, courage, empathy, good faith (integrity), perseverance, reason, and a sense of justice.
- Facione & Facione (1992) suggest that there are seven general thinking dispositions: truth seeking, open-mindedness, analyticity, systematicity, self-confidence, inquisitiveness, and maturity.
- Perkins (1995, pp. 284-285) describes seven core dispositions to clear, broad, deep, sound, curious, strategic, and aware thinking:

  1. *Disposition to be clear,* coherent, precise, specific, and well organized
  2. *Disposition to be broad,* adventurous, flexible, and independent while appreciative of other perspectives and committed to the discovery of connections

3. *Disposition to seek deep understanding* of underlying unities in the form of laws, theories, frameworks, principles, causes, and other governing factors of ideas, things, and events
4. *Disposition to be sound,* accurate, thorough, fair, knowledgeable, logical, and well supported by evidence
5. *Disposition to be curious,* questioning, probing and inquisitive
6. *Disposition to be strategic* and organized in thinking
7. *Disposition to be metacognitively aware* and critical of one's thinking patterns and progress

Aside from an obvious affinity for seven items, the above lists suggest some common themes (e.g., openness to new information and alternative views). It is an understandable distraction, however, that different scholars come to different conclusions about core thinking dispositions. It is, perhaps, even more disconcerting that they use different terms and phrases to describe elements that they do agree on. This dilemma is attributable in part, certainly, to the nature of scholarship, but it also raises an important point about thinking dispositions: It matters not so much the exact thinking skills to be mastered as that they be credible strategies for exercising the resources of intelligence; what matters most is disposition to seek, master, and employ effective thinking strategies. This statement may appear to be a bit reckless at first blush, but it embodies a critical perspective of thinking dispositions. Perkins (1995) captures this relationship in his metaphor of "mindware" (i.e., mental software) programs that are run in the mind to make the best use of intelligence—that is, to solve problems, make decisions, understand difficult concepts, or perform other difficult intellectual tasks. Thinking skills are mindware programs, and there are many such programs. Disposition is the element that interprets the nature and value of a particular thinking-skill program and—most important—determines if, when, and how it will be run.

The Dispositional Difference

Some people are better mental pilots with a more elevated point of view.

—(Perkins, 1995, p. 99)

How important, then, is the dispositional dimension of intelligence? Simply put, it is disposition that holds sway over all other dimensions of intelligence. It is the arena in which intelligent behavior (i.e., the referencing and engagement of multiple-intelligence capacities and strategies) is either advanced or diminished. This is particularly true for the conscious engagement of thinking strategies appropriate to the reflective nature of human intelligence—the dimension that is most defining of the human capacity to acquire and use information to survival advantage. Ultimately, disposition is the means to *grow* capacity for physiological, social, emotional, constructive, and reflective intelligence.

Perkins (1995) is among the theorists who discern a learnable human intelligence as demonstrated by individuals who engage specific strategies for the best use of their minds. Such individuals are more likely to monitor their own thinking and pilot it in effective ways. They cultivate and use more strategies for various intellectually challenging tasks, including dispositions to be proactive, persistent, and creative. The point Perkins makes is that, to a considerable extent, people can learn to think and act more intelligently—good thinkers are made, not born.

As to the matter of thinking strategies that merit dispositional consideration, help is close at hand in the form of composite lists that draw from the collective findings of many scholars.

Winning Dispositions

A mind is like a parachute. To work well, it has to be open.

—(Bumper sticker)

Costa and Kallick (2000) articulate 16 habits of mind that are displayed by intelligent people in response to problems, dilemmas, and enigmas: persisting, managing impulsiveness, listening with understanding and empathy, thinking flexibly, thinking about thinking (metacognition), striving for accuracy, questioning and posing problems, applying past knowledge to new problems, thinking and communicating with clarity and precision, gathering data with all senses, creating and innovating, responding with wonderment and awe, taking responsible risks, finding humor, thinking interdependently, and remaining open to continuous learning.

Covey (1989) advises that habitual dispositions ultimately determine personal effectiveness in all aspects of human existence. In his widely disseminated *Seven Habits of Highly Effective People*, he contends that people become more effective as they progress from dependent to independent and interdependent states through mastery of disposition to:

1. Be proactive
2. Look to the end
3. Put first things first
4. Seek first to understand, *then* be understood
5. Seek win-win solutions
6. Synergize
7. Sharpen the saw through self-renewal in physical, social and emotional, mental, and spiritual domains

Importantly, winning dispositions are not perceived to be exclusive properties of individuals. Rather, organizations are able beneficiaries of such qualities. Senge (1990) speaks to this in his articulation of five disciplines that characterize the dispositions of a learning organization:

1. Systems thinking
2. Personal mastery
3. Mental models
4. Building shared vision
5. Team learning

Endgame: Mindful Disposition

Mental habits, whether good or bad, are certain to be formed.

—(Dewey, 1933, p. 89)

In examining what he terms "the intelligence paradox" (i.e., how can we be so smart and yet so dumb) Perkins (1995, pp. 152-153) concludes that humans are subject to default thinking, that is, they fall into the intelligence traps of:

- Hasty thinking, characterized by impulsiveness and mindlessness—people reacting and acting without thinking about what they are doing
- Narrow thinking, marked by bias and fixed, limited patterns of information
- Fuzzy thinking that fails to seek clarity, precision, and distinctions in information
- Sprawling thinking that wanders in a disorganized way without ever converging

People are most susceptible to falling into these traps when they are not engaged in what Ellen Langer (1989) calls *mindfulness*, that is, a mindful state of being that creates new categories, is open to new information, and is aware of more than one perspective. Mindlessness, on the other hand, is like being on automatic pilot and inattentive.

How, then, shall you be disposed to use and optimize your intelligence? The answer is, it appears, as you wish. What seems more certain, however, is that productive habits of mind are the product of initiative and effort—dispositions that create dispositions. Another way to say this is to once again apply the maxim that if you want a good disposition, *you have to earn it.* Covey (1989) speaks to the nature of habit formation in a similar manner when he stipulates the interactive effects of knowledge, desire, and skill over time in the construction of preferred dispositional behavior. A final exercise in this chapter will illustrate this point:

Scenario: *Amy, Emily, and Abby are each holding an identical plastic cube in their hands at waist height. They all release the cube they are holding at the same time. When they do so, however, Amy's cube descends, Emily's cube ascends, and Abby's cube does not move.*

Question: *What is your explanation for this phenomenon? Three people release three identical plastic cubes at the same time and each cube responds to the release in a different way.*

Reflection Time

Your brief reflection about possible explanations for the above scenario undoubtedly produced a plausible explanation. You may have thought of an explanation immediately, or perhaps you had to think about it for a bit, but you did come up with an explanation—perhaps several explanations? You are now going to be asked to go an extra step in this exercise. Take a minute or two and come up with *one more* explanation for the phenomenon described above. The only requirement is that it must be a different explanation from any you thought of in your first attempt.

Reflection Time

The assumption is that you have now thought of at least two explanations for the described mystery. A further assumption is that if you were repeatedly asked to go back to the scenario and come up with yet another explanation, you could do so. You might even become more analytical and imaginative each time you had a go at it. Indeed, you might become quite good at generating alternatives. Should you happen to be conducting such reflection in the company of others, the explanations might never stop—given the many hundreds of billions of neurons networked in the investigation of all possible alternatives. And that, of course, is the point of the exercise. The goal is not the quick answer—that one person is on land, one person is under water, and one person is on a space shuttle orbiting the Earth . . . or that one person is standing upright, one person is standing on her head, and one person is lying on her side on the ground . . . or that one person is above water and one person is under water, and one person is standing in water at waist depth . . . or . . . The possibilities are endless, are they not, once you start *thinking?*

And what is the product of such thinking? Obviously, it is a means to generate alternatives, a process of problem solving or decision making. But more important, it is an exercise that builds and refines a productive disposition of mind—to be inclined to generate and consider possible alternatives in given situations.

This, then, is the endgame of mindfulness, to be disposed to exercise the physiological, social, emotional, constructive, and reflective qualities of your brain to greatest advantage. This is a worthy goal, one that resonates with the adage that if you give people fish, they will eat for a day. If you teach them how to fish, however, they will eat for the rest of their lives. Thus your brain is served by learned dispositions to think and, thereby, effectively fish the sea of information available to you.

Go fish!

Essence

- The human brain interprets and organizes useful information patterns on all levels of scale. The organization of dispositional intelligence patterns is representative of this patterning at a macrolevel.
- At any given time, a human brain is working to establish a cohesive state of mind among the integrated mental processes that define it. To that end, a brain is disposed to organize and exercise intelligence in a habitual manner that corresponds to valued patterns of internal and external survival information.
- The value of dispositional intelligence is assessed by its contribution to survival (e.g., disposition to be persistent, creative, open-minded, organized, or analytical). Accordingly, a useful disposition is a means for standardizing automatic responses to stimuli—an alternative to having to constantly make moment-to-moment decisions about how to respond to the environment.
- Human disposition toward the establishment and exercise of states of mind is both genetically and environmentally influenced (i.e., the product of nature and nurture).
- Every healthy human brain is genetically disposed to the broad physiological, social, emotional, constructive, and reflective exercise of intelligence—as well as specific thinking behaviors. Yet all individuals are experientially unique in their disposition to exercise such intelligence.
- Beyond basic and individual genetic prescriptions, human disposition to exercise intelligence is malleable and subject to environmental influence (i.e., physiological, social, emotional, constructive, and reflective experience) throughout the life span.
- Sustained states of dispositional intelligence are defining elements of individual and organizational character. Indeed, thinking dispositions are primary influences over the exercise and development of all other dimensions of intelligence (e.g., physiological, social, emotional, constructive, and reflective).

Implications

Only when we do something to keep our thinking in order do we escape the potholes of cognition.

—(Perkins, 1995, p. 154)

- *If* productive dispositions to think, learn, and achieve are established, *then* members of the organization have learned how to "fish" and you, they, we win.
- *If* thinking dispositions are primary influences on learnable intelligence, *then* the cultivation of thinking dispositions in self and others should be the first priority of leadership.

- *If* mental habits, good or bad, are inevitably formed in individuals and organizations, ***then*** it is a responsibility of leadership to discern and promote thinking dispositions that are advantageous to the effective exercise of both individual and organizational intelligence.
- *If* _____,
  then _____.
- *If* _____,
  then _____.
- *If* _____,
  then _____.

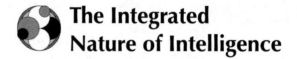

The Integrated Nature of Intelligence

The Gist of It All

> For want of a nail, the shoe was lost;
> For want of a shoe, the horse was lost;
> For want of a horse, the rider was lost;
> For want of a rider, the battle was lost;
> For want of a battle, the kingdom was lost.

—(Anonymous)

What Got Us Here Will Get Us There

What people bring to the table as individuals and members of organizations is the same intelligence package that masters language; creates art and religion; eradicates disease; designs political and economic systems; and enables travel to the moon, planets, and stars beyond. It is this same capacity that holds the promise of solutions for major problems that continue to challenge humankind—problems such as equity, peace, and environmental stewardship. The very existence of this potent capacity is impressive, but for its potential to be realized, it must be understood, engaged, and managed in a productive fashion. Most of all, the integrated dimensions of intelligence must be recognized as the essential forces that underlie all human achievement. Not to be mindful of the nature and nurture of intelligence is, in effect, to be mindless of the nail that enables the shoe that enables the horse that enables the rider that enables the battle that enables the kingdom.

Informed Sailors Have an Edge

If a little bit of knowledge is a dangerous thing, who among us is completely out of danger?

—(Anonymous)

A little bit of knowledge can be dangerous, particularly if that knowledge is either superficial or of questionable validity. It must also be noted, however, that limited knowledge is often what successful human behavior operates on when said knowledge is representative of essential understanding. Thus, as previously argued, people successfully incorporate understanding of such things as electricity, germs, and balanced diet into the conduct of their lives without the extensive knowledge of the physicist, biologist, or nutritionist. Nevertheless, essential understanding is necessarily the product of knowledge distillation, either by an extended time of cultural absorption or by proactive investigation and dissemination of information.

In the event of the dramatic emergence of a new reservoir of knowledge such as that about the human brain, there will be an inevitable transmission of the significance of such knowledge to the general culture. Major breakthroughs in knowledge present a moral imperative for proactive investigation and action, however, to the degree that such knowledge represents an opportunity to improve the conduct of human affairs. Exemplars of such proactive inquiry would be the historic campaigns to translate emerging knowledge about microorganisms into the prevention of diseases such as rabies and small pox.

The point is that individuals in positions of power and influence are not afforded the luxury of having all the answers to all the questions before applying knowledge for the benefit of those whom they serve. As a case in point, leaders at the beginning of the 21st century cannot and will not know all that is known or will be known about the human brain and its capacity for intelligence, yet lead they must—now. What leaders can and must do in this circumstance is proactively engage emerging knowledge about human intelligence and thus construct their personal understanding, understanding that will inform their leadership behavior.

Daunting as the sea may be, the informed sailor stands the best chance of a successful navigation—one that serves the interests of both self and fellow voyagers.

Nurture Nature's Way

Nurture: To nourish; feed; to help grow or develop; cultivate

—(*American Heritage Dictionary*, 2000, p. 1208).

Knowing the nature of something is key to a favorable relationship with it. For example, if you understand the nature of fire, you are in a position to use it to your advantage rather than to be terrorized or victimized by it. Similarly, empowered with a base of essential knowledge about the nature of intelligence, such as that outlined on the previous pages, a leader is in a position to nurture an advantageous relationship. To that end, a leader will reflect on the implications of specific qualities of intelligence for productive leadership behavior. A leader would also be wise, however, to discern strategic interventions that comprehensively actualize the integrated nature of intelligence—major pieces of the puzzle that pull it all together. For example, a leader might work to:

- Develop a physiologically friendly environment amenable to social interactions that promote emotional support, construction of knowledge, and the exercise of reflective and dispositional thinking
- Cultivate an organizational culture that values the dynamic of divergent thinking as a means to maximize the productivity of any subsequent convergence of thinking
- Establish common vision of important purpose as the means to emotionally engage the passion to think, learn, and achieve

Taking the Truman Step

The fantasy film *The Truman Show* (Pleshette, 1998) tells the story of an orphan named Truman who is raised from infancy in a controlled environment contrived by an entertainment enterprise. In this artificial world, all the people other than Truman are actors who play the roles of every imaginable member of a small-town community constructed as the ultimate movie set (e.g., mother, father, friend, teacher, coach, wife, minister, banker, baker, and candlestick maker). The basic storyline of the film is that Truman is the unaware star of *The Truman Show*, the ultimate soap opera. Truman's life is monitored by hidden cameras operating 24 hours a day to capture events prompted by the director of the show—a show that is broadcast to a large and loyal audience in the "real" world. As the film progresses, the adult Truman becomes increasingly suspicious that something is not quite right, which leads to perilous travails and, ultimately, confrontation with the truth and the creators of his contrived existence. The film comes to an end when Truman's sailboat reaches the border of his artificial world. He then must decide whether to return to the security of what has been or to step through the door of the elaborate set to encounter a new but foreign world.

All good stories, of course, aspire to connect with people's sense of the tragedies, joys, and dilemmas of life. *The Truman Show* might hit the mark with its play to confrontation with new ideas and realities. This is not unusual to human experience—ours is a species that is familiar with dramatic shifts in perception about religion, government, and gender roles, to name but a few.

Does the emergence of significant new information about the nature of human intelligence challenge the realty that has been constructed about how people think, learn, and achieve? If a shift in understanding about the nature of intelligence is in progress, does this not, in turn, put pressure on a shift in perception about the nature of leadership? If the answers to these questions are affirmative, it would appear that leaders are poised at the edge of an old reality at the turn of the century. It's a place and moment that require a decision—to adhere to the status quo or, like Truman, open the door and step through to explore a new paradigm of mindful leadership.

Summary Observations

- Specific dimensions or qualities of intelligence never operate independently of each other. A dimensional organization of information about the nature of intelligence is useful to your brain's construction of understanding about a complex phenomenon. The multiple dimensions of human intelligence, however, operate as an integrated whole.
- Human intelligence operates on a biological platform of cells, circuits, and chemicals.
- Social experience is the great provocateur of thinking and learning.
- Emotion is the means by which the brain attends, makes judgments, and is motivated.
- The human brain is a lean, mean, pattern-making machine—a biological system of extraordinary capacity for perceiving and endlessly constructing useful information patterns.
- Reflection is the capacity to consciously manipulate information and rehearse options prior to action—a distinct survival advantage when guessing well is the game and pressure is on the brain.
- The cultivation and exercise of thinking dispositions are the keys to maximizing intelligence.

Reader Reflection

- What are some of the essential qualities of the nature of human intelligence?
- What are some specific examples of leadership behavior that would be compatible with (i.e., nurturing of) what you know about the nature of intelligence?
- Other questions and observations?

Part Two

Accelerating Shift

4

In Search of Leadership

*Older than the Neolithic and newer than
the new millennium, leadership continues
to fascinate and perplex.*

—American Society for Training and Development (2000)

Chapter Orientation

Intrigue and Value

A favorite human pastime is the observation and analysis of leadership. Leadership simply intrigues people. It occupies their attention, finding its way into all manner of conversation and discourse. Leadership is there—at the center or hanging around the edges—in discussions about business, education, government, sports, religion, science, family, history, the environment, the military, a problem, a goal, or a crisis. Whatever the topic, there is often an observation or insinuation or, at the very least, an assumption about what someone did, should have done, is doing, or will do about something that needs doing—be it the boss, a presidential candidate, or a Little League coach. Such proclivity for the analysis of leadership is universally practiced in virtually all human affairs. It is born of an intuitive intrigue and valuation that plays out in countless conversations at dinner tables, water coolers, and corner pubs. As confirmation, you need only to reflect on the content of recent conversations you have been involved in. Was there any reference to the behavior of a director, administrator, official, conductor, chairperson, manager, coordinator, or coach—possibly with some negative or positive judgments cast on the leader's performance?

The value and expectation people hold for leadership cannot be overestimated. There is an assumed connection between leadership and the success of any organization or initiative. This association is so strong that calls to fire the coach, CEO, superintendent, or government official quickly follow perceptions of organizational failure. If stocks rise or fall, the season is won or lost, or productivity improves or diminishes, the leader's behavior is inevitably analyzed—and the leader's tenure is secured or jeopardized accordingly. Leaders are associated with the fulfillment of organizational purpose, be it winning a game, selling a product, or any other achievement goal. Humans know that leadership makes a difference. But is this assumption accurate? If it is true, why is it so . . . and what is a leader to do about it?

Hindsight, Insight, Foresight

The premise of this book is that leaders' influence on the achievement of organizational purpose becomes more effective to the degree that they nurture the intelligence of the members within the organization. To further understand this alignment of leadership to the human brain, it is useful to reference the historical, current, and possible future status of leadership. Accordingly, this chapter will explore leadership as a natural phenomenon that emerges from survival instinct, an elemental phenomenon that is continually forming and maturing in reaction to environmental context, and a nurtured phenomenon that is responsive to the human capacity for conscious reflection and decision making. Specifically, this chapter will do the following:

- Investigate conceptual definitions of leadership
- Review the biological and social roots of leadership
- Exercise hindsight to examine leadership as influenced by historical context
- Exercise insight to describe the evolutionary nature of leadership theory
- Exercise foresight to identify contemporary pressures that are currently encouraging perceptual shifts about leadership theory and practice
- Anticipate a new perspective of leadership theory and practice in the 21st century

Ultimately, it is argued here that it is time for the formulation of a new mental model of leadership, one that is rooted in the past, informed by the present, and responsive to the future. It is proposed that emerging knowledge about the *nature* of intelligence presents an opportunity for leaders to better understand and *nurture* intelligence in themselves and others, thereby enhancing their influence on the achievement *needs* of the systems they lead.

Another Definition in Progress

Of all the hazy and confounding areas in social psychology, leadership theory undoubtedly contends for top nomination.

—(Bennis, 1959, p. 259)

Familiar but Elusive

While the study of leadership has continued to expand in the decades following Bennis's lament, agreement about the nature of leadership remains an elusive goal. This is not unexpected in fields of behavioral science where disagreement and lack of consensus among scholars is pervasive. After all, as Rost (1991) has observed, leadership is a socially constructed reality that cannot be seen or touched but only inferred through observation. And the observation of human behavior, in many social contexts by many scholars, has inevitably generated many interpretations about leadership. The product of this ongoing inquiry is a deepening and broadening of insight about the complex nature of leadership. Definitive clarity about what leadership is, however, is not a reasonable expectation. To paraphrase Stogdill (1974), it is more reasonable to expect the creation of as many definitions of leadership as there are people who attempt to define it.

Leadership, then, like intelligence, is an open concept that will not likely ever be conclusively defined. Yet everyone has a personal understanding, derived from life experience, of what leadership means to them. To demonstrate to yourself the meaning that your brain has constructed for the phenomenon of leadership, it is suggested that you once again pause to complete a sentence stem:

Leadership is _____.

Chances are that your personal interpretation of what leadership is will vary in some manner from that of any other person. On the other hand, it is as likely that your informal definition will generally correspond to statements people commonly make when asked to complete the same sentence stem—statements that suggest leadership is:

- . . . taking charge
- . . . helping others achieve goals
- . . . problem solving
- . . . directing resources to a purpose
- . . . showing the way
- . . . facilitating the actions of a group
- . . . exercising power and influence
- . . . making things happen
- . . . coordinating a collective effort

These informal descriptions generally reflect dictionary definitions that frame leadership in terms of a capacity to command, direct, or guide the actions of others. Such descriptions take on further meaning when interpreted in context, for example, conducting a musical performance, directing a play, or heading a political party. Furthermore, these prevalent perceptions and definitions of leadership are discernable within the scholarship of leadership experts who refine common interpretations to deeper understanding. Consider Burns's (1978) observation:

> Leadership is the reciprocal process of mobilizing by persons with certain motives and values, various economic, political and other resources; in a context of competition and conflict, in order to realize goals independently or mutually held by both leaders and followers. (p. 425)

Thus Burns stresses the dimensions of reciprocity and goal orientation, that is, leadership is an interactive process with others that is engaged in to reach a singular or mutually held goal. More recently, Gardner (1995) offered another perspective in his analysis of the qualities of leaders: "persons who, by word and/or personal example, markedly influence the behaviors, thoughts and/or feeling of a significant number of their fellow human beings" (pp. 8-9).

By attending to the act of influence on behavior, thoughts, and feelings, Gardner acknowledges that leaders sway, inspire, and otherwise modify the thinking and behavior of others.

Taken together, common definitions of leadership coupled with the scholarly interpretations of experts generally describe a phenomenon that engages, influences, and makes things happen.

A Necessary Conceptualization

The effort to conceptualize and classify the nature of leadership is ongoing. Scholars will continue to investigate leadership, construct leadership models and theories, and analyze leadership issues. Such inquiry generates progressive insight and refined understanding about the many contexts and nuances of leadership. But while scholars ponder, practitioners must perform. Accordingly, from a multitude of scholarly conceptualizations, it is important to construct interpretations that capture the basic attributes of leadership—thereby providing a fundamental orientation for practitioners. Northouse (1997, p. 3) demonstrates the construction of such an interpretation through his identification of several central components of the phenomenon of leadership:

1. Leadership is a *process*, between a leader and followers.
2. Leadership involves *influence* that affects followers.
3. Leadership occurs in the context of *groups*.
4. Leadership involves the attainment of *goals*.

These four components are employed by Northouse as the basis for his definition: "Leadership is the process whereby an individual influences a group of individuals to achieve a common goal" (1997, p. 3). Reduced even further, and with acknowledgment that leadership may be exercised by more than one person and is interactive between individuals in a group, a serviceable definition emerges: *Leadership is a process of influencing others to achieve a goal.*

This is a definition that draws from an extensive body of research and theory to render a fundamental interpretation of the essential components of leadership. As such, it is a definition that adequately serves the consideration of leadership-intelligence connections that follows in this text, beginning with a review of the biological and social origins of leadership.

Roots

There is an innate striving in all forms of matter to organize into relationships. There is a great seeking for connections, a desire to organize into more complex systems that include more relationships, more variety. This desire is evident everywhere in the cosmos, at all levels of scale.

—(Wheatley & Kellner-Rogers, 1996, p. 30)

A Natural Occurrence

Nature's propensity for organizing complex and evolving systems has been commented on in prior chapters. It is also important to note, however, that the organization of anything has basic requirements. For example, an initial action, a first step—a lead event—is a necessary attribute in the organization of systems large and small, simple and complex. The organization and transformation of systems also requires progressive encouragement and support. Accordingly, in nature we observe initial bonding, divisions, and transitions that serve to cue, guide, and otherwise influence the behavior of other elements in an environment. In the biological world this is, of course, a matter of survival. Survival requires organization, and organization requires initiation and facilitation. Something or someone must take the lead in getting things rolling, showing the way, setting the pace, sustaining momentum—making things happen. Organic relationships don't just happen, they follow a lead, and one thing *leads* to another. Thus prompted by the genetic code and encouraged by environmental experience, organisms literally construct and operate themselves through cellular interactions that influence the organization of cellular relationships.

Leadership is a natural phenomenon that is observable in the survival behavior of life forms throughout the biological world, from simple cellular structures to complex organisms. Illustrations of such behavior include the lead shoot of a tree or shrub that establishes a path for plant development (similar to the "pioneer" axon fibers that establish pathways for other axons to follow in the neural network development of a brain), the foraging ant scout that leads the colony to a food source, the alpha wolf that sets the pace for the hunt, and the matriarch elephant that guides the migration of the herd. The process of individual biological elements influencing other biological elements in the achievement of a common survival goal is sometimes subtle, sometimes obvious, but always a fundamental and pervasive exercise by which nature conducts its business.

A Social Construction

Nature's affinity for organizing systems became manifest in human development. As described in Chapter 3, the social experience of early humans provided ample opportunity for observing the behavior of others—and to look to others for help, guidance, and example. Most significant, from millions of years of social intimacy, the human brain evolved a capacity for consciousness, an awareness of self in relationship to others. This evolutionary breakthrough enabled reflection about probabilities, possibilities, and options. It is at this point that the natural phenomena of system organization and leadership entered a new arena—that of a brain that was capable of conscious reflection about systems (such as social hierarchies and coalitions) and how individuals influence each other in systems. Thus human awareness of self in relationship to others was accompanied by awareness of the potential of self and others to influence those relationships.

Hindsight:
From Club to Neuron

Some Things Remain Constant, Other Things Change

The central components of leadership remain constant over time and context. Leadership is always a process of influencing others toward the achievement of a goal. But all human behavior evolves within environmental context. Established behaviors continue to be employed until environmental challenges prompt adaptation or alternative practice. As the Durants (1968) observed in *The Lessons of History*, human culture evolves at the influence of experience and context. Through the examination of economic history in three stages, for example, hunter-gatherer, agricultural, and industrial, they observed that the behavioral code of one stage was changed by the next. The practice of leadership is not exempt from such contextual influence. Thus the exercise of leadership in human culture responds to different contexts by making adjustments in the leadership behaviors engaged to influence others in goal achievement. More specifically, adjustments are made in how the leader and followers interact and, subsequently, how the leader exerts influence on group achievement. These adjustments are based on changes in environmental conditions and human needs that inform the leader—and the resulting perceptions about appropriate leadership behavior that subsequently emerge.

From Neolithic to New Millennium

Men, women, and children have been exercising leadership behavior for as long as human beings have banded together and worked cooperatively to survive (Pellicer,

1999). It is possible, therefore, to examine different incarnations of leadership as it evolved in relation to changing social, economic, and technological contexts. Such examination is a means to understand how leadership has been practiced as a mirror of the times.

Before proceeding further, you are invited to reflect about the influence of context on leadership. For example, how did the context of prehistoric times, the agrarian age, the rise of world religion and military empires, feudal society, the industrial age, and the computer revolution inform human perceptions about how to behave as leaders? The following directions will assist your reflection about this question:

1. Select one of the historical time periods referenced above (e.g., prehistoric).

2. Envision yourself as a leader in that time and related space.

3. What is the goal you are trying to help others achieve in that context?

4. What would *inform* your leadership practice in that context (i.e., what significant information would be assailing your senses, what would you be seeing and hearing)?

5. What would be your *perception* of the role of a leader in that context?

6. What leadership *behavior* might you engage in to influence the group in the achievement of the goal?

> Reflection Time

With reference to your own reflection, consider further the disparity of influences on leadership in the following contexts:

- **Leadership in Prehistoric Times.** Driven by the need to gather food, accrue other hard-won resources, and somehow survive with limited defenses against powerful adversaries, prehistoric leadership might have perceived value for influencing an unquestioning compliance through fierce demonstrations of strength. Such perception would perhaps be informed by basic survival instincts and the examples of elders, thus leading to leadership behaviors that favored rule by strength and decisive and unilateral decisions to ensure immediate and swift courses of action in dangerous environments.

- **Leadership in the Agrarian Age.** Perhaps informed by the need to cooperate in the conduct of agricultural activity, a leader in the agrarian age might have been more disposed to exert influence through bargaining and trading of goods and services. The environment was more stable, and goals were more long-term in nature—as represented in the patience required in crop production. Leadership behavior was further informed by a greater sense of community and interdependence. The resulting leadership perceptions likely favored behaviors that influenced achievement through communication skills, coalition building, and patience.

- ***Leadership in an Age of Industrialization.*** Informed by new technologies and increased competition in the marketplace as well as the goals of high productivity and profitability, an industrial age leader might have perceived value for fast-paced, hard-driven decisions with an eye on the bottom line. Further informed by the emergence of efficiency studies and scientific management, the prevailing leadership perception likely favored decision-making behavior aligned to data and quotas.

From your own leadership reflection, as well as those above, it might be concluded that context provides the medium within which leadership is *informed* by prevailing environmental conditions and goals. Thus informed, a leader inevitably forms *perceptions* of leadership *behavior* deemed appropriate to such conditions and goals. In this manner, leadership perception and behavioral mode of influence adapts to context.

Insight:
The 20th Century

In the quest for understanding what causes leaders to lead and followers to follow, the past century has witnessed much pondering and hypothesizing about the attributes of effective leadership. From the great-man theory (leaders are born, not made) to systems theory (leaders are made, not born), the study of leadership has explored many paths. Such exploration, notably, has continued to be subject to the influences of available information and other contextual variables. A brief history of leadership theories that have emerged in the last hundred years illustrates this point.

Trait Theory and the
Measurement Movement

The advent of the 20th century heralded the first systematic attempt to study leadership. The leader was perceived to be the one unquestionably in charge, and the effective leader was one that could get results and loyal followers at the same time through some endowment of certain personality traits. Traits such as intelligence, birth order, socioeconomic status, and even child-rearing practices were examined. This theory coincided with the development of measurement in the field of psychology, providing the impetus for measuring for traits through checklists, tests, rating scales, and interviews. Unfortunately, no single characteristic or set of characteristics emerged as the magic bullet, yet the basic tenet of command and authority suited an industrial age. While trait theory is still alive and well in some attempts to provide benchmarks for leadership, it has been criticized as an input model that is lacking in consideration for outcomes.

Behaviorist Theory and Leadership Style

Henry Ford and the Detroit automakers characterized leadership at the beginning of the last century. Driven by the goal to maximize profit through the use of new technologies, this era of leadership valued efficiency, productivity, and scientific process. Associated goals were to minimize waste, streamline industry, and gain wealth through competition. Theorists such as Frederick Taylor and other proponents of scientific management informed leadership behavior. The perception was that leadership was to manage the worker by the maxim of "don't think, just do" in a humdrum existence of work driven by mechanical technology (Rost, 1991). The belief that what leaders *do* matters most became a far more significant orientation than that of leadership traits, thus creating attention to leadership style.

Bureaucratic Control

Big government characterized leadership by the mid-20th century. Driven by the perceived need for control in an era marked by depression and nationalism, a command mentality took over. This era of leadership valued rank and prestige, rules and regulations, and restrictive boundaries to control information flow. The goal was management of large systems with clear boundaries and direction from the top. Theorists such as Elton Mayo and theories of structural and bureaucratic control informed leadership behavior. The perception of a leader was that of a bureaucrat who functioned within the structural frame of policy and procedure.

Situational Leadership

By the late 1960s and early 1970s, leadership was examined in the context of distinctive characteristics of the setting to which the leader's success could be attributed (Hoy & Miskel, 1987). In the rebellious 1960s, a more egalitarian view of society informed leadership, professing that a person could be a follower or a leader depending on the circumstances. Concerned with both the goal and the needs of relationships with others, leadership theory was beginning to recognize the complexity of leadership. Ultimately, situational leadership was found to be lacking because the theories could not predict which leadership skills would be more effective in which particular situations. Situational leadership did advance leadership perception, however, by highlighting the readiness and capacity of members in an organization to share in leadership influence and responsibilities.

Transformational Leadership

By the 1980s, nonleader leadership, or the concept of many leaders, was proposed as a basic tenet of effectiveness. Barnes and Kriger (1986) suggested that previous theories of leadership were insufficient because they presumed a single leader with multiple followers. For the first time, leadership was examined as a characteristic of the entire organization, in which roles overlap and complement one another. The needs and goals of the organization were seen as shared commodities. Murphy (1988) and others rejected the "hero-leader" framework and helped conceptualize the capacity of leadership that runs throughout an organization. Informed by a rising sense of motivation and morality, empowerment and idealism became popularized as appropriate leadership characteristics. Critics soon appeared on the scene, however, with questions about pragmatism and results. How would a leader go about achieving true transformation?

Systemic and Strategic Leadership

Recent theories of leadership have been characterized by the examination of entrepreneurial information systems. Driven by the free flow of information, the 1980s and 1990s valued teaming, strategic planning, and a combination of bottom-up and top-down decision making. The goal was instant communication to meet the pressing need to succeed in a competitive global marketplace. Management gurus such as Deming, Juran, and Senge proposed theories of systemic thinking to inform leadership behavior. The perception of leadership that emerged was that of a planner and systems thinker who was oriented to systemic responses to the rapid pace of change.

Foresight:
The Times Are Changing

Sergiovanni (1992) suggests that leadership has been viewed too narrowly in the past. He further suggests that a calling to higher purpose has been missing. Most recently, popular theories about servant leadership (Greenleaf, 1996), spirituality in leadership (Block, 1993; Kouzes & Posner, 1995), and empowerment (Heifatz, 1994; Senge, 1994) have made their way into the popular press in the form of articles, videos, and audiotapes. Written primarily for general audiences, these theories balance pragmatism with idealism, focusing on what should occur to make leadership effective. Presented as a behavior that applies broadly to different contexts, both at work and at home, leadership has become an accessible concept for the masses rather than a narrow construct for the elite. Addressing a broader need for contributing to the common good—and informed by value for integrity, trust, honesty, and the like—the goal is described as service within and outside the organization to make a difference in the world. Informed by religious tradition and concepts of stewardship and empowerment, leadership behavior is perceived through the roles of sharing and building capacity within an organization to achieve its moral as well as bottom-line purposes.

The Purpose of Leadership

The search for meaning and desire for connectedness are innate qualities of humans who, by nature, are social animals that form organizations. Throughout

evolutionary history, the human species has become hardwired to cooperate; recipro-
cate; and, ultimately, behave in selfless, generous ways in order to reap the benefit of
cooperative endeavors (Ridley, 1996). Senge (1990) suggests that humans are hungry
for lives that are purposeful. He describes shared vision as a "force in people's hearts"
of impressive power (p. 354). The insightful work of Margaret Wheatley (1992) synthesizes field theory, quantum physics, and social psychology to describe organizational
vision as a by-product of ongoing conversations and "meaning as a strange attractor"
that creates coherence and self-organization in a group (p. 136).

Are workers at the beginning of the 21st century searching for opportunities to
contribute to their organization, their communities, and their world? If this is so,
Rost's (1991) definition of leadership as "an influence relationship among leaders
and followers who intend real changes that reflect their mutual purposes" (p. 102)
falls short of a true sense of collaboration and community to serve a higher purpose.
Accordingly, humankind is past due in developing a theory of leadership that serves
the complexities and challenges of the context of the new millennium.

Construction of a New Mental Model for Leadership

The evolution of the brain teaches us that a high degree of complexity cannot be handled by rigidly organized systems.

—(Goldberg, 2001, p. 222)

At the dawn of a new millennium, humanity can look back at a century that witnessed an incredible convergence of historical events and developments, including cat-
astrophic wars, atomic energy, exploration of the solar system, genetic engineering,
microcomputer technology, global economic and communication systems, major civil
rights movements, the rise and fall of totalitarian governments, and expansion of world
democracy. Moreover, while people are still adjusting to the significant events and developments of past decades, they are entering a new century that promises to be as
eventful and challenging—particularly in prevailing issues of equity, justice, and quality of natural environment.

A thoughtful assessment of the circumstances of challenge and change at the
turn of this new century would understandably place a high premium on the exercise
of human disposition and capacity to "figure it out." One might also conclude that
the circumstances of the 21st century will require even more—that humankind
must become much more adept and disposed in the exercise of intelligent behavior.

The present age, therefore, represents a further contextual influence on leadership in that the convergence of social, scientific, and technological advances create a
press for perceptual shift about appropriate leadership behavior. Recent lessons from
complexity theory, quantum physics, and evolutionary psychology suggest that the
organizations of today cannot be controlled, manipulated, mandated, or charmed.
Leadership theory must speak to the fundamental social and emotional dimensions

of human intelligence, dimensions attuned to the search for meaning, the benefit of collaboration, and connection to a higher purpose. There is a need for leadership theory and perception that rejects the certainty of Newtonian organizations and eschews predictability, a theory of leadership that thrives on uncertainty, that can deal with creativity and rapid change, and that can release the restraints on the potential of human beings who work within organizations (Zohar, 1997).

Leaders in the 21st century need to challenge their old assumptions and examine their ingrained habits of behavior. In *Mindfulness*, Langer (1989) suggests that intelligent behavior has three characteristics: creating new categories of thinking, openness to differing viewpoints and new sources of information, and flexibility and adaptability in resultant actions. Mindlessness, in contrast, is characterized by an entrapment in old categories, by automatic behavior that precludes attending to new signals, and by action that operates from a single perspective (p. 4). The next wave of understanding about leadership would do well to address this issue of mindfulness. Such examination might lead to new understanding in theory that rests on the dual pedestals of purpose and intelligence.

A New Definition

It is time for a new mental model of leadership. Senge et al. (1999) describes mental models as the discipline of developing awareness of attitudes and perceptions that influence thought and interactions. As demonstrated earlier, the concept of leadership is informed and formed by context. Our current context surely calls for a new view of leadership that engages and nurtures the collective intelligence within the organization to achieve significant purpose.

The mental model of leadership advanced in this chapter suggests that *mindful leaders understand and apply their own intelligence to the understanding and application of intelligence throughout their organizations to achieve meaningful purpose.* The assumptions underlying this premise are

1. Organizations exist when two or more people gather together for a common purpose; this has been true since the day of the cave and will be true into the future.

2. The human potential within any organization is its greatest asset; this recognizes the enormous power of human intelligence and unlimited capacity that runs throughout the organization, not just in the "head of the head."

3. In order to take advantage of this asset, the minds within the organization must be fully engaged; organizations have the capacity to be mind numbing or mind expanding. Humans are naturally drawn to engage in endeavors that stimulate and are meaningful, and it is the leader's responsibility to ensure such engagement.

4. Organizational environment influences the extent to which intelligence is fully engaged. Threat and coercion can shut down the creative potential of

the people within any organization, while support and openness enrich the opportunity for creative thinking.

5. Actions of the leader can influence the extent to which an organization can be intelligence friendly; while the leader is not the savior on the white steed, a leader's actions do speak (and influence) louder than words. It is the leader who acts mindfully, nurturing her or his own intelligence and the intelligence of others, who sets the tone for an organization poised to be successful in the new century.

6. We are experiencing an unprecedented era of new knowledge about the brain and how people naturally learn and achieve. Leaders must become judicious consumers of this expanding knowledge base in order to inform their practice. They and their organizations cannot afford to be uninformed about this breakthrough in knowledge.

New Perspective:
The Fundamental Source of Our Problems

A Mindful Moment

Throughout evolution, the emphasis has shifted from the brain invested with rigid, fixed functions (the thalamus) to the brain capable of flexible adaptation (the cortex).

—(Goldberg, 2001, p. 217)

Bateson (1979) has suggested that there is a fundamental and problematic gap between the way humans think and the way nature works—that there is a need for the human mind to establish a much deeper appreciation for how nature conducts its business. The context of the 21st century both requires and accommodates a closing of that gap through the cultivation of a new perspective of leadership, a perspective that consciously aligns leadership behavior to the nature of intelligence and the achievement of goals. A new perspective is required by the escalating complexity of human existence. It is accommodated by emerging knowledge about the human capacity to think, learn, and achieve. The reflective nature of human intelligence, informed by new information about multiple dimensions of intelligence, allows leaders to become more knowledgeable and purposeful in their leadership behavior than ever before.

This is a moment when leaders must break free from prevailing perceptions that selectively nurture the intelligence capacity of individuals in groups. Leaders at the beginning of this new millennium must seize the moment and become mindful practitioners, leaders who are stewards of organizational intelligence. To this end, however, there are no formulas, lists, shoulds, or promises as to how to best respond to the pressing opportunity and need. Rather, leaders must meet this challenge by engaging their brains in proactive reflection about current mental models of leadership. Indeed, just as the human brain has progressively evolved from rigidity to flexibility in function as a means to accommodate increased complexity, leadership in an increasingly complex context must assess the merits of flexible models of leadership.

New Lenses

A new perspective of leadership requires adjustment in the quality and organization of resources that inform understanding. This is not unlike the experience of an adjustment in an eyeglass prescription. In that instance, the introduction of new materials in new configurations results in enhancement of eyesight. The analogy can be made for the introduction of new information about the nature and nurture of human intelligence. If this new information is effectively organized by leaders, it, in effect, provides new lenses through which to see leadership practice (see Figure 4.1). More profoundly, as stated previously and often in this text, the quality of this emerging information is of breakthrough stature, providing unprecedented revelation about human thinking and behavior. Thus informed, leaders are in a position to use these new lenses to great effect in the observation and analysis of leadership—particularly in discerning more effective alignment of leadership behavior to the natural capacity of human intelligence to achieve goals.

The ability to *see* leadership in relationship to the nature of human intelligence is an important development made possible by the organization of new sources of information. What, then, might this alignment look like?

New Alignment

As noted earlier in this chapter, the essence of leadership remains constant across time and contexts. Leadership is always about influencing others in the achievement of a goal.

Context does influence leadership, however, in that it exerts pressure on *how* leaders influence others. Accordingly, to speak of a new alignment of leadership behavior requires an acknowledgment, first, that the basics do not change. Leaders always align their influence on others—whether consciously or subconsciously—by the pursuit of an achievement need, some desirable goal or outcome. This alignment is rooted, of course, in the biological imperative to survive as acted out in social communities. In more primitive settings, it involves leader reflection about how to acquire food or shelter or other basic needs and how, therefore, others might best be influenced to achieve that need. In more sophisticated contexts, a leader is asking the same questions, perhaps in a more refined manner, but it is still a matter of reflection about what need must be addressed to enhance quality of existence and how others can be influenced to resolve it.

What, then, does revelation about the nature of intelligence have to offer leadership alignment of influence to the achievement of needs? Figure 4.2 speaks to this issue. Basically, leadership that is uninformed about the nature of intelligence is still aligned to the achievement of a need through influence on others. A leader in this

Figure 4.1. Perceiving Leadership Through Dimensions of Intelligence

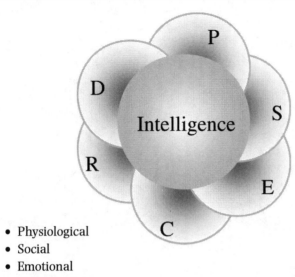

- Physiological
- Social
- Emotional
- Constructive
- Reflective
- Dispositional

circumstance (i.e., the circumstance of leaders until now), however, is dependent on intuition and feedback from trial-and-error initiatives to influence others in the achievement quest. This is not to say that leaders have not been effective in their leadership influence. Examples of effective leaders are, after all, abundant, both in historical and current times. Such leaders, however, are necessarily left shooting in the dark. They may (and do) benefit from astute observation and study of what works and what doesn't in helping people successfully achieve a purpose, but the bottom line is that many leadership initiatives miss the mark or are deflected. Leadership that is informed about the nature and nurture of intelligence enjoys an advantage that has only recently been made possible by brain-intelligence research. A leader in this modern-day context has the benefit of information about the multiple dimensions of the natural human capacity to think, learn, and achieve. This new circumstance brings a new wrinkle to the alignment of leadership influence—*the conscious nurture of the nature of the human capacity to achieve a need.* Such an advantage holds promise for more effective alignment of leadership influence by virtue of the refinement it brings to the leader's classic reflection:

1. What is the *need?*

2. What dimensions of the *nature* of human intelligence are important to the achievement of this need (e.g., requirements for the construction of new

Figure 4.2. The Advantage of Mindful Leadership

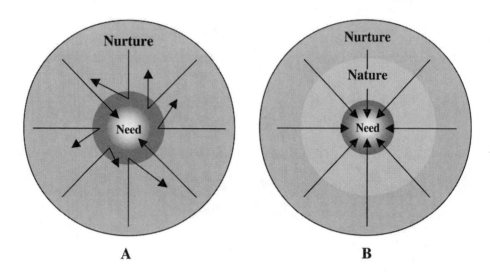

A.   Uninformed about the nature of intelligence, leadership behavior (as represented by the arrows) is susceptible to intuitive trial-and-error attempts to nurture others in the achievement of a specific need.

B.   Informed about the nature of intelligence, leadership behavior (again represented by the arrows) is consciously aligned to the nurture of the natural human capacity to think, learn, and achieve—thereby asserting more efficient and effective influence on others in the achievement of a specific need.

knowledge, reflective reasoning, emotional engagement, social interaction, stress management, exercise of proactive and collaborative disposition)?

3. How might I best *nurture* the nature of intelligence required for the achievement of the need?

The prospects of this orientation to leadership as the nurture of the nature of the human capacity to achieve need (see figure 4.3) will be examined at length in Chapter 6.

Next Steps

The next chapter will describe the process of perceptual shift as a means to challenge current leadership models and behaviors and to consciously change what is thought and what is done. This is a necessary process in the construction of a new mental model for leadership. Most important, the adoption of a behavioral-change strategy that facilitates the translation of thought into action will be introduced. The employment of such a strategy is timely to the promotion of the next evolution in perception about effective leadership practice.

Figure 4.3. New Leadership Alignment: Nurture of Nature's Way to Achieve Need

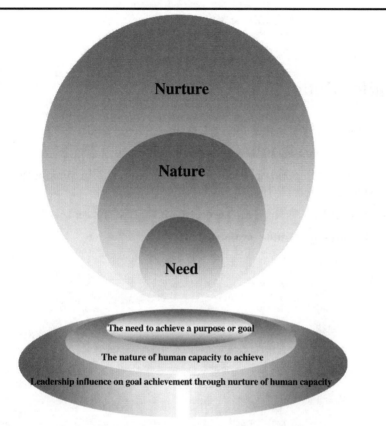

Summary Observations

- Leadership is a natural and highly valued phenomenon in both nature and human societies.
- Leadership is the process of influencing others in the achievement of a goal.
- The essential nature of leadership remains constant, but the nature of how influence is exercised is subject to the specific context that informs leadership.
- Leadership theory has evolved dramatically in the past century to refine understanding of many contributing qualities of effective practice.
- The organization of emerging knowledge about the nature and nurture of intelligence makes it possible to see leadership from a new perspective, one that is informed about dimensions of human capacity to think, learn, and achieve purpose.

- The emerging model of leadership is one in which leaders consciously align their influence to the nurture of the nature of the human capacity to achieve need.

Reader Reflection

- How would you define and explain the nature of leadership to a colleague?
- How does context influence leadership practice?
- What contemporary pressures are influencing shifts in thinking about leadership practice?
- What will leadership practice evolve into in the 21st century?
- Other thoughts and questions?

5

Pushing Perception

On the eve of the third millennium, we are not only aware, and aware of our awareness, but we are now also aware of how and why we are aware and how and why we are aware of our awareness.

—J. Allen Hobson (1999, p. xi)

Chapter Orientation

The Power of Perception

"What you see is what you get." This expression holds more truth than is commonly appreciated, given that what is seen and understood affects what is done and the results achieved. For example, a stick lying on the road may be seen as a splinter of wood or an obstruction in the path and likely ignored or kicked out of the way. If, however, the stick is seen as a tool to dig with, a lever to pry with, a club to hit with, or a toy to toss to your dog, it may be applied to such purposes. Whether the behavior is as simple as throwing a stick or as complex as leading an organization, the choices made and the resultant actions taken derive from a rich mixture of perceiving, reflecting, and selecting behavior in which to engage. Humans are not just creatures of habit, after all, but are continuously influenced by experience, knowledge, and their basic nature to learn and adjust.

Social beings' observations and discoveries of others additionally influence perceptions of appropriate behavior. The story of the titmouse and robin is illustrative:

In the early 1900s, milk was delivered to homes in the United Kingdom in bottles without caps. Two bird species, the titmouse and the red robin, learned to drink the cream that floated to the tops of the bottles. Eventually, dairy distributors began putting aluminum seals on the bottles to solve this problem. In about 20 years, the population of titmice (about 1 million birds) learned how to pierce the seal. In contrast, the red robins did not. Occasionally, one robin would discover how to pierce the seal, but that knowledge never spread. What is the explanation? Titmice are social. They travel in flocks. Robins are territorial and rarely communicate.

—(de Geus, 1997, p. 52)

In this case, group learning changed perception and, subsequently, behavior. Discoveries were attended to and passed on, creating an extraordinarily successful learning process.

Leaders might do well to follow the learning process exemplified by the titmice. At the beginning of the 21st century, there is an exceptional opportunity to engage significant new information about the nature of human capacity to learn and achieve. This information can be a valuable source for refining leadership perceptions and behaviors. Such refinement is most likely, however, if it is conducted in the company of colleagues.

In this chapter, the journey to mindful leadership continues with exploration of:

- The nature of perception—what we see
- The product of perception—what we do
- Perception and the nature of change
- Behavioral change spiral
- An essential shift in perception that is facilitated by emerging knowledge about the brain—an opportunity to proactively construct perception of leadership practice aligned to the nature and nurture of intelligence
- Building the bridge of structures that will facilitate perceptual shifts that connect prior leadership models to new insights about effective leadership behavior

As described in Chapter 4, the context of leadership is changing. Emerging information about the brain presents a unique opportunity to reflect on understanding of the nature of human intelligence within organizations and, consequently, to restructure patterns of leadership behavior. Leaders can either take advantage of these discoveries, like the titmice, and shift their way of seeing and responding to the challenges of leadership, or they can remain closed to this new knowledge, as did the robins, and depend on individuals to discover such insights independently, in their own good time.

In order for leaders to fully engage the emerging knowledge base about the nature of intelligence, proactive reflection is necessary to accelerate a reshaping of our understandings about leadership. Chapter 3 describes the constructive capacity of the brain to detect, construct, store, and retrieve blocks of knowledge that are continually refined and reconfigured to make sense of the world. This chapter explores the process of perceptual shift to establish the power of new information to transform our understanding and, in this case, resultant leadership behavior.

The Nature of Perception

The Box

It is common to hear people admonish themselves or others to "think outside the box." The implication is that old ideas and thinking patterns are trapped inside the box, while new challenges require new ideas, which may emerge from unconventional ways of thinking, that is, outside the box. Perhaps the nature and importance of the box and what it represents in relationship to human intelligence is overly simplistic.

It is more recently understood that relationships and patterns are the currency of our world, even the universe. Complexity scientists propose that order comes out of chaos, indeed, that it is the natural emergence of order that maintains equilibrium in both the immediate and far-removed environments. These new theories imply that as people learn and change, a new order emerges. Wheatley (1992) suggests that information both informs us and forms us, observing that what knowledge is taken in, and how it is made sense of, actually re-creates who people are, what they think, and how they behave.

Perhaps altering the expression "think outside the box" to "think about the box and adjust it accordingly" is more appropriate. The box is fundamental to human nature, because there always have been and always will be mental patterns, or established order, by which the world is understood. There is no option but to create and modify patterns in relation to surrounding influences. Humans have the capacity, however, to reflect on the nature of a particular mental model and to actively structure and restructure it as new information and circumstances inform and reform. Since brain architecture has been handed down over generations and was designed for the exigencies of the prehistoric era, it is, in fact, imperative that a continuous reshaping of the box occurs to adapt to an ever-changing world. It is what the brain does—and does so well.

Definitions Abound

Humans have long sought to understand the process by which they see and understand the world. As a matter of fact, the origins of the word *perception* can be traced to the Latin *percipere, to see wholly* or *see all the way through.* Just as with intelligence and leadership, definitions of perception abound:

- A process through which we make sense out of the world (Runyan, 1977)
- The process by which we receive information through our five senses and assign meaning to it (Wells, Burnett, & Moriarty, 1995)
- A complex process by which people select, organize and interpret stimuli into meaningful pictures of the world (Markin, 1974)

To take it a step further, Wilke (1986) surmises that there are three basic functions that are contained in the definition of perception: seeing a stimuli in the external world, selecting and attending to certain stimuli and not others, and interpreting the stimuli and giving it meaning. Adding yet another important dimension, Forgus and Melamed (1966) make the case that only those stimuli that trigger some kind of reaction or adaptive behavior from an individual should be called information. They, therefore, define perception as the process of information extraction that precedes behavior change.

It is also important to note that perceptions evolve from the natural accumulation and integration of knowledge interacting with current values and behavior patterns. For example, if one lacked prior experience with a stick or any knowledge of leverage, tools or toys as possibilities for its use may not be perceived. On the other hand, if other long, slender objects had been used as a crowbar or a baseball bat, as a weapon or a tossing toy, one would likely be able to generalize and integrate prior knowledge into a new perception for the use of the stick. Compatible with the earlier interpretation of the neural pattern-making disposition of the brain, then perception assumes a deeper influence on human behavior beyond simple pattern making to a process of achieving understanding.

Construction Through Influence

Perceptual psychologists recognize that most raw, unorganized sensory stimuli are almost instantaneously and subconsciously corrected into *percepts*, or usable experience (Kolb & Brodie, 1982). Perception is not a simple matter of organizing direct sensory stimuli into percepts, however. Percepts themselves, constructed from past experience, also become organized, greatly advancing the accuracy and speed of a person's perception. In simple terms, as new information is taken in, it is simultaneously integrated with existing understandings. The translation of the stick into something useful is, therefore, instantaneous and effortless.

Gestalt psychology, holistic in its orientation, takes into account total configurations of mental processes. Experiments by proponents of the Gestalt theory showed that perception of *form*—a mental structure that takes its attributes from a corresponding structure of brain processes—does not depend on perception of individual elements making up the form (Shepherd, 1988). Thus *squareness* can be perceived in a figure made up of four red lines as well as in one of four black dots. Or, as mentioned before, a box can have an inside, outside, or adjustable sides (see Figure 5.1).

Figure 5.1. Construction of Three-Dimensional Perception From a Two-Dimensional Drawing

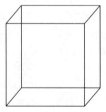

For example, when viewing the box in Figure 5.1, a three-dimensional object is perceived from a two-dimensional drawing. The whole is perceived in order to make sense of the world, based on past experiences with box-like shapes. The process of perception, therefore, is complex and dependent on multiple influences. Wells and colleagues (1995) suggest at least three: the characteristic of the stimuli; the relation of the stimuli to the context; and the condition within the individual, such as experience, attitude, personality, and self-image. In fact, Zaltman (1979) and others suggest that there are few variables that do not influence whether we choose to notice things and how we interpret what we do perceive.

In addition, our environment is explored through a filter of emotions, values, and existing mental models in an attempt to understand. Sylwester (2000) reminds us that emotion drives attention. It is through our emotional filters that we unconsciously decide what is worth perceiving. Thus perceptions are affected by our worldview, defined as our overall perspective from which we see and interpret the world (Gardner, 1983). Composed of experiences, prior knowledge, values, beliefs, social relationships, and context, worldview acts as a powerful filter for incoming information and an equally powerful translator as new patterns of understanding are formed. Combs et al. (1976) suggested that people do not behave according to the facts as others see them. They behave according to the facts as they see them. What governs behavior from this point of view is individuals' unique perception of self and the world in which they live and the meanings things have for them. To sum up, as Fitzgerald (1998) adroitly observed, no two people see the external world in exactly the same way; to every individual, a thing is what he or she thinks it is—not a thing, but a think.

The Product of Perception— "What We Do"

Conclusions Drawn

The product of perception—the conclusions one draws and the priorities one sets—determines the essence of understanding that directs behavior. If one reads the cautions about smoking but continues to smoke, the resultant behavior is inconsistent with the information at hand. If one reads the cautions about smoking, values one's health, believes in one's capability to stop, and lives in a culture of nonsmokers, change in behavior is more likely to occur.

The act of perceiving can portend both good and bad news. As a means to organize and distill meaning from the universe of information that confronts us, perception represents our judgment of useful and important patterns of thinking, that is, mental models.

The good news is that perception enables the construction of positive and serviceable templates for human behavior; humans extend courtesy, exercise, balance our diet, protect individual rights, aspire to fairness, educate the young, engage in hygienic practice, work hard, and so forth. Indeed, the attributes of any human culture represent a common understanding of patterns important to survival and the quality of life.

The bad news is that perception *will* direct behavior, regardless of the quality of the perception. At best, perception is the product of reflective interpretation of both the quantity and quality of available information and the suitable pattern formation with existing worldviews. Mere effort, however, does not provide an assurance that a formulated pattern of understanding is accurate, serviceable, or even good. Argyris (1990) argues that people live in a world of self-generated beliefs, which remain largely untested. Beliefs are adopted because they are based on conclusions drawn from personal observations and past experience. Eventually, action is taken, often misguided and based on faulty beliefs.

It's a dilemma. Humans are dependent on their power to perceive but are limited by lack of information. And when, by virtue of inadequacy of effort, misinformation, or attachment to existing worldviews, faulty perceptions are produced, compatible behavior surely follows. Racism, war, domestic violence, environmental destruction, and economic disparity might be said to be examples of behaviors evolving from the negative incarnations of human perceptions.

Moreover, perception can have another, more subtle downside: rigidity. Barker (1993) described it as the seductive power of a successful mental model or paradigm. The "if it ain't broke, don't fix it" or "we've always done it this way" mind-set is a familiar example of when perception becomes a mental boundary that obstructs new thinking and understanding. Historical examples abound of this phenomenon, such as when monarchy was defended as the best form of government, bleeding patients with leeches was good universal medical practice, and women were not deemed qualified to vote. Hindsight, however, is always a relatively easy exercise. The greater challenge is to be aware of the mental boundaries imposed and the peril these boxes pose for new thinking and understanding.

Behavior Modified

It is valuable to know how perception both informs and compromises behavior. As Argyris (1990) suggests, people do not always behave congruently with their espoused theories or with what they say they believe. They may, instead, behave congruently with what he calls their "theories in use" (mental models). A few examples may illustrate:

- **Reluctant Learners.** In the context of the late 19th century, when Louis Pasteur verified the existence of microbes, which carry both bacteria and viruses, the prevailing worldview was limited in its ability to understand and translate new information into usable behaviors. Even in childhood, our mother's admonitions to wash our hands and rinse off the fruit may have carried little weight. Our mothers most likely modeled washing, through what seemed like endless cleaning of clothes, dishes, furniture, and us. The need for independence, an insufficient understanding of biology, and a limited value for cleanliness probably influenced our childhood worldview. As a result, childhood behavior, limited by insufficient information and a worldview that was not open to modification, was not most likely consistent with the knowledge available. In other words, most of us ignored cleanliness in favor of freedom and fun.

As our knowledge base expanded and we started to believe that things could exist even if we couldn't see them, we became more open to the fact that germs could cause problems. Slowly, behaviors were modified but certainly not with as much vigilance as our mother had shown or warned us to show. One day, a special report on the nightly news presents a kitchen exposé using infrared light to show the rapid and diffuse spread of bacteria from handling raw chicken. With an expanded knowledge base, new and dramatic information, and value for family health, our mental model for dealing with germs matured and the change in behavior finally followed suit.

This natural accumulation and integration of knowledge interacting with values and behavioral patterns ultimately shifted not only perception but also subsequent behavior. This process occurs in every aspect of daily life, including the workplace. Consider the case of a leader caught in an outmoded perception of effective leadership practice:

- **Leader as Reluctant Learner.** Consider the experience of Sam, a superintendent of a suburban school district. His experience and training led him to believe that leaders were strong decision makers, that knowledge and information was to be disseminated on a need-to-know basis, and that subordinates follow the rules set down for them for the good of the organization. In the mid-1980s, when the call for school reform and restructuring was heralded across the nation, his worldview filtered the movement into leadership behaviors that more closely resembled a feudal monarchy. He issued mandates, lost patience with subordinates, and did not get the results he wanted.

    In the early 1990s, Sam had a mutiny on his hands. His principals were disgruntled, teachers were antagonistic, and his board of education was calling for increased accountability. Something wasn't working. With a raised awareness of the need at hand, Sam attended a series of workshops on shared leadership and site-based management. Through a process of introspection, engagement with the knowledge base on transformational leadership, and interaction in a culture in need of change, Sam's mental model for leadership slowly began to change. His behavior soon followed suit in incremental steps. As he gained a sense of confidence through the achievement of results and the praise of colleagues, he became bolder in his new leadership style. He claims today to be a "born-again" superintendent.

In both these cases, the perceptual filters were initially so strong that new information had little effect on changing behavior. Ultimately, with additional information, increased need, and a mounting sense of self-efficacy, behavior followed suit. How does this happen, and what can be done to promote more informed decision making around leadership behaviors? To answer these questions, the relationship between beliefs and behavior must be examined.

Perception and the Nature of Change

Contemporary models of behavioral change at the individual and interpersonal levels suggest three key elements necessary to understand the shift in thought and, ultimately, in deed (Bandura, 1995). As figure 5.2 illustrates,

1. Knowledge is necessary but not sufficient to produce behavior change. Current and changing understandings, motivation, skills, and factors in the social environment also play important roles. As noted earlier, leadership does not occur in a vacuum. Change in leadership behavior not only will be mediated by increased understandings but also will be accompanied by perceived needs and the skills to implement the change as leaders interact with those they lead.

2. Behavior is considered to be mediated through cognition; that is, what we know and think affects how we act. In other words, in order for us to change our leadership behavior, a change in the construction of our understanding must occur first.

3. People and their environments interact continuously, influencing the resultant behavior change. The system and the specific situation influence the leader in deciding which behavior to select.

The Behavior Change Spiral

If knowledge affects perception, but knowledge alone will not change behaviors, it is worth looking at a behavioral-change model to understand the process of putting thoughts into action. Figure 5.3 is our version of a widely used model that explains the integration of new insights and understanding into changed leadership behaviors.

Stage one, **_pre-contemplation,_** is characterized by lack of awareness that new information is available and relevant to one's context. Currently, leaders may not be aware that a wealth of emerging knowledge about the brain exists or has possible implications for leadership behavior. In this stage, behavior remains somewhat static or only slightly modified by factors in the environment that create a need. This type of reactive state can lead to crisis management or, at the very least, missed opportunities to enhance leadership effectiveness. In other words, the box is formed with tight boundaries around thought and behavior. This is the stage superintendent Sam was in for many years.

Figure 5.2. The Relationship Between Information, Perception, and Behavior

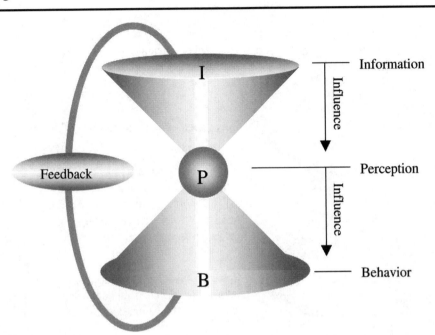

Information processed by the brain influences perception that, in turn, influences behavior.

Contemplation occurs when learning opportunities arise and are seized on for greater effectiveness. As new knowledge about leadership or, in the case here, emerging knowledge about the brain and human intelligence is made available, leaders have the opportunity to acquire new insights and change their perceptions about human capacities within their organizations. This is the information-gathering and processing stage where new knowledge is integrated with prior learning. In other words, the sides of the box are starting to become malleable. Superintendent Sam entered this stage when he actively sought to read about and go to workshops on site-based management.

Proactive reflection is where cognitive dissonance may arise with the realization that past and current understanding, beliefs, and behaviors may not be consistent with emerging insights and understandings. At this point, leaders will find it necessary to critically analyze their current leadership behaviors for alignment with new information. For superintendent Sam this occurred with new information about shared decision making coupled with dissatisfaction about prior performance, both internally and externally perceived. Another critical factor emerges in this state with the leader's sense of self-efficacy, or perceived ability, to make the changes necessary. Sam had to feel comfortable with his ability to make the changes and accept assis-

Figure 5.3. Behavior Change Through Perceptual Shift

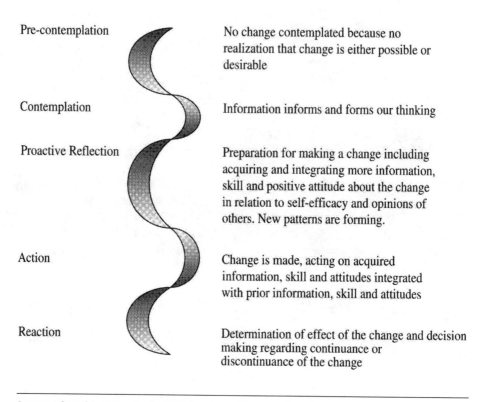

Pre-contemplation — No change contemplated because no realization that change is either possible or desirable

Contemplation — Information informs and forms our thinking

Proactive Reflection — Preparation for making a change including acquiring and integrating more information, skill and positive attitude about the change in relation to self-efficacy and opinions of others. New patterns are forming.

Action — Change is made, acting on acquired information, skill and attitudes integrated with prior information, skill and attitudes

Reaction — Determination of effect of the change and decision making regarding continuance or discontinuance of the change

Source: Adapted from Prochaska, DiClemente, and Norcross (1992).

tance as needed. In other words, the sides of the box are adjusted to fit new understandings and possible new behaviors.

Action and reaction are stages that occur simultaneously as leaders engage in new behaviors and respond to the feedback given as a result. Everyone has likely experienced the process of trying something new, be it a golf swing, a new exercise program, or an adopted professional practice, and watching the results. If the results are as anticipated, the new behaviors are more likely to be continued. On the other hand, if negative feedback is received, the practice is likely discontinued. Fullan (1991) and others caution to beware of the "implementation dip," when things may get worse before they get better. In other words, the box may resist the change and try to return to its former dimensions. In the case of superintendent Sam, the feedback he received from both colleagues and superiors, as well as the concrete positive results of his actions, were enough to keep him on the path to new leadership behaviors.

Some would suggest that we are much more likely to act our way into a new way of thinking than think our way into a new way of acting (Pascale, 2000). Organizations as diverse as Shell Oil and the U.S. Army have put this theory to the test. After simulated maneuvers using new tactics, the army conducts a perceptual shift strategy called After Action Review. Teams of soldiers are asked leading questions to guide them through reflection and feedback on experienced behaviors. At Shell, the use of action learning with feedback in the form of direct interaction with customers served a similar purpose. Both organizations structured the necessary feedback loop to shift perceptions and use behavior to inform thought.

Perceptual shift and accompanying behavioral change are processes that occur over time. The process of learning new information, filtering that information through our worldview, and modifying our existing mental models is fluid and fragile. Fluid in the sense that hundreds and perhaps thousands of connections are being made and reorganized as learning occurs; fragile in the sense that new learning is vulnerable to interference and forgetting.

Necessary Conditions

Behavioral change is, perhaps, the most difficult type of learning to achieve (Caine & Caine, 1999). When we consider the complexity of rearranging our view of the world, in this case, our mental model for leadership, it's really an awe-inspiring occurrence. Generally speaking, it appears that in order for a person to perform a given behavior, one or more of the following must be true:

1. The person must have formed a strong positive intention (or made a commitment) to perform the behavior.
2. There are no environmental constraints that make it impossible to perform the behavior.
3. The person has the knowledge and skills necessary to perform the behavior.
4. The person believes that the advantages (benefits, anticipated positive outcomes) of performing the behavior outweigh the disadvantages (costs, anticipated negative outcomes).
5. The person perceives more social (normative) pressure to perform the behavior than to not perform the behavior.
6. The person perceives that performance of the behavior is more consistent than inconsistent with his or her self-image, or that the performance does not violate personal standards that activate negative self-actions.
7. The person's emotional reaction to performing the behavior is more positive than negative.
8. The person perceives that she or he has the capabilities to perform the behavior under a number of different circumstances (Fishbein, 2001).

Senge (1990) proposes that mental models are "deeply ingrained assumptions, generalizations, pictures, images, or stories, that influence how we understand the world and take action. Very often, we are not consciously aware of our mental models or the effect they have on our behavior" (p. 8). It is time for leaders to become aware of their current mental models of leadership and proactively seek information, add their own personal meaning, and restructure their perceptions and subsequent behaviors. It's time to adjust the box.

The premise of this book is relatively simple. Humans have evolved as a species to a point where they can reconstruct their mental models at will. As knowledge about the human brain and the nature of intelligence is accumulated, leaders can reflect on their current perceptions of leadership and engage in personal change processes that will lead to appropriate behaviors. What emerges is the creation of a new mental model of leadership that is brain compatible and drives leadership behaviors within the organization, ultimately facilitating the accomplishment of its purpose.

An Essential Shift

The story is told about a driver who, lost on a country road, stops to ask a local farmer how to reach the next town.

The farmer responds, "Why, it's just two sees away." "Pardon me. I don't understand," says the driver. "Well, it's easy," says the farmer. "You just go down the road as far as you can see from here, and then turn right, and go again as far as you can see from there."

Perceptual change and resulting modification of leadership behavior is not only possible but essential to the context of leadership in the new millennium. The pressure of accumulating information about human intelligence combined with proactive reflection—and the implications thereof for leadership purpose and practice—hold great promise for generating leadership behaviors that are more compatible with the needs of organizations and the humans who inhabit them.

As described by the two-sees story above, however, perception is incremental. Any understanding that is formulated establishes a new position from which one can, if one chooses, look deeper and farther to formulate the next level of understanding. At the same time, perceptual shift follows the organizing of information into new patterns—thereby facilitating the ability to see things more clearly while simultaneously seeing things differently (de Bono, 2000). Thus perception is the means by which the human quest for understanding is kept "movin' on down the road."

Building the Bridge

In Chapter 6, a framework for creating a coherent mental model of leadership is introduced that takes advantage of the growing knowledge base about the nature and nurture of human intelligence. The framework is intended as a structure that will facilitate perceptual shift about leadership behavior that maximizes human capacity in:

- Self
- Systems
- Situations

The challenge for leaders is to build the bridge between prior mental models of leadership and new possibilities for effective leadership, given the press of new information and rising demands for effective practice. The framework offered capitalizes on the brain's capacity to create new understandings and proactively engage in the construction of resultant mindful leadership behavior.

Summary Observations

- Perception is the process through which the human brain makes sense of the world.
- Perception is a process of constructing understanding that precedes behavior change.
- Perception, how humans understand or "see" the world, both prescribes and compromises behavior.
- Perceptual shifts are constant and inevitable by virtue of the construction and integration of new knowledge over time.
- The good news is that a perceptual shift can be initiated and accelerated through proactive acquisition and refinement of knowledge.
- Proactive alteration of perception through conscious reflection prompts parallel change in behavior.
- The power of perception is used to advantage through understanding its foundational role in enabling intelligence and directing behavior.
- Emerging knowledge about the nature and nurture of intelligence compels leadership reflection about perceptions of compatible leadership behavior.

Reader Reflection

- Perception is . . . ?
- The relationship between perception and behavior is . . . ?
- Perception is altered by . . . ?
- A reason leaders might want to proactively reflect about their perceptions of effective leadership behavior is . . . ?
- Other thoughts and questions?

6

Connecting Leadership to the Brain

Our understanding of the nature and processes of leadership is most likely to be enhanced as we come to understand better the arena in which leadership necessarily occurs—namely, the human mind. Perhaps this characterization should be pluralized as human minds, since I am concerned equally with the mind of the leader and the minds of the followers.

–Howard Gardner (1995, p. 25)

Chapter Orientation

Responding to the Moment

As observed in earlier chapters, there is nothing new about connecting leadership to the brain (CLTB). It is a connection that is natural, historical, and inescapable. Interaction between the neural networks of leaders and followers is the medium for leadership just as it is the medium for any other human interaction—be it parenting, teaching, or conducting commerce. What is new, however, is a dramatic advancement in knowledge about the nature of the human brain and the intelligence it enables. This emerging knowledge is arguably of such magnitude that it will inevitably inform and alter leadership behavior—as well as many other aspects of human affairs. How soon and to what degree this new knowledge favorably influences leadership practice, nevertheless, is a matter of how leaders structure their response to the opportunity that lies before them.

In Lieu of a Miracle

Architects have a useful expression for describing the universal relationship between vision and achievement: First you see it, then you build it. A cautionary addendum to this maxim would be that just because you "see it" does not mean it is going to happen. A comic scenario that is a variation of a famous *New Yorker* cartoon portrays this dilemma of good ideas coming to naught for lack of action:

> A group of executives are standing in front of a large flowchart depicting an intricate project. The project includes extensive description of mission, goals, line and staff relationships, communication routes, and the like. One of the executives points to the spot where the flow chart narrows to an empty box and asks, "And what happens here?" Another member of the group responds, "Then a miracle occurs."

The message is clear. Meaningful change or progress occurs only when what is envisioned is translated into specific action. That is, ideas are not truly potent until they are acted on—because it is only action that produces tangible results. This is a message that merits the attention of leaders who aspire to align their behavior to knowledge about the nature of human intelligence. Simply put, reflection about the import of evolving knowledge does not advance beyond the status of an intellectual exercise if compatible behavior is not determined and enacted as a result. Thus while it is important to first see leadership connections to the brain, the ultimate task is to consciously build such connections in the form of leadership influence on the achievement of goals. To that end, the narrative of this text now turns to the details of a framework for the alignment of the need, nature, and nurture of human achievement—a framework that forgoes reliance on a miracle in favor of structures that support human capacity to figure it out. Accordingly, the content of this chapter will

- Provide orientation to the value of a framework for organizing information and planning action
- Review the foundational premises for a framework that aspires to facilitate effective alignment of leadership behavior to the nature of intelligence
- Propose a framework for interpreting productive relationships between human intelligence, leadership, and achievement of goals
- Provide opportunity for the reader to enter the proposed framework to more directly examine its primary components
- Provide opportunity for the reader to experience applications of the proposed framework to self, systems, and situations
- Encourage leaders to exercise their human capacity to reflect and seek answers to complex questions, that is, to follow the example of Louis Pasteur's disposition to wonder, ponder, and inquire

Why a Framework?

Framework: *A structure for supporting or enclosing something else, especially a skeletal support used as the basis for something being constructed; a set of assumptions, concepts, values, and practices that constitutes a way of viewing reality*

—(American Heritage Dictionary, 2000, p. 697)

The Power of a Framework

It is not difficult to make a case for the contribution of frameworks to human affairs. The words in the definition cited above (e.g., *structure, support*) imply the productive value of a framework. Furthermore, demonstrations of the multiple uses of frameworks abound. For example, it would not be possible to build a house or any other structure without first *framing* it—both mentally and physically. The founders of the United States of America *framed* a national constitution that accommodates amendment. The details of treaties and other formal agreements emerge from preliminary *frameworks* for deliberations. The power of a framework, then, lies in its facilitation of mental and physical endeavors to construct, compose, or adjust something that is important to accomplish. A framework is a means by which to focus and organize resources for a desired effect—including the effect of accelerating perceptual shift.

The Most Powerful Framework on Earth

As previously noted, the business of the brain is survival, and, to that end, it assembles neural networks that organize information to useful purposes. This physical construction of neural networks is perpetuated throughout the human life span as connections are continually refined by ongoing discernment of useful patterns within the richness of available information. Thus your brain continually constructs its understanding of the world and, subsequently, directs your behavior accordingly.

The human brain has become very good at the business of interpreting and organizing patterns of information. Key to this success is the brain's adeptness at using established information patterns to frame the organization and refinement of other patterns. In this fashion, the value of an information pattern becomes more dramatic—it becomes a framework that provides structure for further interpretation of information. It is this capacity to continually frame and reframe the construction of knowledge that qualifies the human brain as the most powerful framework on earth—an unparalleled source of structure and support for the endless formulation of ideas and actions.

Thinking Frameworks We Know and Use

Ultimately, the human brain has evolved to a conscious appreciation for frameworks that facilitate its information-processing needs. It demonstrates this value by creating frameworks to serve its interests in many contexts. Formal information-processing structures, such as scientific method, systems analysis, and lateral thinking, are examples of such frameworks. Human brains also design frameworks to support thinking about specific subjects. Examples relevant to leadership would include Covey's (1989) framework for exploring the habits of highly effective people, Deming's (1988) 14-point structure for organizing ideas about total quality management, and Senge's (1990) framing of learning organizations through five learning disciplines. Similarly, Gardner's (1983) frames-of-mind orientation to multiple intelligences and Sternberg's (1985) depiction of a triarchic intelligence represent frameworks intended to facilitate reflection about human intelligence.

A Framework for Connecting Leadership to the Brain

From the perspective of the value of frameworks in general and the human brain's affinity for frameworks in particular, the following sections present a framework designed to facilitate reflection and perceptual shift about leadership-brain connections. The proposed framework aspires to engage the natural disposition and capacity of the human brain to organize information to useful purpose. To that end, it provides structure for the organization of knowledge about the nature of human intelligence and, thereby, reflection about implications for compatible leadership behavior. The framework also supports the application of such knowledge to leadership practice and the progressive development of a mindful leadership disposition.

The proposed framework for connecting leadership to the brain proceeds from several guiding assumptions:

1. An individual brain constructs its own meaning. Accordingly, leaders must construct their personal understanding (i.e., perception) of the nature of intelligence—as well as the implications therein for leadership behaviors that facilitate the achievement of goals.

2. A framework provides important and necessary structure for the distillation of essential information about human intelligence, the determination of compatible leadership behaviors, and the alignment of the need, nature, and nurture of human achievement.

3. There is no universal prescription for leadership behavior. Effective leaders adapt to both situation and context. Leadership is also influenced by the physiological, social, emotional, constructive, reflective, and dispositional intelligence of the individual leader in a specific situation or context. In this sense, the determination of appropriate leadership behavior becomes kaleidoscopic as it is continually adjusted in the light of changing realities.

To facilitate your construction of personal understanding about the nature of the proposed framework, it will be presented in multiple formats to engage the multiple dimensions of the nature of your intelligence. Specifically, the following sections sequentially will:

- Review the *foundational premises* of the framework, as outlined in Chapters 1-5
- Present a *conceptual description* of four components that constitute the basic structure of the framework
- Provide a *physical orientation* to the framework
- Provide *direct experience* with the framework

The Framework Foundation

Premises considered in Chapters 1 to 5 provide a foundation for a framework by which leadership practice may be consciously aligned to perception of the intelligence capacity of humans to achieve purpose (see Figure 6.1). These foundational premises provide a base for the assembly of a framework that supports the alignment of leadership behavior to the nature of human intelligence and the achievement of goals. The assembly of such a framework is particularly important if leaders are to become consciously competent in the mindful exercise of leadership practice.

The Framework Assembly

A leader need not passively wait for the pressure of new information to affect perceptual shifts about effective leadership practice. In the presence of emerging revelations from brain science, leaders have the option, if not the obligation, to proactively seek out and act on this knowledge. Indeed, leaders at the threshold of the 21st century have an unparalleled opportunity to cultivate shifts in leadership perception and behavior. They can consciously construct personal understanding of brain-compatible leadership behavior that advances the capacity of individuals and organizations to achieve common purpose. A framework composed of four components is useful to this end (see Figure 6.2):

1. **Arousal of brain attention** to the potential of mindful leadership
2. **Acquisition of knowledge** about the nature and nurture of intelligence
3. **Application of knowledge** about the nature and nurture of intelligence to leadership practice
4. **Adjustment of knowledge** about mindful leadership in response to application experience

Figure 6.1. Underlying Premises of a Framework for Connecting Leadership to the Brain

Foundational Premises: Connecting Leadership to the Brain				
Chapter 1	**Chapter 2**	**Chapter 3**	**Chapter 4**	**Chapter 5**
Emerging information about the human brain presents a unique opportunity to inform leadership practice	Information about the nature of human intelligence is of primary value to informed leadership practice	Information about human intelligence must be effectively organized if it is to inform leadership practice	The context of the 21st century requires a conscious tightening of leadership connections to human intelligence	Perception of leadership connections to intelligence is advanced through proactive reflection

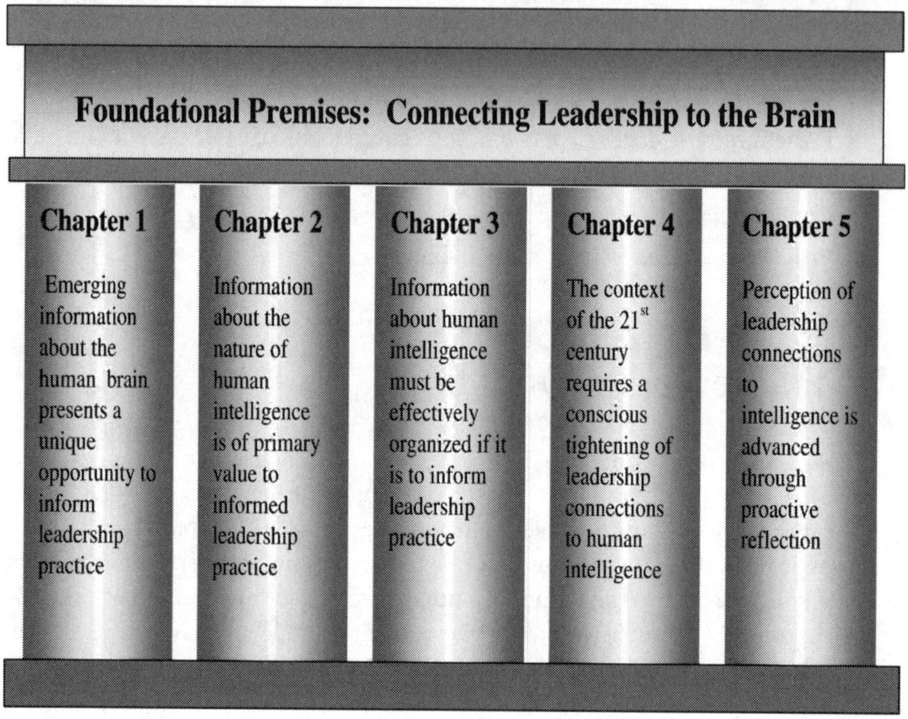

Collectively, these four components make up the necessary structure of a framework for connecting leadership to the brain—a framework that, by design, embraces the natural and powerful operations of the human brain. A conceptual description follows.

Component One:
Arousal of Brain Attention

The comprehensive structure of the brain, in all of its multidimensional-intelligence glory, is the component within which all other components of this framework operate. This is as it must be, given the brain's paramount role in processing information to discern important patterns that guide advantageous behavior. The involvement of this component, nevertheless, must not be taken for granted. It must be consciously brought to the table if any of the other components are to come into play. Specifically, the brain must be aroused to the issue of leadership-brain connections. It is not in its nature to invest its physiological energy—much less its considerable capacities to construct understanding and reflectively manipulate options—if it does not first establish emotional value for the potential benefits of such a commitment.

Figure 6.2. A Framework for Connecting Leadership to the Brain

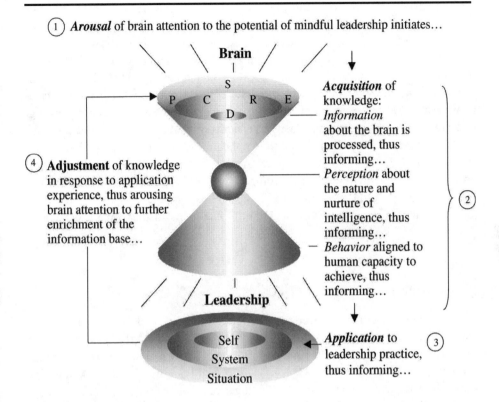

1. **Arousal:** The brain is attentive to the potential of mindful leadership
2. **Acquisition:** The brain processes relevant information to acquire a knowledge base about the nature and nurture of intelligence.
3. **Application:** Knowledge about the nature and nurture of intelligence informs mindful applications of leadership practice to self, systems, and situations.
4. **Adjustment:** Reflection about application experiences adjusts leadership knowledge, skill, and disposition, thereby arousing brain attention to further enrichment of the information base.

The first and foremost component of the proposed framework for connecting leadership to the brain, then, is the brain itself. It is the powerful biological operating system that must be aroused to the potential of intelligence-aware leadership. This may be accomplished by initial encounters with information that establishes value for the merits of the issue—such as the content of the first two chapters of this book. Subsequently, however, the commitment of this primary framework component must be reinforced and maintained by ongoing experience with other framework components.

The good news is that the human brain is, by its very nature, interested in knowing about itself. Furthermore, information processing is the brain's business, a business that is continuously conducted from womb to tomb. The key to this component of a framework that aspires to explore and strengthen leadership-brain connections, therefore, is *conscious* engagement of the information-processing systems of the brain. It is at the conscious level of information processing, after all, that the human brain performs at its best—including its construction of complex knowledge and reflective analysis of behavior options. Conscious engagement of brain information processing, therefore, is the means by which leaders proactively initiate personal understanding about the nature of intelligence and the implications thereof for compatible leadership behavior. In this fashion, component one is the system that underlies and operationalizes the other components of the framework. It is arousal that enables the subsequent acquisition of a knowledge base, application of knowledge to leadership practice, and progressive adjustment of mindful leadership disposition and behavior.

Component Two:
Acquisition of Knowledge

A brief exercise in logic: Given that neuroscientists may find it difficult to keep up with the current research-fueled explosion of information about the brain, and given that the vast majority of people in the world are not neuroscientists, it is safe to assume that most people will not likely master a great breadth or depth of knowledge about the nature of the brain and the intelligence it enables. For the leader who appreciates the need to reference leadership behavior to the nature of human intelligence, then, the challenge becomes one of expeditiously accessing essential knowledge. Component two of the proposed framework responds to this challenge by providing structure for the organization of relevant and practical information—that is, a personal knowledge base about the nature of intelligence and compatible leadership behavior.

The process involved in the exercise of component two of the framework was outlined earlier in Chapter 2, demonstrated in Chapter 3, and elaborated on in Chapter 5. It is a process that involves the steps of:

1. Engaging knowledge sources (e.g., expert, translator, common, summary) about the multiple dimensions of the nature of human intelligence

2. Distilling essential knowledge about specific dimensions of the nature of intelligence (e.g., physiological, social, emotional, constructive, reflective, dispositional)

3. Constructing perceptions about the implications of the nature of intelligence for compatible leadership behavior (i.e., *if* _____ is an essential quality of the nature of intelligence, *then* _____ would be a compatible leadership behavior)

The important point about this second component of the framework is that this is where the rubber begins to meet the road. If the brain's powerful information-processing operations are attentive to the issue, conscious exploration of leadership-brain connections is enabled. This prerequisite commitment does not become productive, however, until exercised in the reflective construction of personal understanding about the nature of intelligence and the implications for leadership behavior thereof. This is the critical aspect of component two. A leader can and should access the understanding of others about advantageous leadership connections to the brain. Leaders must, nevertheless, construct a personal perception of the nature of human intelligence if they are to most effectively discern appropriate bridges to leadership behavior.

Component Three:
Application of Knowledge

The natural business of the human brain is to attend to events that matter, process useful information patterns from the events it is attending to, and apply acquired information patterns to the processing of information about other events that matter. The proposed framework for connecting leadership to the brain mirrors this natural brain activity. Component one arouses the brain to the leadership-brain connection issue. Component two consciously employs the information-processing operations of the brain to the construction of a personal database about the essential nature of human intelligence and compatible leadership behaviors. Component three, then, is where the action is—where knowledge about the nature and nurture of intelligence is applied to leadership practice in three contexts: self, systems, and situations. Specifically, the third component of the framework organizes a sequential process that aligns leadership with the following:

- Clarification of **need:** What is the goal or purpose to be achieved?
- Assessment of the **nature** of intelligence required to achieve the need: What dimensions of intelligence will influence the achievement of the goal?
- Assessment of options that might **nurture** the required intelligence: What behaviors might favorably influence the dimensions of intelligence required for the achievement of the goal?
- Composition of a **narrative** plan of action: What strategic and collective actions will be conducted to influence the targeted dimensions of intelligence?

Component Four:
Adjustment of Knowledge

As described in Chapter 5, the process by which information influences perceptions that direct behavior is a dynamic rather than a linear operation. Thus a leader's interpretation and application of mindful leadership practice in diverse contexts is necessarily adjusted by information that informs and reforms the knowledge base . . . that informs perceptual shift . . . that informs behavior . . . that informs and reforms the knowledge base . . . ad infinitum. Furthermore, the process of consciously aligning leadership behavior to informed understanding of the nature and nurture of human intelligence might be a somewhat mechanical and awkward experience when first attempted. This, then, is the focus of the fourth and final component of the framework: the progressive adjustment of leadership knowledge, skills, and dispositions.

The conscious employment of the brain's neural information-processing system provides the natural structure for the composition of a knowledge base. Once established, however, this base of knowledge must be maintained through the ongoing engagement of the information-processing system that created it. Furthermore, leadership knowledge, skill, and disposition should realize upgraded benefits from the processing of application experiences. To become adroit in the mindful alignment of leadership practice to the nature and nurture of intelligence and the achievement of purpose, then, a leader would both attempt and assess mindful applications of leadership practice—that is, one becomes adept at riding a bike by riding a bike.

This construction and upgrading of expertise need not be onerous, in any case, given the availability of quality information sources (see Resource B) and the natural human affinity for learning from experience. Two strategies in particular, nevertheless, would be useful to the cultivation of mindful leadership capacity:

- **Partnership.** A leader would be well-advised to solicit the collaborative inquiry of colleagues in the quest for more mindful leadership skill and disposition. As considered in Chapter 3, social interaction is a stimulating influence on the constructive and reflective exercise of human intelligence. Collegial inquiry about the nature and nurture of intelligence is also a means to promote mindful leadership throughout an organization—as observed in Chapter 4.
- **Practice.** A leader would also be well-advised to apply the time honored human means for mastering any skill or disposition: Practice, practice, practice. Mindful leadership will evolve only from ongoing upgrading of personal knowledge about human intelligence and applications of that knowledge to self, systems, and situations. In effect, a leader must consciously construct and apply this knowledge until it becomes second nature—second nature, that is, to nurture the nature of human capacity to think, act and achieve purpose.

Entering the Framework

This section invites your brain to move beyond the abstraction of premises and conceptual description to a more physical, real-world construction of what the proposed framework might look like in use—that is, how a leader might engage the framework as a means to consciously align leadership behavior to the nature of intelligence and the achievement of purpose. To that end, you will enter the framework to more directly examine the exercise of its primary components—to examine the structures by which a leader might *turn on, tune in, apply, and adjust* understanding of mindful leadership practice. You will be facilitated in this up-close-and-personal encounter with the framework through reflective question-and-answer dialogues with "Alexis," an experienced investigator of leadership-brain connections.

Step One: Turn On

Engaging the first component of the framework is not unlike turning on a computer for information-processing purposes, such as constructing databases and running application programs. In the case of turning on (i.e., arousing) the brain to the issue of mindful leadership, however, an operating system of virtually unlimited processing and storage capacity is being activated. Accordingly, arousal is the prerequisite component of a framework for connecting leadership to the brain. There is no choice in this matter, because human understanding of anything—including interpretations of relationships between leadership and the nature and nurture of intelligence—is necessarily constructed within the neural networks of the brain. Investment of this knowledge construction capacity, however, must be provoked by a judgment of value. In effect, you must first trip an emotional switch that turns your brain on to the prospects of informed leadership-brain connections. Thus aroused, powerful information-processing mechanisms are available for the construction of a knowledge base about the nature and nurture of intelligence and application programs that align leadership behavior with the nature of the human capacity to achieve purpose.

Reflective Dialogue

A Question for Alexis: How do you turn on—that is, arouse—your brain to the potential of mindful leadership?

Alexis's Response: Generally, my interest in knowing more about the nature of intelligence stems from my interest in being an effective leader. I mean, if understanding more about how people acquire and apply knowledge will give me an edge in my efforts to influence the achievement of group goals, I'm interested. I realize, nevertheless, that I have to be proactive about this issue, because my brain has a lot of things competing for its attention. Accordingly, I make it a point to read articles, books, and other literature about emerging brain research. I also seek out opportunities to participate in professional conferences that present sessions on the topic. Other than that, I make it a point to associate with peers who also are professionally motivated to continually improve their leadership capacity. I figure that, if there is anything happening out there that might make a leadership difference, those who are looking for it are going to discover it first.

A Question for You: How do you or how might you turn on—that is, arouse—your brain to the potential of mindful leadership?

Your Response:

Reflection Time

Step Two: Tune In

A computer is commonly employed to generate and organize data that is subsequently applied to a specific purpose. Similarly, this framework provides structure by which attentive leaders can engage relevant information sources and organize a serviceable body of knowledge about the nature and nurture of intelligence, as modeled in Chapter 3. This is an obvious prerequisite for applications of mindful leadership behavior. A computer without a database is a machine without the information resources required to perform other tasks. A leader who does not construct personal understanding about human intelligence is forgoing acquisition of knowledge that is essential to informed leadership practice in the 21st century. The acquisition of such a knowledge base is facilitated in many ways, such as literature review, seminars, and collegial inquiry—but regardless of how it is established and maintained, it must be acquired if mindful leadership practice is to ensue.

Reflective Dialogue

A Question for Alexis: How do you acquire and organize knowledge about the nature and nurture of intelligence?

Alexis's Response: What helps me attend to the potential of mindful leadership also helps me develop a personal knowledge base about the nature and nurture of intelligence. That is, I read, attend conferences and seminars, and dialogue with colleagues about emerging information about the brain and the subsequent implications of such information for leadership practice. I have to be judicious, however, about my investment of time and effort in the construction of such knowledge. After all, I'm a leader, not a neuroscientist, and I'm responsible for knowing and doing a lot of things. Accordingly, what I find to be expeditious and useful is to read and otherwise access information about the brain and intelligence that is nonexpert friendly—information that has been interpreted, summarized, and organized in a manner that helps me understand the essence of the matter. I also find it important to go beyond just *knowing* things about the brain. By that I mean, for me to really understand something about the nature of intelligence, I find it helpful to interpret it in the context of what I as a leader might do about it. To that end, I'm often asking and answering *if-then* questions. For example, *if* the knowledge construction and complex reasoning capacities of the brain are both stimulated and facilitated by social interaction, *then* leaders should structure frequent opportunities for individuals in an organization to interact with others as they engage new information, attempt to solve problems, plan goals and tasks, and the like (see Figure 6.3).

A Question for You: How do you or how might you acquire and organize knowledge about the nature and nurture of intelligence?

Your Response:

> Reflection Time

Figure 6.3. Construction of Perception About the Nature of Intelligence and Compatible Leadership Behavior

Construction of Perception About the Nature of Intelligence and Compatible Leadership Behavior		
Dimension of Intelligence	**Perception**	**Compatible Behavior**
Physiological	← if—then →	?????
Social	← if—then →	?????
Emotional	← if—then →	?????
Constructive	← if—then →	?????
Reflective	← if—then →	?????
Dispositional	← if—then →	?????

Development of a Knowledge Base: The Nature and Nurture of Intelligence

Information about the brain is engaged and processed to construct a perception (i.e., an understanding) of the essential qualities of the nature of human intelligence it enables and, thereby, implications for compatible leadership behavior.

Step Three: Apply

Leaders engage the proposed framework by turning on and tuning in the powerful information-processing system of their brains to the nature and nurture of intelligence. Thus aroused and focused, the next step is to apply knowledge about intelligence in a manner that informs leadership behavior in the contexts of self, systems, and situations. To advance the computer metaphor further, one might envision software application programs that are informed by a database. When opened by an operating system, such application programs provide structure for the completion of particular tasks—such as plotting the movement of weather patterns, computing economic trends, or synchronizing music with fireworks displays. In the case of connecting leadership to the brain, your brain is the operating system that generates a database of essential knowledge about intelligence. To most effectively apply such knowledge, however, there is need for some manner of application programming—structure that will align leadership behavior to the nature and nurture of intelligence. In effect, then, it is structured application of knowledge about intelligence that represents the mindful exercise of leadership influence on the human capacity to achieve purpose.

What would a leader be doing, then, in the exercise of a framework application program that aligns leadership behavior with the nature of the human capacity to think, learn, and achieve purpose? To engage your brain in its constructing of a physical sense of this component of the framework, envision the four concentric circles of the application program (as depicted in Figure 6.4) laid out on the floor of a familiar room—your office or any room in your home will do. Now picture yourself standing in the center circle. Better yet, stand in the middle of the room you are located in as you read this. (If you are reading this while you are a passenger in a car, plane, or train, however, please forgo the kinesthetic experience and stick with the visualization!) In exercising an application program, then, leadership practice is initially centered by the first of four steps, as described below (see Figure 6.4).

1. *Clarification of need: What is the purpose or goal to be achieved?*

In the case of an application of the scan-and-respond process to self, the answer to this question is always the same by virtue of the very definition of leadership. The purpose of leadership is always to influence others in the achievement of a goal. The real value of asking this question of yourself is that it serves as a valuable reminder. It is a means to reorient oneself and avoid confusion with other purposes—to reaffirm that leadership is the facilitation of others in the establishment and achievement of purpose.

Questions for You: As you stand at the center of the circle—what is the universal purpose of leadership? What is your leadership purpose?

Your Response:

> Reflection Time

Clarification of need in systems or situations is a different matter, as there is no universal answer to the question. In fact, it is critically important to clarify and communicate the unique purpose or goal of any system or situation. This is the prerequisite step too often overlooked, whether by ignorance or neglect, for emotionally committing the resources of intelligence. In the case of a system, need is often described in terms of mission or organizational purpose. The needs of given situations are expressed in terms of goals, such as material gain, performance improvement, or the resolution of a problem or an important decision.

Again, clarification of need is the essential first step in a mindful application of leadership. It is what centers leadership and generates passion for attending to and acting on important purpose. In all cases, be it a matter of self, a system, or a situation, leadership is not leadership unless it influences the achievement of a need.

Questions for You: Think about an organization you are associated with. What is its purpose or mission? What is a current situation confronting that organization (per-

Figure 6.4. CLTB Framework Application Program: Scan-and-Respond Steps

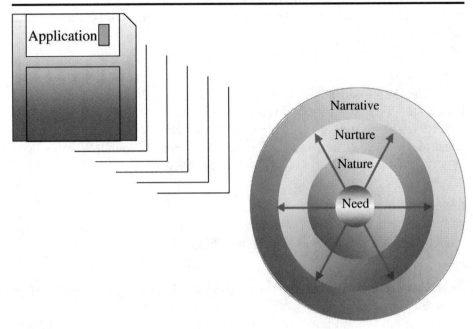

1. **Need:**   Clarify the purpose or goal to be achieved.
2. **Nature:**   Assess the intelligence requirements for achieving the need.
3. **Nurture:**   Assess the behavior options for influencing the nature of the required
                    dimensions of intelligence.
4. **Narrative:**   Compose a plan to nurture the natural capacity to achieve the need.

haps a new project, a specific problem, a unique opportunity)? What is the goal, the preferred outcome for that situation?

Your Response:

Reflection Time

2. Assessment of the nature of intelligence required for achieving the need.
    This step occurs as you move outward from the center to the next ring of the circle. It is the same process whether applied to self, system, or situation—a conscious assessment of knowledge about the nature of intelligence in relation to an achievement need. Specifically, this step in the application process asks questions about the status and requirements of different dimensions of intelligence that may be important to the achievement of an identified purpose or goal: What are the potential physiological demands and effects of the task at hand? What are the requirements and op-

portunities for social interaction? What are the likely and preferred emotional responses to the achievement need? Is there a need to construct new knowledge? Is reflective reasoning required? What thinking dispositions will be important to achieving this need?

A Question for You: Think back to your responses to questions about the purpose of leadership, the mission of an organization you are familiar with, or a goal associated with a situation that is confronting an organization. What are your observations about the status and requirements of different dimensions of intelligence (e.g., physiological, social, emotional, constructive, reflective, or dispositional)? What might be important to the achievement of any of those needs?

Your Response:

> | Reflection Time |

3. Assessment of options for the nurture of the intelligence required to achieve the need.

Moving outward to the next ring of the circle, a leader considers options for favorably influencing dimensions of intelligence deemed relevant to the achievement of an identified need. In a very real sense, leaders at this step in an application program are conducting a neural conversation with themselves. This conversation considers the desired outcome, particular qualities of intelligence that are important to achieving the outcome, and interventions that might nurture said qualities of intelligence. Again, this step accesses the leaders' knowledge about the nature and nurture of intelligence, whether in applications of such knowledge to leadership behavior affecting self, systems, or situations. Hence leaders will draw on personal knowledge about the nature of intelligence to ascertain how it might be nurtured to greatest effect in the context of a particular achievement need. For example, if leaders perceive that a given purpose or goal will place high demand on a group's capacity to exercise emotional intelligence while under pressure to construct new knowledge important to the reflective resolution of a challenging problem, they will explore options for cultivating and supporting those dimensions of intelligence in the group. Such exploration might envision the facilitation of emotional release, direct and collaborative processing of relevant information, and structured strategies for generating innovative alternatives in group problem-solving processes.

A Question for You: Given your prior identification of intelligence requirements for the achievement of leadership purpose, the mission of a system, or a preferred outcome in a particular situation—what are some specific leadership behaviors or actions that might favorably influence the targeted dimensions of intelligence?

Your Response:

Reflection Time

4. *Composition of a narrative plan of action that will nurture the nature of the human capacity to achieve the need*.

One might observe that, thus far, there is a simple logic to this application process. There is basic rhyme and reason in the sequential steps of clarifying a desirable outcome, assessing resources that are important to achieving that outcome, and then exploring means by which such resources might be most effectively secured and deployed. Given clarity of a need and assessment of the nature of the intelligence required to achieve it, it makes sense that leaders would concern themselves with the nurture of the nature that will achieve the need. If left at this stage, however, the application of knowledge process will likely fall victim to the classic demise of many a failed leadership venture—*the failure to act*. It is with this concern that a fourth important step in the application program is added to translate reflection and assessment into action. To that end, step four in the process requires the composition of a narrative plan of action from the intervention options considered in step three. The importance of this step cannot be overstated. All too often, good ideas and insights come to naught for lack of an implementation plan (as observed in the "then a miracle happens" story described at the beginning of this chapter). Accordingly, in step four of the application component of the framework, the leader steps into the outer ring of the circle to compose—either mentally or physically—a comprehensive plan of action for the expeditious nurture of the intelligence required by an achievement need. An example of this particular step would be a leader determining that a long-term commitment to learning and exercising collaborative skills and strategies would comprehensively and favorably influence multiple dimensions of organizational intelligence (e.g., physiological, social, emotional, constructive, reflective, dispositional).

Reflection Time

As leaders step out of the outer circle and look back at the four steps of the application structure, they are in a position to observe the unity of the process. It is not a complicated or unknown process. After all, this is what successful leaders do—be they CEOs, generals, coaches, philosophers, or politicians. It matters not whether the goal is to put the ball in the end zone or resolve a social injustice, the process is the same in the leaders' brain: What is the goal? What knowledge, skills, or attitudes are important to the achievement of this goal? What are my options for influencing the required knowledge, skills, or attitudes? Which options will I act on?

What is different—the new twist in the context of the 21st century—is that leaders have both the motivation and the means to exercise this process more effectively (see Figure 6.5). The opportunity arises at the second and third steps of the described

Figure 6.5. Scan-and-Respond Alignment of Leadership Behavior to the Need, Nature, Nurture, and Narrative Planning of Achievement

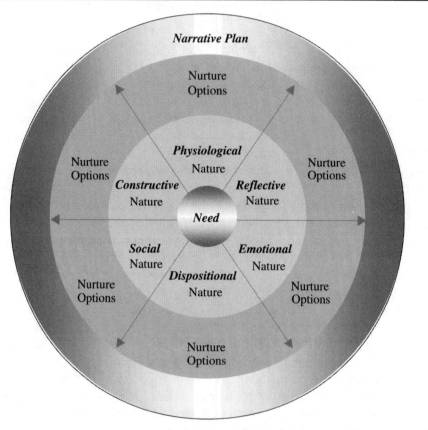

1. Clarify the need.
2. Assess the nature of intelligence required to achieve the need.
3. Assess options for nurturing the required intelligence.
4. Compose a narrative plan of action.

application program. Assuming clarity of purpose and commitment to act, leaders informed about the nature of intelligence are in a position to more effectively align their behavior to the nature of the human capacity to achieve.

Reflective Dialogue

A Question for Alexis: How do you apply knowledge about the nature of intelligence to yourself, systems, and situations?

Alexis's Response: Applying knowledge about the nature of intelligence is, to me, what mindful leadership is all about. It basically means that I consciously reference what I know about the intelligence of people when deciding how I might best influence them in the achievement of a goal. I am being mindful when I sequentially ask myself: What is the goal? How will particular dimensions of intelligence be involved in achieving the goal? What might be done to facilitate the dimensions of intelligence that are important to achieving the goal? Given the options, how will I act to most productively influence the capacities that are important to goal achievement? Simply put, I'm composing a narrative plan in my head about how I might best nurture the nature of human capacity to achieve a specific need.

A Question for You: How do you or how might you apply knowledge about the nature of intelligence to yourself, systems, and situations?

Your Response:

> Reflection Time

Step Four: Adjust

The advantage of the proposed framework, again, is that it provides skeletal structure for the composition and refinement of ideas. A framework should eventually become internalized, however, through experience with the exercise of its components.

Accordingly, a leader who continues to engage this framework as a means to investigate leadership-brain connections—particularly in the construction of knowledge and the application of knowledge to self, systems, and situations—will evolve from a mechanical employment of its components to a level of automatic disposition and skill. In this fashion—referencing the computer metaphor one final time—leaders continually upgrade and adjust the mindful nature of their leadership practice through inquiry and experience.

The integration of feedback from application experiences, then, is most important to the evolution of mindful leadership behavior. It is neural processing of information from such sustained, integrated leadership experience that will lead to mindful patterns of leadership practice (see Figure 6.6). As you are well aware by now, experience informs and reforms the information base that informs the perceptions that inform behavior.

Reflective Dialogue

A Question for Alexis: How do you upgrade and adjust knowledge of mindful leadership?

Alexis's Response: The old maxim "Experience is the best teacher" applies to this question. And, in a way, it is just that simple—you learn by doing. In this case, you

Figure 6.6. The Evolution of Mindful Leadership

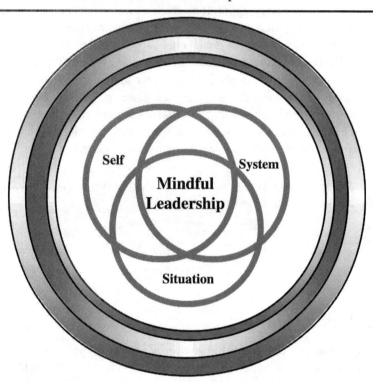

Over time, formal and informal applications of the CLTB framework collectively cultivate mindful leadership disposition and skill. From successive application experience arises an inclination and adeptness for viewing leadership through a lens that aligns behavior to intelligence in self, systems, and situations.

turn your brain on to the potential of mindful leadership, acquire knowledge about the nature of intelligence, and then apply that knowledge in a reflective fashion to your influence on the achievement of goals. One can hardly help but learn about what works and what doesn't work from such experience. The key to this component of mindful leadership, however, is to maximize the learning opportunities within the experience. Generally, there are two simple yet powerful means to that end: (a) Consciously take the time to individually reflect about what is and is not working in an application experience—as it proceeds and after it is completed; and (b) conduct the same reflection process in the company of colleagues—particularly those involved in the achievement of the identified goal or purpose. It comes down to this: the more mindfulness the better. I don't look at mindful leadership as something that I do alone in my organization. If there is one thing I do try to do, it is to involve every member of the group in each component of the framework, particularly the steps of the application process. That way, I have everyone focusing on what needs to get done, the intelligence requirements for getting it done, and what we are going to do to nurture those capacities. As we move through the application process, I also want to access the group's assessment of what is working and what we need to adjust and do differently in the future. In this fashion, we are constantly upgrading our knowledge about the nature and nurture of intelligence in a reality context. Not only does this further inform our knowledge of mindful leadership, it also motivates our continuing attention to how we might learn to exercise it more effectively.

A Question for You: How might you upgrade and adjust your knowledge of mindful leadership?

Your Response:

> Reflection Time

Experiencing the Framework

As you know from your prior review of the constructive nature of intelligence in Chapter 3, direct experience is a most powerful influence on brain capacity to construct understanding. This fact is no less true for the construction of understanding about a framework for connecting leadership to the brain. Accordingly, you are now invited to directly experience the application component of the framework—where the action is.

The following vignettes present opportunities to exercise the application component of the framework in the reality of different leadership contexts. In effect, you will be asked to employ the previously described steps of the application process in three different leadership scenarios (accordingly, you may wish to reference Figure 6.5 as you move through the exercises). Alexis will once again accompany you in this hands-on experience with the framework. In this case, however, you will be the one to take the lead, and Alexis will offer follow-up observations that might have comparison value for your further reflection. Application templates are also provided at the end of the chapter for your further experience with the exercise of the framework in your personal leadership context.

Now . . . slip behind the wheel of the application process and take control.

Application Experience:
A Leader's View of Self

It has been said that leaders must first lead themselves before they can lead others. Accordingly, leadership effectiveness emerges first and foremost from attention to the nature and nurture of one's own intelligence. Four steps guide such an application of knowledge about intelligence:

1. Clarify the **need** (i.e., purpose or goal) to be achieved.
2. Assess the **nature** of intelligence required for achieving the need.
3. Assess options for the **nurture** of the required intelligence.
4. Compose a **narrative** plan to nurture the nature of capacity to achieve need.

A Vignette

The principal of a small suburban school district often seems out of sorts. The impression he leaves with parents, teachers, and students is one of being overworked and understaffed. Small problems grow into large irritants, leaving those around him feeling unsure and insecure about their own jobs. The more overwhelmed this leader feels, the more the quality of his work suffers and the more estranged he becomes from fellow educators. He begins making decisions impulsively and then finds himself in the position of having to clean up the consequences later, adding to his feelings of frustration. The culture of the school and the morale of the staff are beginning to be negatively affected by his behavior.

Reflective Dialogue

Questions for You:

1. **Need:** What is the leader's purpose?
2. **Nature:** What are the dimensions of intelligence required of this leader if he is to serve his purpose effectively?
3. **Nurture:** What might this leader do to nurture the dimensions of intelligence required of him by his leadership purpose?
4. **Narrative:** What plan of action would you recommend to the leader?

> *Reflection Time*

Alexis's Observations: Leadership purpose remains constant, that is, the purpose of a leader is to influence others in the achievement of a purpose or goal. In this case, the purpose of the system is to create a successful learning environment for elementary school children. It would seem obvious from this vignette that the leader is not faring very well within the emotional dimension of intelligence. He appears to be feeling stressed and, therefore, distressed—two factors that may impair his decision-making abilities. It seems that he is involved in a negative downward spiral with one stressful situation leading to another. From the physiological dimension, he may also be suffering from lack of sleep due to increased pressure at school and, therefore, may additionally be impaired in his ability to think clearly. Most likely, he is not eating well and may be neglecting exercise. As a result of his behaviors within the social dimension of intelligence, he is separating himself from productive interactions and the ability to use others as a sounding board—or at the very least, to receive support from those with whom he works. Because he is beginning to make decisions impulsively, he is not allowing himself time to reflect and think through the best course of action, diminishing the reflective and constructive dimensions of his intelligence. Dispositionally, he may have a tendency to look on the bleak side and his interpretation of his own current state is becoming a self-fulfilling prophecy. Accordingly, to nurture the capacities required of his job, this leader might consider

- Taking some time away from the job to rest and relax. The benefit of sleep, exercise, and proper nutrition should not be minimized. Additionally, by reducing the stress levels, this leader may be able to process the needs of his school more effectively.
- Increasing positive interaction with his immediate support group. Accessing the capacity of those around him in an atmosphere of hope and high energy will create new possibilities for creative solutions to old problems.
- Building in time to reflect. The gift of time is one of the first to go when we feel overworked. We begin to work harder, not smarter. By practicing "I need some time to think about this before I make a decision," this leader can begin to offer higher quality responses that won't require further fixing down the road.
- Considering the alternatives. The principal may decide to arrange lunch periods with key staff members to spend time listening to varying perspectives and reflecting on beneficial courses to take. Through thoughtful, two-way communication, relationships can be rebuilt, reflection can be enabled, and some stress reduced.

Of all of these options, it seems that working toward the establishment of a collaborative organizational culture—one of regular and structured problem solving and shared decision making among members of the system—would be the most productive course of action.

Application Experience:
Leadership Influence on System Capacity

Leadership does not occur within a vacuum. Rather, it occurs within a context or system. This application promotes reflection about appropriate leadership behavior that maximizes system potential for achieving organizational purpose. Again, four steps guide this adaptation:

1. Clarify the **need** (i.e., purpose or goal) to be achieved.
2. Assess the **nature** of intelligence required for achieving the need.
3. Assess options for the **nurture** of the required intelligence.
4. Compose a **narrative** plan to nurture the nature of capacity to achieve need.

A Vignette

A start-up technology firm hires a new CEO. She decides that the first order of business is to discover as much as she can about the nature of the company and its workers before she makes any major decisions. On talking to employees, she discovers that people were drawn to work here for the high degree of flexibility and creativity offered in the work environment. Further investigation reveals that the company is borderline anarchistic with few rules, no systemic policies, a mission that is a moving target, and a business plan that has been rewritten five times in the past year. Employees are actively working on their résumés, and an atmosphere of everyone for herself or himself has developed. Several of the initial visionaries have left the company for opportunities in larger, more stable environments. Deadlines have occasionally forced workers to pull all-nighters to get the job done. The new CEO is dismayed to find that the reality of the company is much different from the one painted by the board of directors who hired her.

Reflective Dialogue

Questions for You:

1. ***Need:*** What is the system purpose?
2. ***Nature:*** What are the dimensions of intelligence required of this system if it is to achieve its purpose?
3. ***Nurture:*** What might be done to nurture the required dimensions of intelligence?
4. ***Narrative:*** What plan of action would you recommend?

> Reflection Time

Alexis's Observations: The universal purpose of all commercial enterprises is to provide a good product and achieve profit from doing so. Beyond that, the more specific purpose of the technology firm is most likely to produce products that respond quickly and effectively to the needs of a rapidly changing and competitive marketplace. In order to achieve these purposes, the system needs to be efficient, flexible, and future oriented. To that end, the system requires the comprehensive exercise of multiple dimensions of intelligence. The exercise of such intelligence, however, appears to be compromised by the status of a system in flux. Workers are responding reflexively, rather than reflectively, due to conditions of uncertainty in their workplace. This jeopardizes their ability to apply their constructive and reflective capacities to product and marketplace issues. Due to the lack of stable patterns and predictability within the system, attention is being emotionally diverted to job survival behaviors. The system is generating a climate of uncertainty and uneasiness for its employees, and one might surmise that social interactions are being negatively affected by a watch-your-back mentality. Instead of gravitating toward collaboration and mutual problem solving, workers are likely becoming Balkanized and protective of their own jobs. Accordingly, the leader has her intelligence-nurturing work cut out for her, with particular need to address the social and emotional dimensions. Some options for the leader to consider would be:

- Taking immediate action to lessen uncertainty and confusion. Putting patterns and structures in place will allow workers some practical modicum of predictability. Clear processes, timelines, roles, and procedures may help employees begin to feel more secure and better able to focus on the job at hand.
- Rebuilding relationships among workers. Creating time and processes for productive work teams will increase social interaction and the probability that creative construction of new ideas will occur.
- Clarifying purpose and facilitating the construction of meaning. Workers need to know to what ends they are working. Creating shared understanding and meaning within the workplace will facilitate greater motivation and productivity.
- Arranging opportunities for members of the organization to exercise, relax, and have fun together.

What might be most important for the CEO to consider in her assessment of options and a plan of action is that organizational capacity is very much a product of culture building and that organizational cultures are not built in a day—or a weekend planning retreat. Accordingly, she should be wary of how she approaches the obvious need for some kind of planning procedure that will refocus the company's values, mission, and goals. Such an immediate move in that direction might understandably be interpreted by the members of the organization as a quick-fix maneuver. Indeed, the leader might be well-advised to start with attention to the structures that facilitate inclusion and respect through the structured meetings of minds and planning of consensus actions. Such a beginning will focus attention on social, emotional, and physiological qualities of the human capacity to think, learn, and achieve—a good base from which to then further cultivate the constructive, reflective, and dispositional intelligence qualities of the organization.

Application Experience:
Leadership Response to a Situation

Leaders must adapt their leadership behavior to the unique needs of any given situation. As in the previously described vignettes, four steps guide the leader in making decisions about appropriate leadership behavior applied to a situation:

1. Clarify the **need** (i.e., purpose or goal) to be achieved.
2. Assess the **nature** of intelligence required for achieving the need.
3. Assess options for the **nurture** of the required intelligence.
4. Compose a **narrative** plan to nurture the nature of capacity to achieve the need.

A Vignette

The manager of a branch of a large metropolitan bank has been given day-to-day operational authority over the business of his particular branch. The bank's mission clearly indicates that customer service is a top priority: "Satisfied customers are loyal customers." On this particular Monday morning, the manager was faced with a situation involving a customer who was not only dissatisfied but was downright angry. Waving the last statement from her account, shouting loudly at the teller, and declaring fraudulent practice, the customer threatened to call the FDIC for intervention. In response, the teller became defensive and began to speak loudly and rudely to the customer. On hearing the exchange, the manager intervened.

Reflective Dialogue

Questions for You:

1. **Need:** What is the goal in this situation?
2. **Nature:** What are the dimensions of intelligence required to achieve the goal in this situation?
3. **Nurture:** What might be done to nurture the required dimensions of intelligence?
4. **Narrative:** What plan of action would you recommend?

> Reflection Time

Alexis's Observations: Again, the goal of any for-profit organization is to increase profit. A primary related goal—that certainly applies to this situation—is to satisfy the customer to ensure repeated business. Accordingly, this situation requires attention to the intelligence of both the customer and the teller. The customer is obviously emotionally distraught. From the behavior exhibited, one can surmise that access to the social, reflective, and constructive capacities of the brain have been emotionally diminished. The customer's behavior is also creating a cascading influence of negative emotion on the teller, who also abandons his social, reflective, and constructive intelligence options and begins to respond inappropriately because of feelings of threat and intimidation. Both parties continue in a downward spiral of emotion-reaction-emotion in which their prospects for a rational construction of a positive solution to the perceived problem is improbable. In response to this situation, and in order to nurture the capacities of those involved, the leader might

- Rapidly intervene to change the tone of the interaction. By entering with a calm, mediating tone, the leader can assist both parties in disengaging from their negative emotional spiral.
- Listen actively to the needs being expressed by the customer. Engaging the social intelligence of the customer in an open and frank conversation is a means to redirect emotion and access reflective and constructive thinking.
- Model appropriate problem-solving behaviors for the teller. By remaining calm, taking time to think, and encouraging a positive feeling tone, the leader can provide job-embedded training for the teller.
- Contemplate an employee training program in conflict resolution to better enable employees to engage their cognitive problem-solving abilities in the heat of an emotional situation.
- Confer with the employee after the heat of the battle has passed, and facilitate his exercise of a disposition to analyze the experience and generate creative resolution and customer relations alternatives.

In the big picture, this situation is, of course, all about organizational culture again. So what a leader does to cultivate a mindful organizational intelligence will anticipate situations such as these. The leader should also appreciate, however, that every situation, large or small, represents an opportunity to either reinforce or advance organizational intelligence.

Becoming Louis

At some distant point in prehistorical time, the evolution of intelligence produced the distinct human capacity to think reflectively and, subsequently, to ask and seek answers to complex questions. In Chapter 1, Louis Pasteur's scientific discovery was offered as an example of how advances in knowledge influence shifts in perception and behavior. Pasteur's story is also an example of the human capacity and disposition to wonder, ponder, and inquire. Louis's curiosity about the nature of disease led him to an inquiry of scientific investigation that, ultimately, produced answers beyond his original questions.

The framework that has been presented in this chapter aspires to facilitate the natural capacity of humans to raise and answer important questions. Specifically, the proposed framework provides structure for reflection by leaders about the relationship of their behavior to the capacity of individuals and organizations to achieve purpose. Leaders who engage this framework are thus aggressively exercising their human disposition to find the answer to questions of concern, in this instance, to questions about brain-compatible leadership. To engage in such an exercise is to become, like Louis Pasteur, a seeker of answers to an important question. In this case, the investigator is searching for the keys that will open doors to greater understanding and effect in the practice of leadership.

Summary Observations

- Frameworks, by their nature, provide structure and support for the construction, composition, and refinement of ideas.
- The proposed framework for connecting leadership to the brain is founded on the premises that:
    1. Significant new knowledge about the human brain presents an opportunity to better understand and exercise effective leadership practice.
    2. New information about the nature of intelligence enabled by the human brain is the primary target for improved leadership-brain connections.
    3. Information about the nature of human intelligence must be processed and organized if it is to effectively inform leadership practice.
    4. The context of the 21st century both requires and accommodates a tightening of conscious leadership connections to the powerful and multidimensional intelligence capacity of the human brain.
    5. Perceptual shifts about the nature of human intelligence and compatible leadership behavior can and should be advanced through proactive reflection.
- The proposed framework for connecting leadership to the brain mirrors the natural information-processing operations of the human brain in its employment of four structural components:
    1. Arousal of the powerful information-processing system of the human brain to the potential of mindful leadership
    2. Acquisition of knowledge about the nature and nurture of human intelligence
    3. Application of knowledge about the nature and nurture of human intelligence to leadership practice that affects self, systems, and situations
    4. Adjustment and continual upgrading of knowledge about mindful leadership in response to application experience
- Within the framework, the application of knowledge about the nature and nurture of intelligence to leadership practice is organized by a four-step alignment process:
    1. Clarification of **need** (i.e., purpose of goal)
    2. Assessment of the **nature** of intelligence required for achieving the need
    3. Assessment of options that will **nurture** the required intelligence
    4. Composition of a **narrative** plan of action that will nurture the nature of self and others to achieve needs

- The proposed framework is a structure designed to support reflection about leadership connections to the brain. It is not a source for prescriptive actions or remedies. The only such answers this framework will divulge are those discovered by the intelligence of the leader who enters and experiences its components.
- The endgame for connecting leadership to the brain is a deep, internalized understanding of human intelligence that naturally guides compatible leadership behavior. Until that mindful status is achieved by a leader, the employment of a framework that facilitates the human capacity and disposition to "figure it out" is in order.

Reader Reflection

- What is the value of a framework for connecting leadership to the brain?
- How would I explain the four components of the proposed framework?
- How would I explain the four steps in the application program process?
- How might I organize a personal knowledge base about the nature and nurture of human intelligence (see Template 6.1, page 182)?
- How might I apply knowledge about the nature and nurture of intelligence to leadership practice that affects myself, a system, or a particular situation (see Templates 6.2, 6.3, and 6.4, pages 183-185)?
- Other thoughts and questions?

Template 6.1. Construction of a Knowledge Base About the Nature and Nurture of Intelligence

Wake Up and Smell the Coffee: Constructing a Personal Knowledge Base			
On realizing that he or she is alive and practicing leadership in a *Louis Moment,* a leader processes and organizes information about the brain to construct personal understanding of the nature and nurture of human intelligence and the implications thereof for effective leadership practice.			
Knowledge about multiple dimensions of intelligence	*Perception of the nature and nurture of intelligence*	*Behavior that is compatible with perceptions of intelligence*	*Strategies that influence multiple dimensions of intelligence*
Physiological:	← if—then →		
Social:	← if—then →		
Emotional:	← if—then →		
Constructive:	← if—then →		
Reflective:	← if—then →		
Dispositional:	← if—then →		

Template 6.2. Application to Self: Connecting Leadership to Personal Intelligence

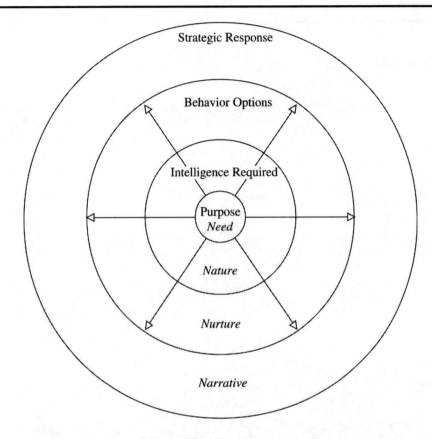

Informed by personal knowledge about the nature of intelligence and compatible leadership behavior, the leader conducts a scan-and-respond process to:

A. Clarify leadership purpose; that is, what is the **need**?

B. Assess the intelligence requirements of self for achieving leadership purpose, that is, what is the status of relevant dimensions of the **nature** of personal capacity to achieve?

C. Assess options for advancing the self-intelligence required for the achievement of leadership purpose; that is, what behavior will **nurture** the nature of personal capacity to achieve?

D. Compose a strategic response that will nurture the natural capacity of self to achieve leadership purpose; that is, what is the **narrative** plan of action?

Template 6.3. Application to Systems: Connecting Leadership to Organizational Intelligence

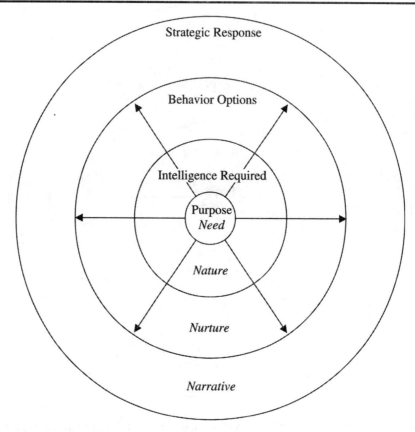

Informed by personal knowledge about the nature of intelligence and compatible leadership behavior, the leader conducts a scan-and-respond process to:

A. Clarify system purpose; that is, what is the **need**?

B. Assess the intelligence requirements of the system for achieving leadership purpose; that is, what is the status of relevant dimensions of the **nature** of organizational capacity to achieve?

C. Assess options for advancing the intelligence required for the achievement of system purpose; that is, what behavior will **nurture** the nature of the human capacity to achieve throughout the organization?

D. Compose a strategic response that will nurture the natural capacity of members to achieve system purpose; that is, what is the **narrative** plan of action?

Template 6.4. Application to Situations: Connecting Leadership to Situational Intelligence

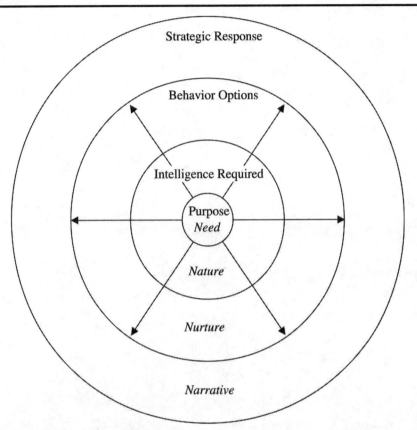

Informed by personal knowledge about the nature of intelligence and compatible leadership behavior, the leader conducts a scan-and-respond process to:

A.   Clarify the situation goal; that is, what is the **need**?

B.   Assess the intelligence requirements for achieving the situation goal; that is, what is the status of relevant dimensions of the **nature** of the human capacity to achieve?

C.   Assess options for advancing the intelligence required for achievement of the situation goal; that is, what behavior will **nurture** the nature of the human capacity to achieve?

D.   Compose a strategic response that will nurture the natural capacity of involved individuals to achieve the situation goal; that is, what is the **narrative** plan of action?

Part Three

An Emerging Paradigm

7

Mindful Leadership

*No complex system can succeed without
an effective executive mechanism.*

—Elkhonon Goldberg (2001, p. 230)

Chapter Orientation

The Wonder of You

Chapter 1 of this book led off with a description of the human disposition and capacity for completing the puzzle, finding the answer, solving the mystery, improving products and processes—*to figure it out*. This chapter brings the exercise of these natural traits back home to you because, in the final analysis, it is your exercise of such disposition and capacity that will determine whether you are indeed mindful of the intelligence compatibility of your leadership behavior. This is an important point, because it speaks to a common trap that human brains are sometimes lured into when investigating new concepts and processes. It is the trap of accepting a model, list, or other prescriptive structure as the answer that merely has to be acted on—rather than thought about. Accordingly, *the wonder of you* is the key to the *mindful you*. Mindful leadership is not the product of a recipe; rather it is a phenomenon that unfolds within the intrigue and questioning of an individual brain. The framework presented in Chapter 6 is a useful tool for such reflection. Ultimately, however, *you* have to figure out the implications of breakthrough information about the nature of intelligence for the conduct of effective leadership behavior.

A Time to Wonder and Ponder

The content of prior chapters collectively describes a unique convergence of events that mandate reflection about effective leadership behavior:

1. Unparalleled growth of new knowledge, rapid change, and complex systems

2. Unprecedented opportunity to understand and engage the human capacity for extraordinary intelligence—within individuals and organizations

This convergence of circumstances creates a compelling case for the consideration of a new mental model of leadership, one that is mindful (i.e., attentive) rather than mindless (i.e., heedless) of the nature and nurture of intelligence.

What, then, must a leader aspire to do during a time that both requires and accommodates more effective exercise of human intelligence? The everyday challenges confronting commerce, medicine, education, government, and other institutions are increasingly complex. Beyond that, the challenges of the 21st century—issues of war, terrorism, the environment, human rights, genetic engineering, and the equitable distribution of resources are a few that come to mind—are of a magnitude and complexity that threaten not only the quality of existence but also the very survival of humankind. Furthermore, the more complex the nature of such problems, the more necessary and beneficial is a collective effort in their resolution. Accordingly, leadership in this new millennium, more so than at any time in the past, requires leaders who understand and effectively apply their own intelligence. This quality of personal intellectual effectiveness is, indeed, a prerequisite of effective leadership, yet is not sufficient in itself. The intellectually aware and adept leader must also engage and nurture the collective intellectual capacity of the affected group. That is, an organization will succeed in achieving important purpose to the degree that the entire membership is also aware of and adept in the exercise of intellectual capacity, both as individuals and as a collaborative group. Contemporary breakthroughs in information about how humans acquire and use knowledge are most timely, therefore, in accommodating a pressing need to more mindfully align leadership to the brain. Indeed, it is an auspicious time to contemplate the *principles, practices, and purpose* of mindful leadership. To that end, this chapter will provide an opportunity for synthesis and reflection about

- Antecedents of mindful leadership
- Four principles of mindful leadership
- Six practices for the engagement of mindful leadership
- Case study analysis of the principles and practices of mindful leadership
- The purposes of mindful leadership
- Attributes of mindful leaders

Antecedents of Mindful Leadership

The organizations that will truly excel in the future will be the organizations that discover how to tap people's commitment and capacity to learn at all levels in an organization.

—(Senge et al., 1994, p. 4)

You have several advantages to draw on in constructing personal perceptions about mindful leadership. First of all, of course, you have the prodigious and multidimensional resources of human intelligence at your command. You also have the advantage of your personal leadership experience—experience that includes people who have influenced your mindful leadership perceptions on a subconscious, if not conscious, level. The following exercise illustrates this point.

Leadership Legacy Exercise:
The Inheritance

1. Reflect for a moment about individuals whom you respect as exemplars of leadership. They might be contemporary or historical figures, members of your family, other people you have had a personal relationship with, or individuals you know from more distant experience. In any case, they should be people whom you judge to be effective leaders—whether in positions affecting family, religious, health, governmental, commercial, educational, or other organizations.

> Reflection Time

2. Select four individuals from the leaders you admire to join you at a council table (see Figure 7.1). Identify each of the invited leaders by name at chairs one to four.

3. Sit yourself at the head of the table in the chair marked "heir to the legacy."

4. Moving from chair to chair, write down one or two distinguishing attributes of the character or behavior of each of the four leaders seated at the table.

> Reflection Time

5. Moving around the table once more, ask each of your distinguished guests to share her or his best advice about leadership. Again, in the space provided, jot down what you think your guests' counsel would be.

> Reflection Time

6. Finally, in the space provided in the middle of the table, record what you have learned about leadership from these leaders—from both their example and their advice. That is, what is your inheritance? What leadership legacy has been passed on to you? How have your perceptions of leadership been influenced by important people in your life experience?

> Reflection Time

Figure 7.1. Leadership Legacy Exercise: The Inheritance

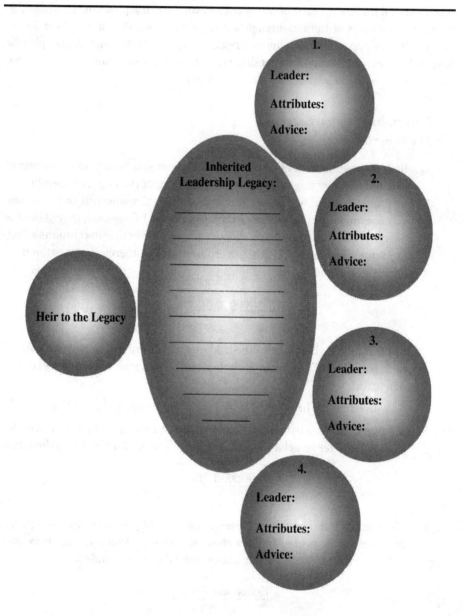

Regardless of the mix of people sitting at your table in the above exercise—your mother, a third-grade teacher, a high school coach, Joan of Arc, Gandhi, whoever—your perceptions of effective leadership can be traced to the influence of core values and behaviors of people you know or know of. Similarly, you have also likely been influenced to some degree by encounters with the general literature about leadership, literature that espouses leadership tenets such as common vision, empowerment, collaborative culture, capacity building, team learning, total quality, and win-win. Indeed, it is somewhat predictable that these leadership themes are not unlike the advice that came forth from those huddled around your council table. For example, were you advised about the importance of clear goals? Did your leadership mentors exhibit value for common vision, empowerment of others, collaboration, commitment to quality, and team learning in their facilitation of group achievements?

In this manner, then, the antecedents of your development as a mindful leader (and indeed as a mindful person) have been established. Your consideration of the merits and means of mindful leadership does not occur in a vacuum. You come prepared for such contemplation by virtue of the accumulated and intuitive experience of self and others. Indeed, the legacy that you described on the council table above most likely describes leadership qualities and behaviors that are compatible with the nature and nurture of human intelligence—qualities and behaviors that favorably influence the physiological, social, emotional, constructive, reflective, and dispositional dimensions of the human capacity to learn, evolve, and achieve. A leadership instinct for connecting to the multidimensional nature of intelligence, therefore, is not new. The opportunity to be consciously informed and mindfully attuned to such connections, however, is.

Principles of Mindful Leadership

Principle: *A basic truth, law or assumption; a rule or standard, especially of good behavior*
—*(American Heritage Dictionary,* 2000, p. 1395)

Chapter 6 introduced a framework that provides structure and support for the alignment of leadership behavior to the nature of the human capacity to achieve. By design, the framework embraces the natural and powerful operations of the human brain as represented in the four components of arousal of attention to knowledge, acquisition of knowledge, application of knowledge, and adjustment of knowledge. These components, in turn, can be incorporated into serviceable principles (i.e., standards of behavior) by which mindful leaders might focus their thinking and growth.

Principle One: *Mindful leaders attend to the potential of mindful leadership practice.*

Argyris (1990) reminds us that it is the job of leaders to surface the power inherent in the human resource of the organization. This advice is all the more important, given the emergent status of breakthrough information about the nature of the human capacity to acquire and apply knowledge. Thus contemporary leaders have both an exceptional opportunity and a responsibility to tap the power inherent in themselves and others to the end of achieving significant purpose. If this is to happen, however, leaders must be mindful of emerging information about the brain in order to progressively construct knowledge, challenge belief structures, and cultivate a repertoire of leadership practices that effectively advances the intellectual capital of their organization.

Principle Two: **Mindful leaders acquire knowledge about the nature and nurture of intelligence.**

A leader who appreciates the need to attend to the potential of mindful leadership will act to construct a personal knowledge base about the nature of intelligence and the implications thereof for leadership practice. A practical approach for acquiring such knowledge is to engage credible knowledge sources to distill essential understandings and, thereby, facilitate the construction of perceptions about compatible leadership behavior. This is a critical aspect of mindful leadership in that a leader must construct a personal perception of the nature of human intelligence if he or she is to effectively discern appropriate bridges to leadership behavior.

Principle Three: **Mindful leaders apply knowledge about intelligence to self, systems, and situations.**

Influencing others to achieve goals requires action. Accordingly, the development of a knowledge base about the nature of intelligence is of little promise if not applied in a manner that creates capacity within an organization. To that end, leaders will be mindful of opportunities to nurture intelligence within self, systems, and situations, thereby progressively enhancing the achievement capacities of individuals and the organization as a whole.

Principle Four: **Mindful leaders adjust their leadership knowledge in response to experience.**

The process of reflection involves the reconstruction, analysis, and synthesis of information. A mindful leader will proactively engage in such reflection to capitalize on the experience of nurturing the nature of the human capacity to achieve needs. In this manner, leaders continuously inform and reform their knowledge base, provoke perceptual shifts about leadership purpose and practice, and add to their repertoire of effective leadership behaviors.

From Principle to Practice: Stages of Competence

While principles act as guideposts for the exercise and development of mindful leadership, it is practical experience that ultimately fulfills the promise of the mindful leader. Practice doesn't always make perfect, but it does, over time, establish the habits—

dispositions if you will—that guide your behavior. Thus in learning any new or modified behaviors, we experience progressive stages of expertise as our knowledge and comfort levels grow with increased thought and application.

Whether riding a bike, conducting brain surgery, or preparing a gourmet meal, various stages of competence are experienced as knowledge and skill evolves from a novice stage to that of expert. Hunter (1982) refers to such stages as ways of knowing. Accordingly, the experience of progressive stages of competency is a most likely scenario for the development of mindful leadership practice. With this orientation, you are invited to consider the following competency stages and to reflect on your competency status as a mindful leader:

- **Unconscious Incompetence.** At this stage, one would be very unaware of emerging knowledge about the human brain and few, if any, leadership decisions would be based on knowledge of individual and organizational intelligence. This is the blissful state of not knowing what you don't know. (You might have been at this stage before reading this book, but you are not there anymore!)
- **Conscious Incompetence.** On becoming aware of information about the human brain and the intelligence it enables, one begins to see implications for behavior. At this stage, leaders might become painfully aware of what they should be doing but, perhaps, feel unprepared to do. This is a distressing stage because you see the discrepancy between where you are and where you want to be. Some call it controlled floundering, others disequilibrium. It is a necessary route brains must take to begin to reorder neural networks into new understandings and practices. (You may be here!)
- **Unconscious Competence.** This is the stage of intuitive knowledge developed through trial and error. This level of expertise is difficult to pass on to others because actions have often become automatic and internalized and one may not be able to articulate the thought processes engaged in creating a result. Furthermore, when behavior is organized and exercised at an intuitive level, replication is not guaranteed. (Your leadership instincts may often serve you well, but instinct likely comes up short when there is a need for consistency and sustained execution of effective practice.)
- **Conscious Competence.** Informed by personal knowledge, one is able to reflect on experience and modify behavior based on results. This is a very mindful state where you are conscious of the translation of your knowledge base into practice. This is a stage of awareness that allows you to consciously replicate and adjust behavior to influence a desired outcome. (This is where you want to be!)

Mindful Leadership Practice

Practice: *A habitual or customary action or way of doing something*
                    —*(American Heritage Dictionary,* 2000, p. 1378)

To assist your journey toward conscious competence as a mindful leader, six mindful leadership practices are presented for your consideration in this section. The caveat is that these practices represent the authors' interpretations of intelligence-compatible leadership perception and behavior. Accordingly, you are invited to modify and add to the suggested practices to make your own "sense" of what mindful leaders might do to influence the success of their organizations.

Mindful Practice One: Nurture the Physiological Platform That Enables Intelligence

 Relevant information: *The physiological nature of intelligence*

- The human brain is a three-pound collection of physiological structures that interactively regulate and operate all human behavior.
- Human intelligence is enabled by a brain physiology of incredible complexity, capacity, and environmental responsiveness.
- The physiological architecture of the human brain is the biological platform on which human intelligence performs its extraordinary feats of information processing at cellular and chemical levels.
- Everything that a human brain experiences through its sensory mechanisms affects electrochemical exchanges and modulations within a network of a quadrillion synapses between the axons and dendrites of approximately 100 billion neurons.
- The capacity of the human brain to process information approaches infinity.
- Neural networks in the human brain are modified by experience, and plasticity in learning continues throughout the life span.
- Human intelligence is not fixed but malleable by quality and quantity of environmental experience.
- Nutrition, hydration, movement, rest, oxygenation, natural light, and stress are influences on brain chemistry and, thereby, the optimal exercise of intelligence.

 Guiding perception: *Human intelligence operates on a biological platform of cells, circuits, and chemicals.*

 Compatible behavior:

Attend to Physiological Needs

An environment that demonstrates care and attention to physiological needs helps people to function more effectively. Balancing work with rest, healthy diet, and complementary exercise reaps payoffs in brain productivity. Accordingly, a mindful leader might contemplate ways to facilitate the following;

√ Access to drinking water, healthy food, fresh air, and natural light

√ Opportunities for physical movement and change of body posture

√ Flexible scheduling of work, recreation, and rest time

√ Humor, joy, and other pleasure-related experiences that induce oxygen rushes and other beneficial chemical alterations in the brain

√ Participation in fitness and wellness programs

√ _____

Stimulate Neural Development

The capacity of an organization to achieve rests on the incredible information-processing capacity of the brain. A leader is well-advised, therefore, to appreciate and capitalize on the unlimited capacity that lies within an organization. It is particularly important for a leader to appreciate how the quality and quantity of environmental experience throughout the life span modify brain capacity. Routine and repetitious tasks performed in a consistent environment are not stimulating to neural development. An environment that is rich in novelty and range of sensory stimulation, on the other hand, encourages neural development—the cultivation of bushy dendrites. Such development is enhanced, both within individuals and the collective neural capacity of an organization, when opportunity to learn and grow becomes a seamless ingredient of organizational life. Accordingly, a mindful leader might contemplate ways to facilitate

√ Meaningful and challenging work

√ All manner of social interaction in the processes of planning, performing, evaluating, and resolving

√ Diversity of experience and character in the composition of work teams

√ Cross-department task groups

√ Access to multimedia information

√ Flow of information and ideas laterally and vertically throughout the organization

√ Variety of roles and responsibilities imbedded within job descriptions

√ Range of responsibilities within job categories

√ Professional-growth opportunities for individuals and groups through on-site workshops, seminars, and study groups and off-site conferences, retreats, and sabbaticals

√ Opportunities to learn outside individual or organizational expertise

√ Opportunities to read books about the nature and nurture of intelligence

√ Individual and group goal setting and self-assessment of progress

√ Sensory enrichment within the design and appointment of the physical environment (e.g., varied color, music, artwork, furnishings, space arrangements)

√ _____

Protect Against Stress

Environmental experience either stimulates or diminishes neural development by virtue of biochemical effects on the brain. Sensory stimulation by novelty and other rich experience arouses and motivates neural development. Excessive and prolonged emotional response to stressful stimuli (e.g., physical or psychological harassment, overwhelming workloads, pressure for change, confusing directives), however, generates negative effects on neural health and efficiency of operation. It is important, therefore, for leaders to nurture environments that are psychologically and physiologically supportive of the members of an organization. Accordingly, a mindful leader might contemplate ways to facilitate

√ Physically safe facilities and surroundings

√ Open, honest, and frequent communication

√ Zero tolerance for harassment

√ Value for positive and proactive disposition

√ Work that is meaningful and challenging but not overly stressful

√ Collaborative team structures

√ Celebration of individual and group achievements

√ Fun

√ _____

Mindful Practice Two:
Promote Social Relationships

 Relevant information: *The social nature of intelligence*

- A human organism is composed and maintained as a system of interactive molecular and cellular relationships.
- The human brain is disposed by nature to replicate the pattern of its own interactive molecular and cellular organization by establishing interactive relationships with other brains, thus forming social systems.
- Social existence is a survival strategy that is common to all animals, and it is a strong environmental influence on the evolution of intelligence.
- Human intelligence is endowed by eons of social evolution with unparalleled neural capacity for constructing and storing patterns of information, awareness of the emotional states of self and others, language, and reflective reasoning.
- Human consciousness and moral perspective of what is good and bad is born of the evolution of social awareness of emotional states in self and others.
- The unfolding of human intelligence is expectant of and dependent on the same social experience that constructed it—the critical attribute of environmental experience by which neural circuitry is activated, reinforced, and refined.

- Social interaction provokes the cognitive dissonance essential to emotional arousal, knowledge construction, reflective reasoning, mindful disposition, and, thereby, physiological plasticity of neural networking.
- The overarching human need and disposition to connect and interact in a society of mind is extended beyond face-to-face encounters by technological mediums such as print, radio, television, and computer networks.
- Whether direct or indirect, social interaction engages a flow of energy and information through a collective intelligence that maximizes the human potential to think, learn, and create.
- Communities of mind emerge from social networking to solve difficult problems, create better systems, and invent new technologies.
- Social interaction remains a force in the advancement of intelligence capacity during the present age of human evolution and activity.

 Guiding perception: ***Social experience is the great provocateur of thinking and learning.***

 Compatible behavior:

Create Opportunities for the Meeting of Minds

Human intelligence expects and depends on social experience as a primary means for the unfolding of its potential. Simply put, when one brain meets another brain, the exercise of intelligence—in its multiple dimensions—inevitably follows. Accordingly, a mindful leader might contemplate ways to facilitate

- √ The organization of teams, cohorts, and other groups as appropriate to general responsibilities and specific tasks and interests
- √ Periodic or incidental alteration of group compositions to change the dynamics of experience and perception
- √ Training in group processes and interactive meeting structures that access and involve all the brains in the group (e.g., processes and structures that facilitate the ordered processing of divergent ideas to convergent perceptions)
- √ Interaction between departments
- √ Time and format structures that support dialogue
- √ Free flow of information throughout the organization
- √ Access to distant brains (e.g., news media, books, the Internet)
- √ Access to on-site and off-site professional growth experiences in the company of colleagues
- √ Collaboration in the resolution of problems, decisions, or other challenging tasks
- √ Mentoring of members new to the organization
- √ Peer coaching of performance goals and assessments
- √ _____

Cultivate Shared Vision

Social interactions between brains most effectively expand organizational capacity if focused by a shared vision of meaningful purpose. Such vision strengthens a culture of collaboration in which common purpose transcends individual ambition. Making a contribution to the common good, therefore, is what counts. Thus the collective capacity of human intelligence is tapped when the brains within the organization are enticed into collaborative relationships by clear, compelling, and mutually held goals. Accordingly, a mindful leader might contemplate ways to facilitate

√ Formal and informal conversations about purpose and progress
√ Organizational visioning
√ Strategic planning
√ Quality circles
√ Action research and planning
√ _____

Invite Diversity to the Table

The strongest ropes are woven from a diverse blend of fibers. Similarly, the greater the diversity of experience and perspective represented in social interactions between brains, the greater the prospects of strong and productive thinking—particularly in instances of the most challenging problems and tasks. Two or more heads are literally better than one when operating in socially adept collaborative groups. Such benefit to an organization, however, will not be realized unless every brain feels comfortable and valued in its contributions of information and ideas. Accordingly, a mindful leader might contemplate ways to facilitate

√ Zero tolerance of divisive comments or actions
√ Active pursuit of different viewpoints
√ Diversity of backgrounds and perspectives in task groups
√ Diversity training
√ Training in group skills
√ _____

Mindful Practice Three:
Harness the Power of Emotion

 Relevant information: *The emotional nature of intelligence*

- Emotion is a survival mechanism that evolved in life forms that move and have need to quickly screen, judge, and react to an array of environmental information.

- The purpose of emotion is to ensure the survival advantage of reflexive action prior to reflection—to act first, think later.
- Emotion has been highly refined in humans by the influence of a rich environmental experience born of social existence and high mobility over a long evolutionary period.
- Emotion involves the processing of sensory information through neural and glandular systems that alter mind and body states while arousing the prefrontal cortex to what is worth thinking about.
- Emotion is designed for limited engagement and can become unhealthy if sustained over time, due to the adverse effect of associated chemical releases.
- The intelligence capacity of the human brain is challenge motivated and threat inhibited.
- Humans are aware of and able to mediate emotional responses, a capacity referred to as emotional intelligence.
- Emotion is intimately involved with the arousal and operation of the physiological, social, constructive, reflective, and dispositional dimensions of the nature of human intelligence.
- Emotion is a means for initiating attention and focusing capacity for constructing understanding and resolving problems.
- As an old and proven survival system by which humans attend, make judgments, and are motivated—emotion is still very much in charge of human behavior.

 Guiding perception: *Emotion is the means by which the brain attends, makes judgments, and is motivated.*

 Compatible behavior:

Cultivate a Climate of Trust and Support

The emotional mechanisms of the brain arouse and focus mind and body states by judgment of survival interests. This arousal and focusing is strongly influenced by social experience. The brain does its best work, therefore, when challenged within safe and supportive social environments. Accordingly, the mindful leader might contemplate ways to facilitate

- √ A spirit of collaboration
- √ Inclusive participation in solution seeking
- √ Camaraderie and collegial relationships through team building, mentoring, interpersonal-skills training, and social rituals and events
- √ Zero tolerance for harassment, intimidation, or other anti-social behavior
- √ Individual and organizational confidence in the capacity to learn and achieve
- √ Value for diversity in perspective and experience

√ Support and reward for risk taking

√ Value for trial and error

√ A no-blame policy

√ Compassion and caring for individuals or groups within the organization during situations that are particularly challenging and stressful

√ Honoring and celebrating positive events and achievements—both individual and organizational

√ Value for civility and positivism

√ _____

Cultivate a Climate of Challenge and Passion

The brain continually screens sensory information to emotionally determine what is worthy of the attention and commitment of its considerable resources. Simply put, if the brain does not become emotionally excited about something, it is not going to efficiently and effectively engage in social interaction, construction of knowledge, reflective reasoning, or productive thinking dispositions—all of which are stimulating to the physiological growth and refinement of neural networks. The arousal and focusing of the multidimensional capacity of human intelligence, therefore, is responsive to a clear and meaningful sense of purpose. The engagement of intelligence is also emotionally motivated and maintained by novel and challenging tasks that are related to significant purpose. Again, there is a strong tie between emotion and social experience here, in that clarity of shared purpose becomes an emotional rallying point for collaborative endeavors, and collaboration sparks a contagious exercise of intelligence. Accordingly, a mindful leader might contemplate ways to facilitate

√ Dialogue about beliefs and values related to personal and organizational purpose

√ Inclusive organizational visioning and planning

√ Frequent and direct communication about individual and organizational purpose

√ Formal and informal conversations about progress toward the achievement of purpose

√ Referencing of organizational purpose in the process of decision making and problem solving

√ Modeling of passion for personal and organizational purpose

√ Involvement in the construction of new knowledge relevant to the achievement of purpose

√ Involvement in creative and analytic reflection about the challenges and means to achieving purpose

√ Involvement in the planning, implementation, and assessment of specific actions designed to serve the achievement of purpose

√ _____

Cultivate a Culture of Emotional Intelligence

Emotional intelligence is represented in the capacity to be aware of one's emotional state and to apply that knowledge in a manner that contributes to the welfare of self and others. Accordingly, a mindful leader might contemplate ways to facilitate

√ Awareness of the motivating role of emotion in arousal and commitment to the achievement of purpose

√ Reflection about the emotional state and response of self in relation to issues and events

√ Awareness of the emotional state and response of others in relation to issues and events

√ Structures and strategies for the processing of emotional states and responses

√ Skill in conflict resolution

√ _____

Mindful Practice Four:
Facilitate the Construction of Meaning

 Relevant information: *The constructive nature of intelligence*

- To survive, organisms must recognize and remember information patterns, and the more mobile the organism, the higher the premium placed on pattern recognition.
- The human brain is a lean, mean, pattern-making machine in residence within the most mobile organism on earth.
- Human brain capacity for constructing meaning and memory is enabled by the organization of neural network alliances and the dynamic manipulation of information variables that connect new information patterns to established patterns.
- The capacity to detect, organize, and store information patterns is genetically installed in the brain during prenatal development, but the brain is expectant of and dependent on environmental experience to construct meaning and memory of useful informational patterns.
- The richer and more direct the sensory experience, the stronger the construction of meaning and memory.
- Emotion is a critical element of experience enrichment in the construction of meaning and memory.
- Social interaction is a primary means for providing emotional context and other information enrichment in environmental experience.

- The construction of strings of patterns of information into ever more complex relationships is the cognitive process that underlies the most sophisticated work of the human brain.
- The capacity to construct useful mental models presents a double bind when the brain becomes comfortable with familiar patterns and openness to alternative patterns is ignored or resisted.

 Guiding perception: *The human brain is a lean, mean, pattern-making machine—a biological system of extraordinary capacity for perceiving and endlessly constructing useful information patterns.*

 Compatible behavior:

Provide Sites and Structures for the Construction of Knowledge

The brain has a phenomenal capacity for discerning, organizing, storing, and retrieving information patterns. This capacity for organizing a body of information (i.e., knowledge) is, however, expectant of and dependent on a quality of sensory stimulation from environmental experience. The acquisition of knowledge is also a brain-by-brain process of connecting new information to prior knowledge. Information is physically constructed through connections within the neural networks of an individual brain as the result of sensory experience. Providing the time, place, and structure for such construction, therefore, capitalizes on human capacity to organize, challenge, and restructure knowledge of concepts and procedures important to the achievement of purpose. Accordingly, a mindful leader might contemplate ways to facilitate

- √ Access to rich information sources through print, video, news media, the Internet, workshops, seminars, and interactive conferencing
- √ Direct experience with new concepts or procedures
- √ Visualization of concepts and procedures through graphic representation and model construction
- √ Metaphor and analogy
- √ Study teams
- √ Quality circles
- √ Reciprocal teaching, peer coaching, and mentoring of new concepts and procedures in pairs and small groups
- √ Open dialogue and feedback sessions
- √ Conference rooms, commons areas, workrooms, gardens, nature trails, and other environments that support dialogue
- √ _____

Construct Knowledge That Matters

The brain is emotionally motivated to construct meaning and memory by its judgment of the value of specific information. Providing access to information throughout the organization and encouraging dialogue about the meaning of such information promote the construction of understanding. It is also important to discern what information is pertinent or irrelevant to organizational purpose and, thereby, worthy of the brain's knowledge construction efforts. Accordingly, a mindful leader might contemplate ways to facilitate

√ Alignment of knowledge acquisition to a shared vision of organizational purpose and goals

√ Decentralized decision making to promote personal judgments about what is worth knowing

√ _____

Challenge Knowledge Constructions

The brain's survival business is predicated on the discernment of valuable information patterns. The double bind within the extraordinary human capacity to perform this task is the danger of reliance on information patterns that have proved to be reliable in the past. Thus seduced, the brain may resist exploring new information—to its ultimate disadvantage. It is important, therefore, to challenge conventional knowledge and to entertain the construction of new and refined perceptions. Accordingly, a mindful leader might contemplate ways to facilitate

√ Novelty of experience

√ Creative thinking

√ Debate

√ Devil's advocates

√ Design teams

√ _____

Mindful Practice Five:
Build a Culture of Reflection

 Relevant information: *The reflective nature of intelligence*

- Human capacity to reflectively review and endlessly reconfigure relationships within and between established patterns of information represents the essence of human intelligence—the defining quality of being able to engage in neural dialogue to decide, resolve, create, plan, analyze, hypothesize, deduce, and invent.

- The reflective nature of human intelligence arises from the social evolution of brain capacity for information patterning, emotional awareness, and language.
- The effective exercise of the reflective nature of human intelligence is both dependent on and demanding of physiological health, social interaction, emotional tension, knowledge construction, and mindful disposition.
- The exercise of analysis, imagination, improvisation, and foresight in thought and action is the key to human versatility and, thereby, survival success.

 Guiding perception: *Reflection is the capacity to consciously manipulate information and rehearse options prior to action—a distinct survival advantage when guessing well is the game, and pressure is on the brain.*

 Compatible behavior:

Supply Time, Space, and Structure for Thinking

The human brain spontaneously responds to problems and opportunities by retrieving and contemplating information relevant to action options. It does its best reflective work, however, when provided with the time, place, and tools for the deliberate exercise of reasoning skills. Such calculated information processing is essential for complex learning, problem solving, and creativity. Accordingly, a mindful leader might contemplate ways to facilitate

√ Regularly scheduled time for reflection about problems and issues relevant to purpose

√ Journal writing

√ Dialogue

√ Case study analysis

√ Quality circles

√ Structured information sharing and processing (e.g., ordered processing, normative processing)

√ Metaphor and analogy

√ Formal thinking structures and processes (e.g., articulated steps for problem solving, decision making, conflict resolution, systems analysis, investigation, analysis of perspective, debate, comparison, inductive or deductive reasoning, experimental inquiry, etc.)

√ Environments that are conducive to reflection (e.g., natural light, fresh air, comfortable and utilitarian furniture, access to information resources, opportunity for movement, freedom from distractions, etc.)

√ _____

Provoke Thinking Otherwise

Supplying time, space, and structure for thinking demonstrates value for human capacity to understand, resolve, and create. It also communicates the message that reflective capacity is distributed throughout the brains of all of the members of an organization. Such capacity is further maximized by the deliberated provocation of critical and creative thinking. Provoking analysis and creativity engages natural ability to detect causal relationships, link seemingly unrelated information, generate alternative views, and construct new understanding and original products. Accordingly, a mindful leader might contemplate ways to facilitate

√ Social interaction over controversial and challenging issues and problems

√ Systems thinking

√ Analysis of errors in positions and ideas

√ Construction of support for positions and ideas

√ Value for innovation

√ Divergent and lateral thinking

√ Improvisation

√ Invention

√ Play

√ _____

Mindful Practice Six:
Cultivate Mindful Dispositions

 Relevant information: *The dispositional nature of intelligence*

- The human brain interprets and organizes useful information patterns on all levels of scale, and thinking dispositions are representative of such pattern organization at a macro level.
- The human brain strives to organize and exercise intelligence in a habitual manner that corresponds to valued patterns of internal and external information.
- The value of human dispositional intelligence rests on its contribution to survival (e.g., disposition to be persistent, creative, open-minded, organized, or analytical) Accordingly, a useful disposition is an alternative to having to constantly make moment-to-moment decisions about how to respond to the environment.
- Human disposition in the exercise of intelligence is both genetically and environmentally influenced (i.e., the product of nature and nurture).
- Every healthy human brain is genetically disposed to the broad physiological, social, emotional, constructive, and reflective exercise of intelligence—as well as the exercise of specific thinking behaviors.

- Every human brain is experientially unique and malleable in its disposition to exercise intelligence throughout the life span.
- Sustained states of dispositional intelligence define human capacity to think, learn, and achieve by influencing the exercise and development of other dimensions of intelligence (e.g., physiological, social, emotional, constructive and reflective).

 Guiding perception: **The cultivation and exercise of thinking dispositions are the keys to maximizing intelligence.**

 Compatible behavior:

Proactively Exercise the Multiple Dimensions of Intelligence

A capacity for intelligence does not automatically translate into intelligent behavior. Humans are genetically programmed to exercise physiological, social, emotional, constructive, and reflective dimensions of intelligence. The multifaceted nature of intelligence must be consciously and regularly engaged, however, if its potential is to be realized. One might say that intelligence is developed and refined to the degree that there is a disposition to use it. Accordingly, a mindful leader might contemplate ways to facilitate the following:

√ Propensity for exercise, healthy diet, novel environmental experience, and other means to optimize the physiological base on which intelligence operates

√ Propensity for seeking and structuring social opportunities for collaboration and the sharing and challenging of ideas

√ Propensity for the analysis and management of emotional states and the motivational value of meaningful purpose

√ Propensity for direct and rich information experience as the means for constructing personal understanding

√ Propensity for the reflective engagement of specific thinking strategies

√ Propensity for metacognition

√ _____

Target Productive Thinking Dispositions

Beyond broad dispositions to engage and cultivate the multiple dimensions of intelligence are the more specific qualities and behaviors of effective thinkers. Such thinkers are disposed to tendencies in their thinking that are particularly productive. Accordingly, a mindful leader might contemplate ways to facilitate the following:

√ The use of data and research

√ Seeking and using diverse viewpoints

√ Creativity

√ Open-mindedness

√ Persistence

√ Analysis

√ Accuracy and precision

√ Clarity and coherence

√ Empathy

√ Curiosity and questioning

√ Speculation and hypothesis

√ Inductive and deductive reasoning

√ Advocacy

√ Listening

√ Risk taking

√ Metacognition

√ Collaborative inquiry

√ Humor

√ _____

Strategic Practices

Divide and Conquer, but . . .

As stated repeatedly in this text, you will find it useful to employ a multidimensional approach to understanding and engaging the complex nature of intelligence. To that end, the previous chapter section describes mindful leadership practices that might emerge from mindful leadership principles to be compatible with six dimensions of intelligence (see summary presented in Figure 7.2). Such alignment of leadership behavior to the nature of intelligence seeks the advantage of focusing on specific and important qualities of intelligence—qualities that might escape understanding and attention if not thus proactively profiled. The dimensions of human intelligence, however, work in concert to acquire and apply knowledge to survival advantage. Accordingly, while it is productive to reflect on the nature and nurture of a specific dimension of intelligence when reviewing and planning leadership behavior, it is also important to maintain the perspective of the integrated nature of intelligence.

Figure 7.2. Example: Organization of Mindful Leadership Principles and Practices

Mindful Leadership Principles
- Attend to the potential of mindful leadership practice.
- Acquire knowledge about the nature and nurture of intelligence.
- Apply knowledge about intelligence to self, systems, and situations.
- Adjust leadership knowledge in response to experience.

Mindful Leadership Practices
1. Nurture the physiological platform that enables intelligence:
   a. Attend to physiological needs.
   b. Stimulate neural development.
   c. Protect against stress.
2. Promote social relationships:
   a. Create opportunities for the meeting of minds.
   b. Cultivate shared vision.
   c. Invite diversity to the table.
3. Harness the power of emotion:
   a. Cultivate a climate of trust and support.
   b. Cultivate a climate of challenge and passion.
   c. Cultivate a culture of emotional intelligence.
4. Facilitate the construction of meaning:
   a. Provide sites and structures for the construction of knowledge.
   b. Construct knowledge that matters.
   c. Challenge knowledge constructions.
5. Build a culture of reflection:
   a. Supply time, space, and structure for reflection.
   b. Provoke thinking otherwise.
6. Cultivate mindful dispositions:
   a. Proactively exercise the multiple dimensions of intelligence.
   b. Target productive thinking dispositions.

. . . Seek Actions That Matter

In reviewing specific leadership actions as described under suggested practices of mindful leadership, patterns inevitably emerge across the dimensions of intelligence, patterns that suggest strategic practices that favorably influence the integrated nature of intelligence. Examples of leadership interventions that comprehensively stimulate the multiple dimensions of intelligence include actions that facilitate social interaction, cooperation, common vision, inclusive planning, direct and enriched information experience, novelty and challenge, and metacognition. The significance of these strategies lies in the span of intelligence they engage. For example, leadership actions that facilitate social interaction or novelty and challenge will comprehensively engage physiological, social, emotional, constructive, reflective, and dispositional dimensions of intelligence. In this fashion, a full complement of human intelligence qualities is brought to bear on goal achievement in a natural, integrated manner.

When in Doubt, Reverse Perspective

A story: Early in the process of writing this book, the authors were at a hotel conference center presenting to a group of leaders a session entitled "The Mindful Leader: An Alternative to Brainless Leadership." Prior to the session, two hotel cleaning-staff members were heard laughing at the title. When asked what they found funny, the elder of the two, a gentleman somewhat advanced in years, gave a weary smirk and replied, "Brainless leadership, there's just so much of it!"

To more fully appreciate the value of mindful leadership practices, particularly that of strategic actions that broadly influence the multidimensional nature of intelligence, you will find it useful to contemplate the alternative to proactive alignment of behavior to informed perception. As suggested by the gentleman quoted in the story above, might ignorance be less blissful than commonly credited? What is the cost to the achievement of organizational purpose—not to mention the frustrations for all the individuals involved—when leadership is mindless of the nature and nurture of human capacity? Consider the qualities and effects of leadership that, either out of ignorance or ill-informed perception, engages in practices that facilitate isolation, lack of collaboration, conflicting and confusing perceptions of purpose, top-down planning that denies the participation of affected parties, limited and passive opportunities to access information, absence of novelty and challenge, and discouragement of reflection.

A reflection exercise will facilitate your assessment of leadership behavior that is either mindful or mindless of strategies that comprehensively influence the multidimensional nature of human intelligence. With reference to Figure 7.3, reflect for a moment about how you would personally respond to the following:

A. An organization in which leaders are mindful of strategic practices that comprehensively engage the multidimensional qualities of intelligence

B. An organization in which leaders are mindless about strategic practices that comprehensively engage the multidimensional qualities of intelligence

Figure 7.3. Reflection Exercise: Assessment of Strategic Practices That Comprehensively Influence the Multidimensional Nature of Human Intelligence

A. Mindful leadership promotes	B. Mindless leadership promotes
1. Physical and Mental Health and wellness	1. Physical and mental stress and decline
2. Social interaction	2. Isolation
3. Cooperation	3. Lack of collaboration
4. Common vision	4. Confusion about purpose
5. Inclusive planning	5. Top-down planning
6. Direct and rich access to information	6. Limited and passive access to information
7. Novelty and challenge	7. Redundancy and complacency
8. Metacognition	8. Discouragement of reflection

Case Studies:
The Rubber Meets the Road

Reality is the ultimate test of theory. To further your perception of mindful leadership, then, you are invited to consider the relevance of mindful practices associated with the concept within reality contexts of leadership influence on the achievement of organizational goals—including a leadership context of personal interest.

The cases that follow present three instances in which leaders of various types of organizations have intuitively been mindful (or mindless) of the nature and nurture of human potential within their realm of influence. As you to read the cases, analyze the ways in which leadership behavior either enhanced or inhibited the physiological, social, emotional, constructive, reflective and dispositional nature of human intelligence in organizations. You might also reflect about the overall effect of the leader's behavior on the ultimate accomplishment of organizational purpose.

A Tale of Two Schools

The Case:

Educators dream, it would seem, of opening their own school. The idea of designing a facility, recruiting staff, establishing curriculum, and building a shared vision of student success is enough to make almost any teacher or school administrator salivate. Recently, two principals and their staffs had such an opportunity. One fared well and one poorly. This is their story.

Two years ago, Dave and Carol each received calls from their respective district administrators. "How would you like the job of opening a new elementary school in our district? We are planning a referendum, and if all goes well, a year from now you'll be drawing up the plans."

Carol's reaction was one of disbelief. What an honor to be selected from all the principals in her large, urban school district. In her usual thoughtful style, she asked for more information and time to think before she said yes to the proposal. She wanted to know how much freedom she would be given in recruiting her own staff and in establishing a leadership team of teachers, parents, and students to work with her on the planning. With an awareness of her own strong core values, Carol also wanted to know how much latitude would be given to her in developing a community vision for the new school. She understood how important it would be to build an inclusive culture from many diverse groups and to reassure all involved that they would be listened to and valued in the creation of a new school. She focused her energies on reflection, listening, learning, and proactive planning.

Dave's immediate reaction was to say yes and wonder later if he had made the right decision. His concerns focused on passage of the referendum and selection of an architect. Selected for his quick and decisive management style, he was ready to roll up his sleeves and get down to the business of building a school. He asked for guidance from human resources about staying within the contract in transferring teachers to his school. He met with the business office to draw up a budget for supplies for the school and with the transportation company to discuss boundaries and busing. Dave knew how important it would be to take care of basic needs. His motto was first things first, and that's what he intended to do. Dave focused on action and decision making.

Once Carol received the answers and freedom she sought to lead the new school effort in a manner compatible with her knowledge and beliefs about effective school reform, she proceeded to carefully design a process to build a new system for teaching and learning. She considered the needs of those who would be joining her in the next year of planning, including a new team of teachers, parents, students, and community residents. She knew that there would be a need for a sense of belonging to a newly developed team and that there would be emotional uncertainties about the venture. She also wanted to capitalize on incorporating diverse strengths and insights into a new school vision. Her first order of business was to carefully interview interested people who wanted to join the adventure. She looked for people who were committed to similar core values. She also sought individuals who were energized by the new initiative, creative in their approach to challenges. and willing to take risks. Once the team was formed, she spent time building relationships with and within the leadership team. As part of the planning process, the team was facilitated in developing consensus around their core beliefs related to teaching and learning. From that focus on what really mattered, the team proceeded to create the beginnings of the new school's vision. One dramatic outgrowth of the process was the extension of the school from a K-5 to a K-8 grade configuration. This stemmed from a common belief that cross-generation learning held benefits for all students and that a home-school community could be established better with relationships built over a longer period of time.

Dave spent the year in advance of the opening of the new school drawing up plans with the architect and ensuring a strong budget base for supplies and capital outlay. He also focused on decisions about bus routes, teacher transfers, school policies and procedures, wiring for technology, and the drafting of new parent-teacher organization (PTO) officers. Almost as an afterthought, Dave scheduled a half-day, team-building workshop for the teachers the day before school started.

One year after the opening of her new school, Carol was holding her third all-faculty retreat to discuss and celebrate the alignment of school initiatives with the core values created by everyone before school started. Her staff was feeling upbeat about multiple successes and their strength as a faculty that shared problems, expertise, and achievements. They were working to refine their discipline procedures to ensure student responsibility for the school values. Plans were under way to include more parents in the next phase of mission development and shared vision for the school. The atmosphere was one of high energy, trust, and collegiality. Staff members were accepting ownership for new initiatives and spent time reflecting on areas in need of improvement. Consensus on school goals for the second year of operation was easily reached, and everyone on staff volunteered for an action team.

One year after the opening of his new school, Dave was in trouble. Lack of trust, low morale, and an attitude of demoralization characterized his school. During an end-of-year faculty meeting designed to set goals for the following year, staff members complained about lack of ownership, poor schoolwide discipline, no appreciation of their efforts, a sense of blame when things went wrong, and multiple hidden agendas. The staff wanted the principal to protect them from demanding parents and to assume control of unruly students. Dave was bewildered at the vociferous response and felt he had done everything he could to ensure that the school would run smoothly the first year. He had formed an advisory team, dubbed the A-team by the rest of faculty, to give input about problems and decisions beforehand if time allowed. Due to time pressures, however, he felt he most often had to make decisions without consultation. He had also tried to intervene in parent complaints rather than take up teacher time with such matters. Dave felt as demoralized as his staff and requested help to facilitate a conflict resolution session with his faculty.

Your Analysis of the Case:

With reference to previously suggested principles, practices, and strategies of mindful leadership (e.g., Figures 7.2 and 7.3), use the lined space below to analyze how Dave and Carol were either mindful (i.e., attentive) or mindless (i.e., heedless) of personal and organizational capacity relevant to the opening of a new school. Specifically, in what manner did they attend to the following:

1. The nature and nurture of the physiological platform that enables intelligence?
2. The nature and nurture of social relationships?
3. The nature and nurture of the power of emotion?
4. The nature and nurture of the construction of meaning?
5. The nature and nurture of a culture of reflection?
6. The nature and nurture of mindful dispositions?

Evidence of mindful practice?

_____
_____
_____
_____
_____

Evidence of mindless practice?

_____
_____
_____
_____
_____

Servants of the People

The Case:

National health issues are alternately treated as political footballs, matters of utmost concern, or mysteries yet to be solved. National volunteer agencies have been formed to address such issues; and governmental agencies are charged with related research, regulation, and safety. In recent years, both types of agencies have attempted to become more proactive in the sponsorship of activities that are more preventive than reactive in nature. The following case contrasts the leadership of a national volunteer agency with that of a federal government agency when given the opportunity to plan such activities.

Proposals were presented to two agencies, one private and one governmental, to sponsor a national leadership-training opportunity that would prepare staff members in local school districts with the skills and knowledge to be advocates for coordinated school health programming. The proposals emanated from the state level but were designed to cast a wide net across the nation for proactive, preventive health promotion. The CEO for the governmental agency (hereafter dubbed NDH) was acutely aware of the political ramifications of such a program. Before making a decision, she gathered information about political leanings in the state from which the proposal came, national precedence for such a proposal, and the preferences of her superiors. She wondered about the career consequences of such a high profile, long-term effort that might be controversial at the local school district level, thereby possibly sending ripples of discontent up the political ladder. Ultimately, on discerning that her superiors thought it would be a profitable move to be seen as proactive and cutting-edge in national health promotion, she reluctantly agreed to approve the proposal. She then immediately delegated all responsibility to an agency director with the idea that, if something went wrong later on, she could direct blame away from herself. If, however, things went well and good press resulted, it was still her agency, and she could take the credit and accolades.

The CEO of the national volunteer agency was very curious when he received the proposal. It was unprecedented in the history of his agency. He called together his think tank, a diverse group of directors, assistants, and volunteers whom he often turned to for brainstorming and creative problem solving. The conversation that ensued was high-spirited, with pros and cons debated and creative alternatives proposed—all of which was frequently referenced to the mission of the agency (hereafter referred to as SPA). The discussion was characterized by one participant as sounding a bit like the old Mickey Rooney and Judy Garland "let's put on a show" movie dialogue. Great enthusiasm and energy filled the room. Ultimately, a consensus was reached that this was a great opportunity to have nationwide impact on preventative health education. It was a go!

The head of NDH, having delegated the proposal to an underling, sat back and watched what happened next. Because her agency was run on the dual premises of political connectedness and competition, she watched and waited for the cream to rise to the top—or for the milk to curdle. The director whose lap the project landed in pulled together his assistants for a planning session. The reaction was less than enthusiastic, with much jockeying for how to delegate further into the bowels of the agency where accountability could be traced if things went wrong. Generally, the individuals involved were afraid to take risks in uncharted territory, especially since the CEO had essentially divorced herself from the process. A standard conference-planning committee emerged with little knowledge of the original intent of the proposal, limited resources with which to proceed, and no understanding of the link of their work to the mission of the agency. Two staff members who had originally vied to chair the committee (for career advancement purposes) quickly dropped out when they discovered this project was an orphan and unlikely to succeed.

The head of SPA, on the other hand, was not only enthusiastic about the project but also was beginning to feel like the proud parent of a gifted child of unlimited potential. He left the initial meeting with his think tank and immediately proceeded to carefully design a process to build the necessary support structure for this huge training effort. After careful deliberation, he handpicked the team within his agency that would take leadership over the project. He looked for people who would be committed to the purpose of the project and who were good at networking within and outside the agency. He opted for people who were willing to skate along the cutting edge, knowing they would have his full support for the new venture. Finally, he looked for a team that was predisposed to systems thinking and to look at problems as opportunities, knowing that this would be a project that required comfort with ambiguity and a steep learning curve. Once the team was formed, relationships were quickly built around a common understanding of the mission—which created meaning and positive emotion for all involved.

One year later, SPA was celebrating one of the most successful training events sponsored in the history of the agency. The CEO had personally kicked off the event with an impassioned speech to participants and had modeled risk taking by allowing his speech to be critiqued as a training activity for the conferees. His hands-on approach, positive feeling tone, and obvious commitment made a real difference to the initial climate set at the institute. Due to his fostering a planning process that built ownership and commitment, the team that designed the training felt pride in their accomplishment. Due to his modeling a tone of care and concern for the project, participants felt well treated and respected as professionals. An increased sense of self-efficacy was one of the most often cited elements on the evaluation. The project was planned for a five-year commitment and almost immediately viewed as a huge success.

By contrast, the CEO of NDH was furious when she received the dismal reviews of the initial training efforts. The planning team was plagued with micromanagement and indecisiveness, which resulted in a training design that lacked meaning and connectedness to the participants' job roles. The infighting and vying for position on the part of agency planners created a competitive environment that left everyone feeling ill at ease. Rather than viewing negative comments during the course of the first training institute as information to be used in redesign, fingers were pointed and blame laid with no agreement about what to do to fix it. Bad became worse, and the final reviews caused the CEO to pull the plug on the entire project. As expected, she fired the chairperson of the committee, and the rest of the members of the planning team slunk back into their cubicles, hoping never to be involved in such a venture again. Unfortunately, they felt reaffirmed in their belief that no one was to be trusted and their jobs were on the line at any given time.

Your Analysis of the Case:

With reference to previously suggested principles, practices, and strategies of mindful leadership, use the lined space below to analyze how the CEOs of the two agencies were either mindful (i.e., attentive) or mindless (i.e., heedless) of personal and organizational capacity relevant to the development of a training program. Specifically, in what manner did they attend to:

1. The nature and nurture of the physiological platform that enables intelligence?
2. The nature and nurture of social relationships?
3. The nature and nurture of the power of emotion?
4. The nature and nurture of the construction of meaning?
5. The nature and nurture of a culture of reflection?
6. The nature and nurture of mindful dispositions?

Evidence of mindful practice?   *Evidence of mindless practice?*

_____   _____
_____   _____
_____   _____
_____   _____
_____   _____
_____   _____

Come Fly With Me

The Case:

The nation's airlines have come under close scrutiny in recent years due to horror stories presented in the media about poor service, unwarranted delays, and borderline inhuman treatment of passengers. Such events prompted Congress to address a passengers' bill of rights. The following case tells the story of two airlines that represent a stark contrast in their service to passengers, service that is revealing of the leadership philosophy that permeates the two organizations. One airline is a major player in the industry, referred to here as *Debilitated*. The other airline is a primarily regional, midsize organization that specializes in direct flights, referred to here as *Dairyland Direct*.

Nick was given the opportunity to transform a private airline owned by a manufacturing company into a public carrier in the early 1970s. He was chosen for the task because his leadership of the small private enterprise was credited by company executives for its high quality of performance and service orientation. His personable manner made the phrase "welcome aboard" sound authentic. His high standard for excellence, often complemented by a smile and pat on the back, made him universally admired and liked by employees of the company. When asked to take the airline to the public and expand its service tenfold, he felt humbled by the trust put in him. He also felt assured, however, that the team he had assembled could pull it off. With trust and confidence in his employers and employees, he eagerly said yes.

Conversely, Fred already was the CEO of a large and profitable carrier that had been plagued by strikes. Because he was recognized for efficiency at cost cutting and tough-minded employee relations, Debilitated wooed him away with major stock options to become head of one of the nation's largest and most successful carriers. Debilitated was starting to lose profit margin due to increased competition from some new upstarts, and the board of directors wanted an aggressive leader who was able to make the hard decisions.

Nick's mantra was "service, service, service." He grounded his actions in the belief that people want to be served kindly, respectfully, and efficiently. He also firmly believed that, because most of the weekday market was business oriented, his clients wanted seamless travel that did not add to the hassle of their jobs. Rather, his clients wanted a travel experience that facilitated their work and doing their job well. Early on, Nick instituted a remarkable training program for all Dairyland employees that focused on service to the customer. The program emphasized that every point of contact was to be both pleasant and convenient for the traveling public. Nick looked at all other systems within the airline and had teams design processes and accoutrements that would add to the flight experience. With quick check-in to nonstop flights, wide leather seats, caring attendants, gourmet meals, and free champagne and wine, Dairyland Direct soon began to garner a reputation for establishing a new industry standard of quality. Travelers from both coasts actually started to envy the region for its start-up carrier.

Frank, on the other hand, immediately began to look for ways to cut costs and abbreviate systems. Layoffs and shortcuts became the name of the game. Check-in lines became longer and slower because fewer attendants were available at the counters. Tempers flared, and employees gained a reputation for being impatient with customers. Food on flights deteriorated to a joke in the industry, and delays became the norm. Slowdowns in service began to set in as disgruntled employees rebelled at being shorthanded and treated disrespectfully by corporate headquarters. Things deteriorated to a point where pilots began to question the company's commitment to safety.

Recent flights on both airlines were revealing of the impact leadership has had on organizational response to challenging situations. In both experiences, the flights were delayed due to mechanical difficulties, causing the passengers to deplane and move to different aircraft before a delayed departure. While the circumstances presented an unpleasant situation for both carriers, their responses were markedly different.

The Debilitated crew provided limited information to the passengers, waiting until anger built to a point where a response became necessary. First class passengers were treated differently from coach passengers, with more information, access to other flights, and beverages provided during the long wait. Attendants at the counters were hassled and hurried as they tried to make alternative connections for angry passengers. Tempers flared, rumors abounded, and service took a nosedive. No alternative compensation was offered, and when asked, the response was, "Write to the company."

In contrast, on Dairyland Direct, all passengers were kept informed about every development at every step as events unfolded. The affected travelers knew what had happened, what would happen, and what to expect. There was no first class since the philosophy of the airline is that everyone is first class and should be treated as such. Free wine and fresh-baked cookies were offered during the wait. Problem solving for connections to other airlines became an opportunity for creative thinking. Attendants kept their sense of humor and engaged passengers in conversation to pass the time. Ultimately, the airline offered a half-price discount to all passengers on their next flight, as a small token of apology for the inconvenience caused. Same problem, but very different response, and very different effect.

Your Analysis of the Case:

With reference to previously suggested principles, practices, and strategies of mindful leadership, use the lined space on page 221 to analyze how Nick or Frank was either mindful (i.e., attentive) or mindless (i.e., heedless) of personal and organizational capacity relevant to the operation of an airline. Specifically, in what manner did they attend to the following:

1. The nature and nurture of the physiological platform that enables intelligence?

2. The nature and nurture of social relationships?

3. The nature and nurture of the power of emotion?

4. The nature and nurture of the construction of meaning?

5. The nature and nurture of a culture of reflection?

6. The nature and nurture of mindful dispositions?

Evidence of mindful practice?　　　　　　*Evidence of mindless practice?*

_____　　　_____

_____　　　_____

_____　　　_____

_____　　　_____

_____　　　_____

_____　　　_____

Close to Home

In reading the above cases, one may be struck by the strong contrast between leader perceptions of appropriate leadership behavior and the ways in which those beliefs and understandings were acted out. Such contrasts in leadership orientation and practice may not always be quite so stark, but the preceding cases are rooted in real circumstances with the names changed to protect the innocent—and the guilty. The ultimate reality test for your perception of mindful leadership practice, however, lies in reflection about a leadership case that you have more intimate knowledge about. To that end, you are now encouraged to shift your thinking to your own organization or an organization you are very familiar with. In identifying such an organization, your reflection about mindful leadership practices is brought closer to home, and the final case to be analyzed is yours.

The Case:

Reflect for a moment about an instance when a leader attempted to engage the members of your organization in the achievement of a goal. Take a few moments to describe for yourself the important components of the leadership story. What was the challenge or problem to be resolved? What did the leader do, and how did she or he do it? How did members of the organization respond to the challenge or goal and to the behavior of the leader?

Your Analysis of the Case:

With your personal leadership case in mind, and with reference to previously suggested principles, practices, and strategies of mindful leadership, use the lined space on page 222 to analyze how the leader was either mindful (i.e., attentive) or mindless (i.e., heedless) of personal and organizational capacity relevant to the achievement need. Specifically, in what manner did the leader attend to the following:

1. The nature and nurture of the physiological platform that enables intelligence?
2. The nature and nurture of social relationships?
3. The nature and nurture of the power of emotion?

4. The nature and nurture of the construction of meaning?
5. The nature and nurture of a culture of reflection?
6. The nature and nurture of mindful dispositions?

Evidence of mindful practice?	*Evidence of mindless practice?*

Mindful Purpose

Purpose: *The object toward which one strives or for which something exists*
—*(American Heritage Dictionary, 2000, p. 1423)*

The Power of Purpose

Purpose is that deepest dimension within us—our central core or essence where we have a profound sense of who we are, where we come from, and where we are going. Purpose is the quality we choose to shape our life around. Purpose is a source of energy and direction.

—(Leider, 1997, p. 1)

Perception of purpose is key to the construction of a paradigm of mindful leadership. Indeed, without orientation to a compelling purpose, a leader would lack the emotional motivation to pursue relevant principles and practices. Moreover, purpose influences mindful leadership on multiple levels:

- A *focused purpose*, such as a mission or goal associated with a specific system or situation, provides reason for a leader to align leadership behavior to perceptions of intelligence. Accordingly, as described at some length in Chapter 6, clarification of an achievement need for a system, a situation, or self is the preliminary step within a framework for leadership applications of knowledge about the nature and nurture of intelligence. Orientation to a focused purpose is thus motivating to the acquisition and application of knowledge about the human capacity to achieve.
- A *fundamental purpose* contemplates an expansive big-picture role for mindful leadership, one that aspires to shape both individual and organizational ca-

pacity beyond an immediate mission or goal. Contemplation of such purpose is encouraged by the contextual challenges that confront leaders at the beginning of the 21st century. Accordingly, a leader might consider that the purpose of leadership is to be mindful of the cultivation of intelligence itself, to nurture the multidimensional nature of human capacity—in self and others.

In the game of life, the rule is that those who figure it out get to move on to the next challenge. Intelligence is the means to figure it out—to resolve problems and achieve goals—and leadership is the means to maximize intelligence in organizations, whether that intelligence is applied to focused or fundamental purpose. Consider further that the challenges of the future are largely unknown to humanity and that the only certainty is that intelligence is the means that will influence the outcome of any and all forthcoming challenges. This circumstance would appear to place a premium on the cultivation of this powerful resource that is at the disposal of all human beings. Accordingly, while mindful leadership attention to nurturing the nature of intelligence, required of the achievement of focused purposes, is appropriate and necessary, there is the more fundamental purpose of being mindful of the mind itself—to nurture intelligence to ultimate survival advantage. Such an orientation might perceive mindful purpose as the nurture of a mindful organizational culture—a culture in which every member is knowledgeable and adept about the nature and nurture of intelligence and, thereby, collectively and continuously engaged in the cultivating of organizational intelligence. Within such an orientation, intelligence itself becomes the purpose of leadership.

The Path to Purpose

Mindful purpose, whether focused or fundamental, establishes the necessary emotional and rational orientation for the exercise of mindful principles and practices. It is important to consider the path to achieving such purpose, however, lest a leader fall into a trap that will dissipate leadership energy and effect. Specifically, while purpose provides the motivating target for the investment of time and effort, progress toward the achievement of purpose is the product of adherence to mindful principles and cultivation of mindful practices. Adherence to a framework composed of principles that arouse, acquire, apply, and adjust leadership knowledge about the nature and nurture of intelligence is a means to develop both depth and substance in mindful leadership practice. In this fashion, investment in mindful principles and practices is the means to expand leadership influence on the achievement of purpose (see Figure 7.4). This is of particular import if a leader is committed to the fundamental purpose of nurturing a mindful organizational culture that maximizes a collective organizational intelligence. The trap to avoid lies in mindless circumvention of principles and practices. A leader who invests time and energy in pursuit of purpose in an unprincipled and unstructured manner runs the great risk that the effort will be superficial, unproductive, short-lived, ineffective, and abandoned—most likely in that order.

Figure 7.4. The Influence of Mindful Principles and Practices on Mindful Purpose

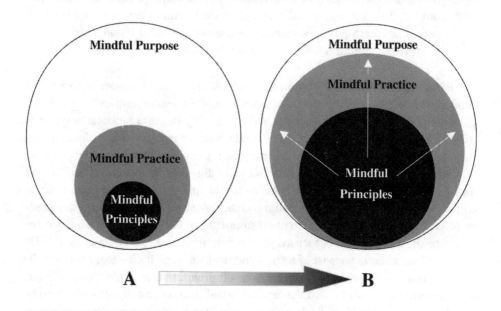

A. Attributes of a Mindful Leader	B. Principles, Practices, and Purpose
1. Adherence to mindful principles	A leadership focus on principles and prac-
2. Cultivation of mindful practices	tices expands leadership influence on the
3. Orientation to mindful purpose	achievement of purpose.

The Mindful Leader

> No leader is ever fully realized; at most, one can observe individuals who are
> in the course of attaining greater skills and heightened effectiveness.

> —(Gardner, 1995, p. 36)

A Journey in Progress

Howard Gardner's observation, as quoted above, is apropos to a panoramic view
of human experience. Few would challenge the assertion that humanity has yet to realize its potential. Similarly, most would concur that there is reason to acknowledge
progress in the journey from the cave to the exploration of the universe and DNA.

Thus the human condition is a story in progress, an ongoing journey to be aware of from both a perspective of the distance that has been covered and the promising destinations that lie ahead. What is most certain, moreover, is that leadership will remain a critical variable in how and to what extent humanity moves forward. The question, then, is, what leadership attributes are most appropriate for facilitating human progress in the context of the challenges of the near future?

Attributes of the Mindful Leader

The qualities of a mindful leader are necessarily constructed in the individual mind. The intent of this text is to provide information and structure by which such construction is facilitated. The brain appreciates the opportunity to examine models, however, as it goes about its perception construction business. To that end, a representation of mindful leadership has been progressively described in the preceding chapters and sections. The portrait that emerges is that of a leader who adheres to mindful principles, cultivates mindful practices, and is oriented to mindful purpose. More specifically, the attributes of a mindful leader might be defined by

1. Adherence to a framework (see Figure 6-2) of four principle components:
   a. Arousal of attention to the potential of mindful leadership
   b. Acquisition of knowledge about the nature and nurture of intelligence
   c. Application of knowledge about the nature and nurture of intelligence
   d. Adjustment of knowledge in response to experience
2. Cultivation of mindful leadership practices within an applications structure (see Figure 6.5) that aligns
   a. Clarification of need (i.e., goals)
   b. Assessment of the nature of intelligence
   c. Assessment of ways to nurture intelligence (e.g., Figures 7.2 and 7.3)
   d. Composition of a narrative plan of action
3. Orientation to the compelling purpose of maximizing intelligence

In the final analysis, when an individual brain has constructed its perception of the concept, all the narrative about mindful leadership might be reduced to a simple statement that articulates personal understanding. For example, a simple definition might propose that *a mindful leader is attentive to the nature and nurture of intelligence in the process of influencing others to achieve a goal.* In any case, mindful leadership will remain an open concept, much like the evolving conceptualizations of intelligence and leadership. What is, perhaps, more important is that, like intelligence and leadership, the concept of mindful leadership will become valued—thereby encouraging further investigation and understanding of its potential merits. There is, moreover, one instance in which abstract understanding of mindful leadership can become very concrete—the instance of self.

The Mindful You

The evidence says that we are entering a period that will require transformation—fundamental structural changes in how we live and work, how we think about ourselves, and how we conduct our politics, economics, and technologies. If we can get through those changes well, or well enough, humanity will be able to live on this planet without destroying the environment, and our children's children will have a future worth living.

Achieving this end will mean not just traveling *in* the great transition period but negotiating our way *through* it.

—(Ray & Anderson, 2000, p. 233)

Setting Out

Some might caution leaders to wait until more is known about the nature of intelligence before they begin to formally align their leadership behavior to it. This position is not without merit, as knowledge about the brain and intelligence is evolving at a rapid pace, with new discoveries often contradicting prior understanding. The paradox would appear to be that one must wait to act as an intelligence-aware leader until one is certain as to what it is to be intelligent. This is a false paradox in that there is no choice in the matter. To be a leader, one must necessarily exercise and engage intelligence—and being mindful about what is known about intelligence as it is known can only be an asset to the exercise. Nevertheless, the journey to mindful leadership requires a proactive disposition to step beyond the comfort of existing norms.

Ray and Anderson (2000, pp. 48-58) describe a process that individuals might go through in a transition to a new cultural perspective:

- *Inner departure:* Previously accepted explanations and practices are found to be questionable and unacceptable.
- *Setting out:* New understanding and ways of doing things are created while beginning to act on what has been found to be unsatisfactory.
- *Confronting the critics:* Emerging perceptions are inevitably challenged—both by self and others.
- *Turning new values into a way of life:* Established patterns and views are let go in favor of thinking in new and creative ways and seeing the big picture.

At the close of this text, consolidate your thoughts about mindful leadership. In doing so, you might assess the status of your perceptions by your sense of having departed in some manner from a traditional perspective of leadership. You might also reflect about where you are in constructing a new understanding of leadership, critically analyzing emerging concepts, and turning new values into a new way of leadership life.

Reflection Time

The above brief reflection should be of some value in judging the perceptual effect of this particular investigation of leadership. To provide a more definitive assessment of your interpretation and integration of the concepts presented, however, you are invited to submit your general assessment of your mindful leadership status to a contextual test. Specifically, return to the council table that you visited at the beginning of the chapter, but this time reverse the procedure with reference to Figure 7.5 and the given directions for a second leadership legacy exercise.

Leadership Legacy Exercise:
The Defense

1. Invite your leadership exemplars back to the council table and have them sit in the four chairs marked judge.
2. Join these leaders at the table by sitting in the chair marked "leader."
3. Assume that the purpose of your meeting with this collection of esteemed leaders is to describe and defend your attributes as a mindful leader. Specifically, you are to lay it on the table, to present for the critical review of the assembled judges your following:
   a. Framework of guiding principles for leadership that is mindful of the nature and nurture of intelligence
   b. Specific leadership practices that are mindful of the alignment of leadership behavior to the nature and nurture of intelligence
   c. Fundamental leadership purpose that is mindful of the nature and nurture of intelligence

> Reflection Time

On completing the above exercise, you should have a clearer understanding of the meaning your brain has constructed about how a leader might mindfully connect leadership to the brain. In articulating mindful principles, practices, and purpose, you are also describing how you are incorporating personal perceptions of leadership with the legacy that you inherited from your council of advisers. In this manner, you are further refining your personal wisdom about leadership—and the leadership legacy that you will pass on to those who call you to their council table.

Bon Voyage

If a breakthrough in knowledge about intelligence equates to an opportunity for breakthroughs in perceptions about leadership, this is a moment to be mindful about the purpose such a perceptual shift might serve. The human story has been, after all, an ongoing saga about a species that has continually evolved in its capacity to exercise intelligence. You might say that humans have always been engaged in a process of getting smarter. Indeed, the evolution of the human capacity to acquire and apply knowledge is evident in a progression from handheld tools and communal shelters to

Figure 7.5. Leadership Legacy Exercise Two

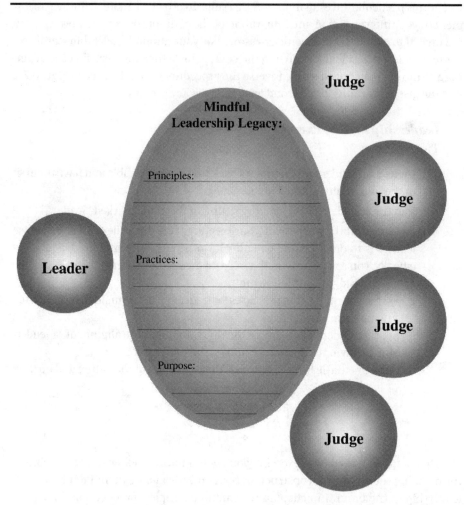

the harnessing of the power of atoms and the creation of complex social structures. The question that always looms, however, is, will humankind get smart enough soon enough to respond to the next challenge? At the beginning of a new century and a new millennium, it is impossible to anticipate the events and challenges of the coming decades. It is clear, however, that the stakes are high. One might necessarily conclude that the circumstances of the future will require more of intelligence—that it will be necessary for humankind to collectively move to a next level and become more adept and consistent in the exercise of intelligent behavior. Enter the mindful leader.

On completing this reflective exploration of leadership-brain connections, two observations might be of some comfort as you look forward to an uncertain future. The story of human intelligence is that of a continuous journey of evolving capacity to acquire and apply knowledge. Similarly, the story of leadership is that of an ongoing journey of refinement in understanding and skill at the influence of ever-changing environmental contexts. The simple message of the preceding pages is that this is a moment in which conscious awareness and convergence of these voyages is enabled. Whatever the future holds in store, it is a safe bet that it will place greater demands on both leadership and intelligence—and the connections therein. It would appear, then, that humanity had better continue to get better at both. Thus your journey to mindful leadership continues. Bon voyage!

Summary Observations

- Mindful leadership is a concept that, like all others, is necessarily constructed by the individual brain.
- An example of a perceptual construction of mindful leadership is represented in this statement: A mindful leader is attentive to the nature and nurture of intelligence in the process of influencing others to achieve a goal.
- Attributes of mindful leaders are represented in adherence to principles, cultivation of practices, and orientation to purposes that are mindful of the nature and nurture of intelligence.
- Adherence to mindful principles and cultivation of mindful practices represent the path by which a leader influences the achievement of mindful purpose.
- The mindful leader will seek strategic practices that effectively engage multiple dimensions of the nature of intelligence.
- Mindful leadership will always be a work in progress.

Reader Reflection

- Examples of strategic leadership practices that comprehensively nurture the multidimensional nature of intelligence are . . . ?
- A specific action I will take to further my attributes as a mindful leader is . . . ?
- Other thoughts and questions?

Resource A: Glossary

acetylcholine.　A neurotransmitter involved in long-term memory and muscle movement.

adrenaline.　A hormone released from the adrenal gland into the bloodstream during times of stress, stimulating the release of glucose for rapid energy.

amygdala.　An almond-shaped structure, connected to the hippocampus, that processes sensory information, catalogs emotional memories, and initiates emotional responses.

automatic memory.　Our reflexive memory that is located in the part of our brain called the cerebellum, the lower area of the brain that coordinates and integrates balance, posture, coordination, and muscle movements.

axon.　Long fibers, extending out of brain cells called neurons, that carry signals away from one neuron to another. There is only one axon per neuron, but axons connect with many dendrites.

brain stem.　The lowest and earliest-formed part of the brain at the top of the spinal cord; often referred to as the lower brain. It receives sensory input and monitors vital functions.

Broca's area.　Area in the left frontal lobe where thoughts are converted into sounds and spoken words.

cell.　The smallest unit of an organism capable of functioning independently.

central nervous system.　Composed of the brain plus the spinal cord.

cerebellum.　A cauliflower-shaped structure located in the hindbrain; coordinates and integrates balance, posture, coordination, and muscle movements.

cerebral cortex.　Neocortex, the quarter-inch-thick outer layer of the cerebrum, which is densely packed with neurons (gray matter) and divided into four lobes: frontal, temporal, parietal, and occipital.

cerebrum. The largest part of the brain, consisting of the brain's right and left hemispheres. It has frontal, parietal, temporal, and occipital lobes.

cingulate gyrus. Lying directly above the corpus callosum, it is the part of the brain that facilitates communication between the midbrain and the cortex.

corpus callosum. A four-inch-long, thick band of axon fibers that connects the right and left hemispheres of the brain.

cortisol. A hormone released from the adrenal glands during times of stress. The release of too much cortisol can cause damage to the hippocampus, a part of the brain involved in learning and long-term memory.

dendrite. A branched fiber extension from a neuron that receives impulses from another neuron or axon through a synaptic connection. A single neuron has many dendrites.

dopamine. A neurotransmitter associated with movement and pleasure.

endorphin. A neurotransmitter that protects against excessive pain.

epinephrine. Adrenaline.

episodic memory. Memory that involves location; stored in the hippocampus.

excitatory neurotransmitter. The chemical in the brain that causes neurons to fire.

explicit memory. Type of memory that involves memories of words, facts, and places; associated with the hippocampus.

frontal lobe. One of the four main areas of the cerebrum; controls voluntary movement, verbal expression, planning, problem solving, decision making, and willpower.

gamma-aminobutyric acid (GABA). A neurotransmitter that prevents electrical impulses from moving down the axon of a neuron.

glial cells. Supporting cells in the brain and nervous system that help maintain neurons by providing oxygen and nourishment; 90% of the brain's cells are glial.

glutamate. An amino acid found in every cell in the brain; used in the nervous system as a fast-excitatory neurotransmitter.

gray matter. Areas of the brain and spinal cord where neurons and dendrites are abundant.

hemisphere (cortical). Half of the cerebral cortex; each half is subdivided into four lobes.

hindbrain. Lower brain emerging from the spinal cord that consists of the medulla, pons, and cerebellum.

hippocampus. The part of the brain that encodes working factual memory to long-term storage; located under the temporal lobes.

hormone. A substance produced by one tissue and sent into the bloodstream to affect a physiological activity such as growth or metabolic rate.

hypothalamus. Located in the forebrain and concerned with basic acts and drives such as eating, drinking, and sexual activity. The hypothalamus plays an important role in emotional behavior through its influence on the pituitary gland.

implicit memory. Memory that is not voluntary and occurs automatically, such as procedural, emotional, and automatic memories.

inhibitory neurotransmitter. A chemical in the brain that prevents neurons from firing.

limbic system. A description of the midbrain area associated with memory and emotion. The limbic system includes the hypothalamus, amygdala, thalamus, hippocampus, and cingulate gyrus.

long-term memory. Process by which the brain stores memories for weeks, months, or longer.

lower brain. Also known as the hindbrain; the lower portion of the brain composed of the upper spinal cord, medulla, pons, and the reticular formation. The lower brain sorts information from our senses and regulates functions of survival such as breathing and heart rate.

magnetic resonance imaging (MRI). technology that produces an image of the brain by using a large magnetic field used to map the structure of the brain.

medulla. Located in the hindbrain; controls heart rate and respiration.

melatonin. Neurotransmitter associated with the cycles of waking and sleeping.

midbrain. Associated with vision and located between the hindbrain and the forebrain.

myelin. A fatty shield that covers and insulates axons for smoother and faster transmission of messages.

neural pruning. The removal of synapses that are not being used.

neuromodulator. A chemical substance released at a synapse that causes biochemical changes in a neuron.

neurons. Cells that compose the neuron system, consisting of the cell body, axons, and dendrites.

neuropeptides. Small proteins, released at synapses, that act as neuromodulators.

neuroscientist. A scientist who studies the structure and function of the brain.

neurotransmitter. A chemical substance released in a synapse by the electrical impulse of a neuron to carry a coded message to another neuron.

noradrenaline. A neurotransmitter primarily involved in states of fight or flight, metabolic rate, blood pressure, emotions, and mood.

occipital lobe. The lobe of our brain that processes vision; located in the rear of the cerebrum.

parietal lobe.   Region of the cerebral cortex found between the frontal and occipital lobes; concerned primarily with the processing of sensory information such as pain, pressure, temperature, and touch.

peptides.   Hormones that travel and carry messages throughout the body.

pineal gland.   Gland that regulates the release of neurotransmitters that regulate sleep.

pituitary gland.   Located at the base of the brain, a gland that releases a variety of hormones into the bloodstream and runs the endocrine system.

pons.   A structure that is a critical relay station for sensory information; located in the hindbrain. The pons relays information from the cortex to the cerebellum.

positron emission tomography (PET) scanning.   Technology that detects increases in activity levels in parts of the brain by tracing the metabolism of glucose.

reptilian brain.   Brain stem.

reticular activating system (RAS).   System that controls and regulates the amount and flow of information that enters the brain.

reticular formation.   Responsible for attention, arousal, sleeping and waking, and consciousness; located at the upper brain stem and bottom of the midbrain area.

semantic memory.   Memory of words, concepts, and numerical systems.

serotonin.   Neurotransmitter that regulates mood and sleep and causes relaxation.

short-term memory.   Temporary memory where information is processed briefly and subconsciously.

synapse.   The gap across which a nerve impulse passes from an axon of one neuron to a dendrite receptor of another neuron or to a muscle or gland cell.

temporal lobes.   Located in the middle of the upper brain near our ears and responsible for hearing, senses, listening, speech, language, learning, and memory.

thalamus.   Located in the forebrain and responsible for relaying and sorting incoming information to the cerebral cortex.

triune brain.   A model of the brain that describes three systems: forebrain, midbrain, and hindbrain.

Wernicke's area.   Located in the temporal lobes and responsible for the comprehension of language necessary for reading, spoken language, and writing.

white matter.   Areas of the brain and spinal cord where there is an abundance of myelinated axons, giving this area of the brain a white appearance.

working memory.   A process in which information is temporarily processed consciously until it is either dropped or stored in long-term memory.

Resource B: Annotated Bibliography

Blum, D. (1997). *Sex on the brain.* New York: Penguin Putnam.

> *Sex on the Brain* is a report on a broad range of animal and human studies intended to provide insight into issues such as aggression, nurturing behavior, infidelity, homosexuality, hormonal drives, and sexual signals. The book is easily readable and filled with stories and scientific data. Paperback, 352 pages. ISBN: 0-140-26348-9.

Brothers, L. (1997). *Friday's footprint: How society shapes the human mind.* New York: Oxford University Press.

> Brothers, a psychiatrist, provides a thorough tour of current research on the social functions of the brain. She argues that humans are evolved to be social animals and that the human mind can only be said to function in a social context. Brothers also provides an interesting discussion of psychoanalysis, which she uses as an example of how thought is molded by conversation. Hardcover, 224 pages. ISBN: 0-195-10103-0.

Bruer, J. T. (1999). *The myth of the first three years: A new understanding of early brain development and lifelong learning.* New York: Free Press.

> John Bruer provides a solid review of what is known and what is not known about early brain development and lifelong learning capacity. In the process, he encourages careful analysis and debate when drawing conclusions based on emerging information from brain research and cognitive science. Hardcover, 244 pages. ISBN: 0-684-85184-9.

Caine, G., & Caine, R. (1999). *Mindshifts.* Tucson, AZ: Zephyr.

The text is designed in a workbook format that is organized into three parts with seven chapters. Part 1 focuses on interconnectedness of problems and approaches to solve them. Part 2 discusses 12 principles of brain-mind learning. Part 3 describes the shift in mental models necessary for change. Throughout the chapters, the reader may interact by answering reflective questions in the space provided. Paperback, 221 pages. ISBN: 1-569-76091-8.

Caine, R., & Caine, G. (1991). *Making connections: Teaching and the human brain.* Alexandria, VA: Association for Supervision and Curriculum Development.

This book explores the implications of recent brain research for teaching and learning. The authors propose 12 principles of "brain-based" learning that should guide the creation of learning experiences. The framework is well defined, with suggestions for orchestrated immersion, relaxed alertness, and active processing. Paperback, 180 pages. ISBN: 0-871-20179-8.

Caine, R., & Caine, G. (1997). *Unleashing the power of perceptual change.* Alexandria, VA: Association for Supervision and Curriculum Development.

The authors unveil what they refer to as perceptual orientations, differing views of reality that frame the ways people think about education and teaching. This book documents the voyage of perceptual exploration as the Caines watched teachers change from individuals who used traditional teaching and beliefs about learning to those who are at home with messy, rich, complex learning environments. Their approach provides a glimpse of the many options open to educators. Paperback, 220 pages. ISBN: 0-871-20287-5.

Calvin, W., & Ojemann, G. (1994). *Conversations with Neil's brain: The neural nature of thought and language.* New York: Addison-Wesley.

This book tells the story of neurosurgery undertaken to end the seizures of epileptics who cannot be helped with conventional drug therapy. In a novelistic style, the story of Neil is detailed before, during, and after his surgery. The book is written by the surgeon and neuroscientists as they explore the intricate landscape of the brain and, in so doing, reveal the mystery of human memory, thought, and language. Hardcover, 330 pages. ISBN: 0-201-63217-9.

Calvin, W. H. (1996). *How brains think: Evolving intelligence, then and now.* New York: Basic Books.

Calvin, a neurophysiologist, suggests that physicists reduce the mind to subatomic particles and mathematical equations, whereas those in his specialty see the seat of consciousness and intelligence in higher levels of brain physiology—the neurons, synapses, and cortex. He argues that the unique level of human consciousness is the product of evolutionary forces that began with the ice age 2 million years ago. Paperback, 192 pages. ISBN: 0-465-07278-X.

Carter, R. (1998). *Mapping the mind.* Berkeley: University of California Press.

Mapping the Mind uses the latest brain scans and computer-generated drawings of the brain to take the reader on a journey through the human brain. Carter, a British science writer, explains in clear language how the brain develops and the factors that influence it. The book also contains short articles written by well-regarded neuroscientists on their areas of study. Hardcover, 234 pages. ISBN: 0-520-21937-6.

Conlan, R. (Ed.). (1999). *States of mind: New discoveries about how our brains make us who we are.* New York: John Wiley.

This collection of essays by preeminent scientists peers into the workings of the brain to reveal recent findings about mental health, behavior, feelings, emotion, memory, dreams, temperament, and identity. The insights of these eight pioneering researchers thus enables the reader to participate in the thrill and wonder of the latest explorations into the nature and function of the human mind. Hardcover, 214 pages. ISBN: 0-471-29963-4.

Costa, A. L., & Kallick, B. (Eds.). (2000). *Discovering and exploring habits of mind.* Alexandria, VA: Association for Supervision and Curriculum Development.

Costa and Kallick define and describe 16 types of intelligent behavior—"habits of mind"—that enable both children and adults in the resolution of problems, dilemmas, and enigmas when the answers are not immediately apparent. The authors maintain that a critical attribute of intelligence is not only having information but also knowing how to act on it. Paperback, 108 pages. ISBN: 0-87120-368-5.

Crick, F. (1994). *The astonishing hypothesis: The scientific search for the soul.* New York: Simon & Schuster.

Applying the methodology of science to the search for the soul, the winner of the Nobel Prize for the discovery of DNA explores the fundamental questions of human consciousness while challenging science, philosophy, and religion. Paperback, 200 pages. ISBN: 0-684-80158-2.

Damasio, A. (1994). *Descartes' error: Emotion, reason and the human brain.* New York: Avon.

Damasio draws on his experiences with neurological patients affected by brain damage and shows how the absence of emotion and feeling can break down rationality. He explains how emotions contribute to adaptive social behavior and offers a novel perspective on the nature of feelings as a direct sensing of our own body states. The book includes intricate diagrams and detailed descriptions of neurological processes. Hardcover, 336 pages. ISBN: 0-380-72647-5.

Damasio, A. (1999). *The feeling of what happens.* New York: Harcourt Brace.

This work reveals the neurobiological foundations of the self in an explanation of the mystery of consciousness—how we know that we know and how our conscious and private minds have a sense of self. Hardcover, 386 pages. ISBN: 0-15-100369-6.

Davis, J. (1997). *Mapping the mind: The secrets of the human brain and how it works.* Secaucus, NJ: Birch Lane.

Davis is a science writer who describes the recent revolutionary breakthroughs in solving the brain's mysteries. In a readable fashion, he discusses new brain-imaging techniques, emotions, learning, memory, and language, and how the brain processes, stores, and uses the data received from the senses. Hardcover, 289 pages. ISBN: 1-55972-344-0.

de Bono, E. (1996). *Serious creativity: Using the power of lateral thinking to create new ideas.* London, UK: HarperCollins Business.

This book is a widely read source for direction about how to access creativity on demand. De Bono's work establishes that creativity is not merely a matter of old-fashioned brainstorming and hoping that ideas will somehow happen. Serious creativity provides formal tools that can be used to deliberately and systematically engage the creative capacities of the human brain. Paperback, 388 pages. ISBN: 0-00-637958-3

Diamond, M., & Hopson, J. (1998). *Magic trees of the mind: How to nurture your child's intelligence, creativity, and healthy emotions from birth through adolescence.* New York: Dutton-Penguin Putnam.

Written for educators and parents, this book takes the reader through the evolutionary journey of the child's brain. It is based on Diamond's pioneering work on enriched environments and their effects on the brain, and on interviews with other noted scientists in the field. An added bonus is a comprehensive resource guide of related books, products, organizations, Web sites, and learning centers. Hardcover, 465 pages. ISBN: 0-525-94308-0.

Dowling, J. E. (1998). *Creating mind: How the brain works.* New York: Norton.

Creating Mind is a lucid introduction to the study of the brain. Dowling describes the mechanisms underlying memory, vision, and language. The many illustrations are clear and work well with the text to explain points best understood visually. Dowling has written an overview that will inspire laypeople and budding neuroscientists alike. Hardcover, 212 pages. ISBN: 0-393-02746-5.

Gardner, H. (1983). *Frames of mind: The theory of multiple intelligences.* New York: Basic Books.

Frames of Mind will definitely broaden the ways readers perceive the concept of intelligence. Gardner takes something we take for granted (a logical-mathematical way of thinking that has shaped Western civilization) and explains how it is inadequate in describing the mind. He goes on to describe a total of seven intelligences that shape our experiences, perceptions, worldview, and thinking. This book is a definite must for every educator and leader. Paperback, 440 pages. ISBN: 0-465-02510-2.

Gardner, H. (1991). *The unschooled mind: How children think and how schools should teach.* New York: Basic Books.

In *The Unschooled Mind,* Gardner draws on the current state of cognitive research and provides practical, well-grounded advice to school reformers who seek not rote learning but deep understanding. Hardcover, 300 pages. ISBN: 0-465-08895-3.

Gardner, H. (1995). *Leading minds: An anatomy of leadership.* New York: Basic Books.

In this book, Gardner applies a cognitive lens to leadership to examine the critical, but most often neglected, components of the mind of the leader and the minds of followers. Through study of the qualities of a wide spectrum of leaders, the author focuses on the nature and importance of what occurs between the minds of leader and follower. Paperback, 400 pages. ISBN: 0-465-08280-7.

Gardner, H. (1999). *Intelligence reframed.* New York: Basic Books.

In *Intelligence Reframed,* Gardner synthesizes the historical development of the measures and meanings of intelligence. The author also shares his observations about the influence of his theory of multiple intelligences on current understanding of education and human development. Paperback, 292 pages. ISBN: 0-465-02611-7.

Gazzaniga, M. (1998). *The mind's past.* Berkeley: University of California Press.

Cognitive neuroscientist Gazzaniga shows in this book how our mind and brain accomplish the amazing feat of constructing our past, a process that is clearly fraught with errors of perceptions, memory, and judgment. This book is a provocative look at how the unconscious brain informs the conscious brain, making *us* the last to know. Hardcover, 200 pages. ISBN: 0-520-21320-3.

Goldberg, E. (2001). *The executive brain: Frontal lobes and the civilized mind.* New York: Oxford University Press.

Goldberg explores the most "human" region of the brain, the frontal lobes. It is this region that enables human engagement in complex mental processes, control, and judgment and determines social and ethical behavior. *The Executive Brain* provides insights from the emerging brain research into the human capacity to reflect, imagine, project, and decide. Hardcover, 251 pages. ISBN: 0-19-514022-2.

Goleman, D. (1995). *Emotional intelligence: Why it can matter more than IQ.* New York: Bantam.

In this book based on brain and behavioral research, Goleman argues that our IQ-idolizing view of intelligence is far too narrow. Instead, Goleman makes the case for emotional intelligence being the strongest indicator of human success. He defines emotional intelligence in terms of self-awareness, altruism, personal motivation, empathy, and the ability to love and be loved by friends. Paperback, 352 pages. ISBN: 0-553-37506-7.

Goleman, D. (1998). *Working with emotional intelligence.* New York: Bantam.

In *Working With Emotional Intelligence*, Goleman takes the concepts from *Emotional Intelligence* into the workplace. Goleman contends that business leaders and workers should not be defined by their IQs or even their job skills but by their emotional intelligence: a set of competencies that distinguishes how people manage feelings, interact, and communicate. This book details 12 personal competencies based on self-mastery, and 13 key relationship skills, all of which Goleman claims lead to or thwart success. Paperback, 383 pages. ISBN: 0-553-37858-9.

Greenfield, S. (1997). *The human brain: A guided tour.* New York: Basic Books.

This accessible book by Greenfield, a British author, follows her earlier, illustrated book on the same topic. It is useful in helping one to view the brain from many different perspectives and in understanding why it is dangerous to view the brain too simplistically by assigning functions to single areas. It takes the reader through the brain's development, from fertilized egg to fully developed organ, looking at the changes and adaptations that occur along the way. Hardcover, 160 pages. ISBN: 0-465-00725-2.

Greenspan, S. I. (1997). *The growth of the mind: The endangered origins of intelligence.* New York: Addison-Wesley.

Greenspan focuses on the early development of emotion and its role in the growth of the mind, intellectually and emotionally. Especially interesting is his discussion of autism and the work he and his colleagues have done to ameliorate the symptoms of this disorder. This book is pertinent for all educators but especially those who work in early childhood. Hardcover, 350 pages. ISBN: 0-201-48302-5.

Hart, L. (1983). *Human brain and human learning.* Village of Oak Creek, AZ: Books for Educators.

Hart's book is somewhat of a classic in the field of the applications of cognitive research to teaching and learning. Unlike many books written about the brain, this one contains many practical suggestions on how to create school environments that help all learners to achieve. Paperback, 206 pages. ISBN: 0-582-28379-5.

Howard, P. J. (1994). *The owner's manual for the brain.* Austin, TX: Leorrian.

Howard has assimilated an assortment of brain research results and created what he hopes is a practical reference work for consumers. Targeting an audience of lifelong learners, educators, and managers, he has selected research on intelligence, stress, learning, creativity, memory, and the emotions. Paperback, 831 pages. ISBN: 1-885-16741-5.

Hutchison, M. (1996). *MegaBrain: New tools and techniques for brain growth and mind.* New York: Ballantine.

Hutchison captures the drama, excitement, and adventure that surround the mystery of the source of human culture. He looks at the recently developed machines and devices that may soon allow us to increase brain size and intelligence; regenerate brain cells; trigger specific brain states; and control the brain's electrical activity in order to alter involuntary mechanisms such as blood pressure, heart rate, and the secretion of hormones. This book is an account of where the pioneers of brain research are headed. Paperback, 380 pages. ISBN: 0-345-41032-7.

Kotulak, R. (1996). *Inside the brain.* Kansas City, MO: Andrews & McMeel.

This revised, updated edition of a highly praised book takes an in-depth look at the latest scientific findings about the brain. Pulitzer Prize-winning author Kotulak reveals new understandings about how nature builds the brain and then develops it during early life. In easy-to-understand text he explains how scientists have changed their once-held belief that brains learn from a preset and unchangeable set of rules. Paperback, 185 pages. ISBN: 0-836-23289-5.

Langer, E. J. (1989). *Mindfulness.* Reading, MA: Addison-Wesley.

Harvard psychology professor Langer seeks to dramatize the rigid conditions and mindsets that often result in mindless human behavior. This book explores the concept of mindlessness: What causes it, what we can do about it, and what difference it makes. This is a great book for people who desire to be more creative in their work, experience more aliveness and alertness, and stay mentally young. Langer's work is effective and important on both personal and societal levels. Paperback, 221 pages. ISBN: 0-201-52341-8.

LeDoux, J. (1996). *The emotional brain: The mysterious underpinnings of emotional life.* New York: Simon & Schuster.

LeDoux begins this book by discussing the history of efforts to understand emotions and how they relate to cognition. He explores the origins of emotions, how some are hardwired into the brain's circuitry and how others are learned through experience. This state-of-the-art research is presented in a highly readable fashion. It is highly recommended. Hardcover, 384 pages. ISBN: 0-684-80382-8.

Mamchur, C. (1996). *Cognitive type theory and learning style.* Alexandria, VA: Association for Supervision and Curriculum Development.

Mamchur provides a practical explanation of cognitive type theory and learning style that will help teachers meet the needs of others while also discovering their own strengths as teachers and colleagues. The theory of psychological type preferences is introduced, along with a case study of each preference that shows that preference typically influences classroom practice. Paperback, 191 pages. ISBN: 0-871-20278-6.

Mithen, S. (1996). *The prehistory of the mind: The cognitive origins of art, religion and science.* London, UK: Thames & Hudson.

The prehistory of the mind presents a reconstruction of how the human mind has evolved over millions of years. Drawing from a depth of archaeological knowledge, the author synthesizes a general evolutionary model of how human cognitive capacities emerged to take their present form. Paperback, 288 pages. ISBN: 0-500-28100-9.

Perkins, D. (1995). *Outsmarting IQ: The emerging science of learnable intelligence.* New York: Free Press.

Perkins begins with a summary and criticism of classic and current theories of intelligence. He contrasts the neurological, experiential, and reflective types of intelligence, emphasizing the importance of the latter for creative thinking and problem solving. His ideas are multidisciplinary and a must for serious educators and anyone interested in intelligence. Hardcover, 390 pages. ISBN: 0-029-25212-1.

Perkins, D. (2000). *Archimedes' bathtub: The art and logic of breakthrough thinking.* New York: Norton.

In *Archimedes' Bathtub,* Perkins articulates how and why breakthroughs occur in human thinking. In doing so, the author explores the common logic behind breakthroughs in many fields, historical periods, and evolutionary epochs. The book also presents the reader with opportunities to experience and build break-through thinking capacity. Hardcover, 292 pages. ISBN: 0-393-04795-4.

Pert, C. B. (1997). *Molecules of emotion: Why you feel the way you feel.* New York: Scribner.

Pert, a neuroscientist whose career began with her 1972 discovery of the opiate receptor, provides answers to such questions as these: Why do we feel the way we feel? How do our thoughts and emotions affect our health? Are our bodies and minds distinct from each other or do they function together as parts of an inter-connected system? Pert's pioneering research and groundbreaking book should be read by all who are challenged by such questions, which have been pondered for centuries. Hardcover, 368 pages. ISBN: 0-684-83187-2.

Pinker, S. (1997). *How the mind works.* New York: Norton.

How the Mind Works presents the big picture of what the mind is; how it evolved; and how it allows us to see, think, feel, laugh, interact, enjoy the arts, and ponder the mysteries of life. It is a substantial synthesis of explanations of the mental life of humans from cognitive science and evolutionary biology. Hardcover, 660 pages. ISBN: 0-393-04535-8.

Ratey, J. J. (2001). *A user's guide to the brain: Perception, attention and the four theaters of the brain.* New York: Pantheon Books.

Ratey describes the basic structure and chemistry of the brain and how its sys-tems shape human perceptions, emotions, actions, and reactions. *A User's Guide to the Brain* also explores how knowledge about the brain can enable under-standing of how to improve one's life and how the brain responds to the guid-ance of its user. Hardcover, 404 pages. ISBN: 0-679-45309-1.

Ridley, M. (1996). *The origins of virtue: Human instincts and the evolution of cooperation.* New York: Penguin.

This book interprets the latest research in the emerging field of evolutionary psychology to answer the age-old question, is human nature cooperative or competitive? Vivid examples of both animal and human behavior examine why humans tend generally to cooperate with one another. Paperback, 295 pages. ISBN: 0-140-26445-0.

Rubinstein, M. F., & Firstenberg, I. R. (1999). *The minding organization: Bringing the future to the present and turning creative ideas into business solutions.* New York: John Wiley.

Being able to adapt, Rubinstein and Firstenberg argue, is the key not only to cop-ing with a continuously changing environment but also to addressing the prob-lems that arise within that environment with innovative, successful solutions. In assessing how leaders can creatively manage the chaos and uncertainty in business, they provide examples for innovative strategies that facilitate both internal and external changes within the organization and the people who work there. Hardcover, 224 pages. ISBN: 0-471-34781-7.

Sapolsky, R. (1994). *Why zebras don't get ulcers: An updated guide to stress, stress-related diseases, and coping.* New York: Freeman.

In a fascinating look at the science of stress, biologist Sapolsky presents an intriguing case that people develop some diseases partly because our bodies are not designed for the constant stresses of a modern-day life. *Why Zebras Don't Get Ulcers* makes understanding the science of stress an adventure in discovery. Paperback, 434 pages. ISBN: 0-716-73210-6.

Schacter, D. (1996). *Searching for memory: The brain, the mind, and the past.* New York: Basic Books.

This excellent book describes new breakthroughs in the study and understanding of memory. It contains information on how and why the new research on the brain may change our understanding of everything from false memory to Alzheimer's disease. Schacter uses well-known works of art to illustrate many of his points. Hardcover, 398 pages. ISBN: 0-465-02502-1.

Senge, P. M. (1990). *The fifth discipline: The art and practice of the learning organization.* New York: Doubleday Currency.

In *The Fifth Discipline*, Senge describes five learning disciplines that enable the learning organization, an organization that is continually expanding its capacity to achieve its goals. It is through the mastery of the five disciplines that organizations most effectively tap the capacity of people to achieve at all level of the organization. Hardcover, 424 pages. ISBN: 0-385-26094-6.

Senge, P., Kleiner, A., Roberts, C., Ross, R., Roth, G., & Smith, B. (1999). *The dance of change: The challenges to sustaining momentum in learning organizations.* New York: Doubleday Currency.

The Dance of Change addresses behavior that facilitates and sustains meaningful change in organizations with particular focus on processes that enable change and forces that constrain change. Readers are introduced to multiple strategies for building personal and organizational capabilities for responding to the challenges of change. Paperback, 596 pages. ISBN: 0-385-49322-3.

Senge, P., Cambron-McCabe, N., Lucas, T., Smith, B., Dutton, J., & Kleiner, G. (2000). *Schools that learn: A fifth discipline fieldbook for educators, parents, and everyone who cares about education.* New York: Doubleday Currency.

Schools That Learn focuses on the importance of developing and reclaiming effective learning systems that meet the learning needs of children and society. To that end, the book describes practices and provides strategies that are meeting success throughout the world, as schools attempt to learn, grow, and reinvent themselves using the principles of organizational learning. Paperback, 592 pages. ISBN: 0-385-49323-1.

Senge, P., Kleiner, A., Roberts, C., Ross, R., & Smith, B. (1994). *The fifth discipline fieldbook: Strategies and tools for building a learning organization.* New York: Doubleday Currency.

The Fifth Discipline Fieldbook is a pragmatic guide to actions that help create and sustain a learning organization. It is a book of extensive examples and activities for promoting the five learning disciplines of personal mastery, mental models, shared vision, team learning, and systems thinking. Paperback, 593 pages. ISBN: 0-385-47256-0.

Siegel, D. J. (1999). *The developing mind: Toward a neurobiology of interpersonal experience.* New York: Guilford.

In *The Developing Mind,* Siegel presents an integrative framework for understanding the interface of the brain and the social environment, with a focus on the ways interpersonal relationships influence the genetically programmed unfolding of the human mind. Hardcover, 394 pages. ISBN:1-57230-453-7.

Snowdon, D. (2001). *Aging with grace: What the nun study teaches us about leading longer, healthier, and more meaningful lives.* New York: Bantam.

Snowdon's book shares the story of brain research applied to the study of aging members of the School Sisters of Notre Dame. Over a period of 15 years, the study has revealed important insights into the importance of linguistic ability early in life, good nutrition, and positive disposition to brain health and performance. Hardcover, 242 pages. ISBN: 0-553-80163-5.

Sousa, D. (2001). *How the brain learns.* Thousand Oaks, CA: Corwin.

This is a reader-friendly book for teachers, staff developers, and administrators. Sousa presents an excellent explanation of the brain's learning systems as well as a host of practical applications. A companion learning manual is also available. Paperback, 248 pages. ISBN: 0-7619-7765-1

Sternberg, R. J. (1996). *Successful intelligence: How practical and creative intelligence determine success in life.* New York: Simon & Schuster.

One of the foremost experts in the field of human intelligence shows why creative and practical intelligence, not IQ, are the best predictors of success in life. Sternberg offers a new definition of intelligence that includes the willingness to take risks and overcome obstacles. His definition predicts how students will fare in problem solving in both their personal and professional lives. Paperback, 304 pages. ISBN: 0-452-27906-2.

Sylwester, R. (1995). *A celebration of neurons: An educator's guide to the human brain.* Alexandra, VA: Association for Supervision and Curriculum Development.

This book is a comprehensive, relatively nontechnical overview of current research findings in neuroscience. Sylwester uses metaphors as he helps the lay reader understand not only the research but also the educational implications. Paperback, 167 pages. ISBN: 0-871-20243-3.

Sylwester, R. (2000). *A biological brain in a cultural classroom: Applying biological research to classroom management.* Thousand Oaks, CA: Corwin.

In *A Biological Brain in a Cultural Classroom,* Sylwester applies the latest brain research and theory to classroom management practices. In doing so, the author bridges key biological concepts and research findings about the brain to compatible classroom leadership behaviors. Hardcover, 160 pages. ISBN: 0-8039-6745-4.

Von Oech, R. (1990). *A whack on the side of the head: How you can be more creative.* Stamford, CT: U.S. Games Systems.

This book is a rich resource of specific strategies and activities that provoke engagement of the creative capacities of the human brain. Paperback, 196 pages. ISBN: 0-88079-479-8.

Weisinger, H. (1998). *Emotional intelligence at work.* San Francisco: Berrett-Koehler.

In *Emotional Intelligence at Work,* Weisinger, a leading expert in the application of emotional intelligence, shows the reader how to master the core competencies of emotional intelligence. He shows how these competencies can be applied in such things as negotiation, dealing with a difficult coworker, improving morale and motivation, or adapting to change. Using true-life examples, Weisinger demonstrates how individuals can increase and apply their emotional intelligence in work situations. Paperback, 272 pages. ISBN: 0-787-95198-6.

Wolfe, P. (2001). *Brain matters: Translating research into classroom practice.* Alexandria, VA: Association for Supervision and Curriculum Development.

Brain Matters makes it clear that matching teaching practice to brain functioning requires understanding of how the brain functions. Part 1 is a minitextbook on brain anatomy and physiology. Part 2 describes how the brain encodes, manipulates, and stores information. In Part 3, the author provides examples of practical applications of brain-compatible teaching strategies. The book also includes a useful glossary of brain-related terms. Paperback 207 pages. ISBN: 0-87120-517-3.

Zohar, D. (1997). *Rewiring the corporate brain: Using the new science to rethink how we structure and lead organizations.* San Francisco: Berrett-Koehler.

Applying concepts of quantum and chaos theory to the working world, consultant and educator Zohar offers advice for achieving transformation in the workplace. Zohar argues that businesses should operate like brains, using stimuli on mental, emotional, and spiritual levels. Unfortunately, contends Zohar, businesses usually ignore the latter two and rely solely on one third of the "corporate brain." Hardcover, 250 pages. ISBN: 1-576-75022-1.

References

American Heritage dictionary of the English language (4th ed.). (2000). Boston: Houghton Mifflin.

American Society for Training and Development. (2000). *Training and Development, 54*(3), cover.

Argyris, C. (1990). *Knowledge for action: A guide to overcoming barriers to organizational change.* San Francisco: Jossey-Bass.

Bandura, A. (1995). *Social foundations of thought and action: A social cognitive theory.* Englewood Cliffs, NJ: Prentice-Hall.

Barker, J. (1993). *Paradigms: The business of discovering the future.* New York: HarperCollins.

Barlow, H. (1987). Intelligence: The art of good guesswork. In R. L. Gregory, assisted by O. L. Zangwill (Eds.), *Oxford companion to the mind* (pp. 381-383). New York: Oxford University Press.

Barnes, L. B., & Kriger, M. P. (1986). The hidden side of organizational leadership. *Sloan Management Review, 28*(1), 15-26.

Bateson, G. (1979). *Mind and nature: A necessary unity.* New York: Bantam.

Bennis, W. G. (1959). Leadership theory and administrative behavior: The problem with authority. *Administrative Science Quarterly, 4,* 259-301.

Bennis, W. G. (1992). *On becoming a leader.* New York: Addison-Wesley.

Block, P. (1993). *Stewardship: Choosing service over self-interest.* San Francisco: Berrett-Koehler.

Blum, D. (1997). *Sex on the brain.* New York: Penguin Putnam.

Bransford, J. D., Brown, A. L., & Cocking, R. R. (Eds.). (2000). *How people learn: Brain, mind, experience, and school.* Washington, DC: National Academy Press.

Brothers, L. (1997). *Friday's footprint: How society shapes the human mind.* New York: Oxford University Press.

Bruer, J. T. (1999). The myth of the first three years: A new understanding of early brain development and life-long learning. New York: Free Press.

Burns, J. M. (1978). *Leadership.* New York: Harper & Row.

Caine, G., & Caine, R. (1999). *Mindshifts.* Tucson, AZ: Zephyr.

Caine, R., & Caine, G. (1991). *Making connections: Teaching and the human brain.* Alexandria, VA: Association for Supervision and Curriculum Development.

Caine, R., & Caine, G. (1997). *Unleashing the power of perceptual change.* Alexandria, VA: Association for Supervision and Curriculum Design.

Calvin, W., & Ojemann, G. (1994). *Conversations with Neil's brain: The neural nature of thought and language.* New York: Addison-Wesley.

Calvin, W. H. (1996). *How brains think: Evolving intelligence, then and now.* New York: Basic Books.

Carter, R. (1998). *Mapping the mind.* Berkeley: University of California Press.

Combs, A. W., Richards, A. C., & Richards, F. (1976). *Perceptual psychology: A humanistic approach to the study of persons.* New York: Harper & Row.

Conlan, R. (Ed.). (1999). *States of mind: New discoveries about how our brains make us who we are.* New York: John Wiley.

Costa, A. L., & Kallick, B. (Eds.). (2000). *Discovering and exploring habits of mind.* Alexandria, VA: Association for Supervision and Curriculum Development.

Covey, S. R. (1989). *The seven habits of highly effective people: Restoring the character ethic.* New York: Simon & Schuster.

Crick, F. (1994). *The astonishing hypothesis: The scientific search for the soul.* New York: Simon & Schuster.

Damasio, A. (1994). *Descartes' error: Emotion, reason and the human brain.* New York: Avon.

Damasio, A. (1999). *The feeling of what happens.* New York: Harcourt Brace.

Davis, J. (1997). *Mapping the mind: The secrets of the human brain and how it works.* Secaucus, NJ: Birch Lane.

Dawkins, R. (1991). *The selfish gene.* Oxford, UK: Oxford University Press.

de Bono, E. (1970). *Lateral thinking.* New York: Harper & Row.

de Bono, E. (1996). *Serious creativity: Using the power of lateral thinking to create new ideas.* London, UK: HarperCollins Business.

de Bono, E. (2001). *New thinking for the new millennium.* New Millennium Press.

de Geus, A. (1997, March-April). The living company. *Harvard Business Review,* 51-59.

Deming, W. E., & Walton, M. (1988). *Deming management method.* New York: Perigree.

Dewey, J. (1933). *How we think: A restatement of the relation of reflective thinking to the educative process.* Boston: Houghton Mifflin.

Diamond, M., & Hopson, J. (1998). *Magic trees of the mind: How to nurture your child's intelligence, creativity, and healthy emotions from birth through adolescence.* New York: Dutton-Penguin Putnam.

Diamond, M. C., Krech, D., & Rosenzweig, M. R. (1964). The effects of an enriched environment on the histology of the rat cerebral cortex. *Journal of Comparative Neurology, 123,* 111-120.

Dowling, J. E. (1998). *Creating mind: How the brain works.* New York: Norton.

Dunbar, R. I. M. (1993). Coevolution of neocortical size, group size and language in humans. *Behavioral and Brain Sciences, 16,* 681-735.

Durant, W., & Durant, A. (1968). *The lessons of history.* New York: Simon & Schuster.

Ekman, P. (1984). Expression and nature of emotion. In K. Scherer & P. Ekman (Eds.), *Approaches to emotion* (pp. 319-343). Hillsdale, NJ: Erlbaum.

Facione, P. A., & Facione, N. C. (1992). *California critical thinking dispositions inventory.* Millbrae, CA: The California Academic Press.

Fishbein, M. (2001). Developing effective behavior change interventions: Some lessons learned from behavioral research. In *Reviewing the behavioral science knowledge base on technology transfer, NIDA research monograph 155.* Retrieved July 13, 2001, from the National Institute on Drug Abuse from the World Wide Web: www.nida.nih.gov/pdf/monographs/download155.html

Fitzgerald, P. (1998). *The gate of angels.* New York: Houghton Mifflin.

Forgus, R. H., & Melamed, L. E. (1966). *Perception: A cognitive-stage approach.* New York: McGraw-Hill.

Fullan, M. (1991). *The new meaning of educational change.* New York: Teacher's College Press.

Gaarder, J. (1996). *Sophie's world: A novel about the history of philosophy.* New York: Berkley.

Gardner, H. (1983). *Frames of mind: The theory of multiple intelligences.* New York: Basic Books.

Gardner, H. (1991). *The unschooled mind: How children think and how schools should teach.* New York: Basic Books.

Gardner, H. (1995). *Leading minds: An anatomy of leadership.* New York: Basic Books.

Gardner, H. (1997). *Intelligence: Multiple perspectives.* San Diego, CA: Harcourt Brace.

Gardner, H. (1999). *Intelligence reframed.* New York: Basic Books.

Gazzaniga, M. (1998). *The mind's past.* Berkeley: University of California Press.

Goldberg, E. (2001). *The executive brain: Frontal lobes and the civilized mind.* New York: Oxford University Press.

Goleman, D. (1995). *Emotional intelligence: Why it can matter more than IQ.* New York: Bantam.

Goleman, D. (1998). *Working with emotional intelligence.* New York: Bantam.

Gopnik, A., Meltzoff, A. N., & Kuhl, P. K. (1999). *The scientist in the crib: Minds, brains, and how children learn.* New York: William Morrow.

Gould, J. L., & Gould, C. G. (1995). *The animal mind.* New York: Scientific American Library.

Green, T., Neinemann, S. F., & Gusella, J. F. (1998). Molecular neural biology and genetics: Investigation of neural function and dysfunction. *Neuron, 20,* 427-444.

Greene, B. (1999). *The Elegant universe: Superstrings, hidden dimensions, and the quest for the ultimate theory.* New York: Random House.

Greenfield, S. (1997). *The human brain: A guided tour.* New York: Basic Books.

Greenleaf, R. K. (1996). *On becoming a servant leader.* San Francisco: Jossey-Bass.

Greenough, W. T., & Black, J. E. (1992). Induction of brain structure by experience: Substrates for cognitive development. In M. R. Gunnar & C. A. Nelson (Eds.), *Minnesota symposia on child psychology: Vol. 24. Developmental behavioral neuroscience* (pp. 155-200). Hillsdale, NJ: Erlbaum.

Greenough, W. T., Black, J. E., & Wallace, C. S. (1987). Experience and brain development. *Child Development, 58*(3), 539-555.

Greenspan, S. I. (1997). *The growth of the mind: The endangered origins of intelligence.* New York: Addison-Wesley.

Harmin, M. (1994). *Inspiring active learning: A handbook for teachers.* Alexandria, VA: Association for Supervision and Curriculum Development.

Hart, L. (1983). *Human brain and human learning.* Village of Oak Creek, AZ: Books for Educators.

Healy, J. M. (1990). *Endangered minds: Why our children don't think.* New York: Simon & Schuster.

Hebb, D. O. (1949). *The organization of behavior.* New York: John Wiley.

Heifetz, R. A. (1994). *Leadership without easy answers.* Cambridge, MA: Belknap, Harvard University Press.

Hobson, J. A. (1999). *Consciousness.* New York: Scientific American Library.

Howard, P. J. (1994). *The owner's manual for the brain.* Austin, TX: Leorrian.

Hoy, W. K., & Miskel, C. G. (1987). *Educational administration: Theory, research, and practice* (3rd ed.). New York: Random House.

Humphrey, N. (1976). The social function of intellect. In P. P. G. Bateson & R. A. Hinde (Eds.), *Growing points in ethology* (pp. 303-317). Cambridge, UK: Cambridge University Press.

Humphrey, N. (1983). *Consciousness regained: Chapters in the development of mind.* Oxford, UK: Oxford University Press.

Hunter, M. (1982). *Increasing Teacher Effectiveness.* Presentation at Cardinal Stritch University, June 20, 1982.

Hutchison, M. (1996). *MegaBrain: New tools and techniques for brain growth and mind.* New York: Ballantine.

Kagan, J. (1998). *Three seductive ideas.* Cambridge, MA: Harvard University Press.

Kauffman, S. (1995). *At home in the universe: The search for chaos, self-organization and complexity.* Oxford, UK: Oxford University Press.

Kipling, R. (1968). *The jungle books.* Norwalk, CT: Heritage Press.

Kolb, L. K., & Brodie, H. K. (1982). *Modern clinical psychiatry.* Philadelphia: W. B. Saunders.

Kotulak, R. (1996). *Inside the brain.* Kansas City, MO: Andrews & McMeel.

Kouzes, J. M., & Posner, B. Z. (1995). *The leadership challenge: How to keep getting extraordinary things done in organizations* (2nd ed.). San Francisco: Jossey-Bass.

Langer, E. J. (1989). *Mindfulness.* Reading, MA: Addison-Wesley.

Langer, E. J. (1997). *The power of mindful learning*. Reading, MA: Addison-Wesley.

LeDoux, J. (1996). *The emotional brain: The mysterious underpinnings of emotional life*. New York: Simon & Schuster.

LeDoux, J. (1999). The power of emotions. In R. Conlan (Ed.), *States of mind: New discoveries about how our brains make us who we are*. New York: John Wiley.

Leider, R. J. (1997). *The Power of purpose: Creating meaning in your life and work*. San Francisco, CA: Berrett-Koehler.

Lennon, J. (1971). Imagine. On *Imagine* [Record]. Hollywood, CA: EMI Records.

Mamchur, C. (1996). *Cognitive type theory and learning style*. Alexandria, VA: Association for Supervision and Curriculum Development.

Markin, R. J. (1974). *Consumer behavior: A cognitive orientation*. New York: Macmillan.

Mithen, S. (1996). *The prehistory of the mind: The cognitive origins of art, religion and science*. London, UK: Thames & Hudson.

Motluk, A. (2001). Read my mind. *New Scientist, 2275*(169), pp. 22-26.

Murphy, J. T. (1988). The unheroic side of leadership: Notes from the swamp. *Phi Delta Kappan, 69*, 654-659.

National Cancer Institute. (1995). *Theory at a glance: A guide for health promotion practice*. Retrieved July 21, 2001, from the National Cancer Institute from the World Wide Web: http://oc.nci.nih.gov/services/Theory_at_glance/HOME.html

Northouse, P. G. (1997). *Leadership, theory and practice*. Thousand Oaks, CA: Sage.

Parry, T., & Gregory, G. (1998). *Designing brain-compatible learning*. Arlington Heights, IL: Skylight Learning & Publishing.

Pascale, R. T. (2000). *Surfing the edge of chaos: The laws of nature and the new laws of business*. New York: Crown Business.

Paul, R. W. (1990). Critical thinking: *What every person needs to survive in a rapidly changing world*. Rohnert Park, CA: Center for Critical Thinking and Moral Critique at Sonoma State University.

Pellicer, L. O. (1999). *Caring enough to lead*. Thousand Oaks, CA: Corwin.

Perkins, D. (1995). *Outsmarting IQ: The emerging science of learnable intelligence*. New York: Free Press.

Perkins, D. (2000). *Archemedes' bathtub: The art and logic of breakthrough thinking*. New York: Norton.

Pert, C. B. (1997). *Molecules of emotion: Why you feel the way you feel*. New York: Scribner.

Piaget, J. (1990). *Child's conception of the world*. New York: Littlefield Adams. (Original work published 1923)

Pinker, S. (1997). *How the mind works*. New York: Norton.

Pleshette, L. (Executive Producer), & Weir, P. (Director). (1998). *The Truman show* [Film]. Hollywood, CA: Paramount Pictures.

Prochaska, J. O., DiClemente, C. C., & Norcross, J. C. (1992). In search of how people change. *American Psychologist, 47*(9), 1102-1114.

Ratey, J. J. (2001). *A user's guide to the brain: Perception, attention, and the four theaters of the brain*. New York: Pantheon Books.

Ray, P. H., & Anderson, S. R. (2000). *The cultural creatives: How 50 million people are changing the world.* New York: Harmony Books.

Ridley, M. (1996). *The origins of virtue: Human instincts and the evolution of cooperation.* New York: Penguin.

Rost, J. C. (1991). *Leadership for the twenty-first century.* Westport, CT: Praeger.

Rubinstein, M. F., & Firstenberg, I. R. (1999). *The minding organization: Bringing the future to the present and turn creative ideas into business solutions.* New York: John Wiley.

Runyan, K. E. (1977). *Consumer behavior and practice of marketing,* Columbus, OH: Merrill.

Sagan, C. (1996). *The demon-haunted world: Science as a candle in the dark.* New York: Ballantine.

Sapolsky, R. (1994). *Why zebras don't get ulcers: An updated guide to stress, stress-related diseases, and coping.* New York: Freeman.

Schacter, D. (1996). *Searching for memory: The brain, the mind, and the past.* New York: Basic Books.

Schaie, K. W., & Willis, S. L. (1986). Can decline in adult intellectual functioning be reversed? *Developmental Psychology, 22*(2), 223.

Searle, J. R. (with Dennett, D. C., & Chalmers, D. J.). (1997). *The mystery of consciousness.* New York: New York Review of Books.

Senge, P. M. (1990). *The fifth discipline: The art and practice of the learning organization.* New York: Doubleday.

Senge, P., Cambron-McCabe, N., Lucas, T., Smith, B., Dutton, J., & Kleiner, G. (2000). *Schools that learn: A fifth discipline fieldbook for educators, parents, and everyone who cares about education.* New York: Doubleday Currency.

Senge, P., Kleiner, A., Roberts, C., Ross, R., Roth, G., & Smith, B. (1999). *The dance of change: The challenges to sustaining momentum in learning organizations.* New York: Doubleday Currency.

Senge, P., Kleiner, A., Roberts, C., Ross, R., & Smith, B. (1994). *The fifth discipline fieldbook: Strategies and tools for building a learning organization.* New York: Doubleday Currency.

Sergiovanni, T. J. (1992). *Moral leadership: Getting to the heart of school improvement.* San Francisco: Jossey-Bass.

Shepherd, G. M. (1988). *Neurobiology.* New York: Oxford University Press.

Siegel, D. (1999). *The developing mind: Toward a neurobiology of interpersonal experience.* New York: Guilford.

Slavin, R. E. (1990). *Cooperative learning: Theory, research, and practice.* Englewood Cliffs, NJ: Prentice Hall.

Smith, F. (1990). *To think.* New York: Teachers College Press.

Snowdon, D. (2001). *Aging with grace: What the nun study teaches us about leading longer, healthier, and more meaningful lives.* New York: Bantam.

Sousa, D. (2001). *How the brain learns.* Thousand Oaks, CA: Corwin.

Sternberg, R. (1985). *Beyond IQ: A triarchic theory of intelligence.* New York: Cambridge University Press.

Sternberg, R. J. (1996). *Successful intelligence: How practical and creative intelligence determine success in life.* New York: Simon & Schuster.

Stogdill, R. M. (1974). *Handbook of leadership: A survey of theory and research.* New York: Free Press.

Sylwester, R. (1995). *A celebration of neurons: An educator's guide to the human brain.* Alexandra, VA: Association for Supervision and Curriculum Development.

Sylwester, R. (2000). *A biological brain in a cultural classroom: Applying biological research to classroom management.* Thousand Oaks, CA: Corwin Press.

Tishman, S. (2000). Why teach habits of mind? In A. L. Costa and B. Kallick (Eds.), *Discovering and exploring habits of mind.* Alexandria, VA: Association for Supervision and Curriculum Development.

Von Oech, R. (1990). *A whack on the side of the head: How you can be more creative.* Stamford, CT: U.S. Games Systems.

Vygotsky, L. (1978). *Mind in society: The development of higher psychological processes.* Cambridge, MA: Harvard University Press.

Weisinger, H. (1998). *Emotional intelligence at work.* San Francisco: Berrett-Koehler.

Wells, W., Burnett, J., & Moriarty, S. (1995). *Advertising: Principles and practice.* Englewood Cliffs, NJ: Prentice Hall.

Wheatley, M. J. (1992). *Leadership and the new science: Learning about organization from an orderly universe.* San Francisco: Berrett-Koehler.

Wheatley, M. J., & Kellner-Rogers, M. (1996). *A simpler way.* San Francisco: Berrett-Koehler.

Wilke, W. L. (1986). *Consumer behavior.* New York: John Wiley & Sons.

Wolfe, P. (2001). *Brain matters: Translating research into classroom practice.* Alexandria, VA: Association for Supervision and Curriculum Development.

Wright, R. (2000). *Nonzero: The logic of human destiny.* New York: Pantheon Books.

Zaltman, G. (1977). *Dynamic educational change models, strategies, tactics and management.* New York: Free Press.

Zohar, D. (1997). *Rewiring the corporate brain: Using the new science to rethink how we structure and lead organizations.* San Francisco: Berrett-Koehler.

INDEX